Learning To Walk With God

Twelve Steps To Christian Growth

CHARLIE RIGGS

WORLD WIDE
PUBLICATIONS
1303 HENNEPIN AVE., MINNEAPOLIS, MN 55403

Acknowledgements

Unless otherwise marked, Scripture quotations are from the *Holy Bible: New International Version,* copyright 1973, 1978, 1984 The International Bible Society; *The Amplified New Testament* (TAB), copyright 1954, 1958 The Lockman Foundation; *The New King James Version* (NKJ), copyright 1979, 1980, 1982 Thomas Nelson Inc., Publishers; *The Living Bible* (TLB), copyright 1971 Tyndale House Publishers, Wheaton, IL; *The New Testament in Modern English* (Revised Edition) by J.B. Phillips (Phillips), copyright 1958, 1960, 1972 J.B. Phillips; *The King James Version* (KJV). Used by permission.

LEARNING TO WALK WITH GOD by Charles Riggs

Library of Congress Catalog Card Number 86-50541
ISBN 0-89066-082-4

Printed in the United States of America.

1 2 3 4 5 6 7 8 9 10 / 86 87 88 89 90 91 92 93 94 95

CONTENTS

FOREWORD

In my first area ministry with The Navigators during World War II, I started a Bible class for military personnel. Lt. Charles Riggs was the first and for a while the only member of that class.

Like so many of us, Charlie had trusted Christ as Savior some years earlier but had no idea how to grow as a Christian and become established in a rewarding relationship with God. But he began to faithfully study and memorize Scripture and to spend more and more time in the early mornings with God.

Charlie has ministered as a member of the Graham Team for many years now, responsible for counseling and follow-up for those who respond to the Gospel in Billy Graham's meetings all over the world. I know of no one anywhere better qualified than Charlie to write this book on *Learning To Walk With God* as a follower of Jesus Christ.

For Charlie does not speak theoretically. He shares from his continuous experience of walking with God how a Christian can live a meaningful and significant life.

If you are one who has recently or not so recently committed your life to Christ as your Lord and Savior, you will want this book to refer to every day along with your Bible. Its chapters steer you around the pitfalls and lead you over the hills as you discover God's unfolding plan for your life. They contain the godly wisdom of a man who has walked the path you have taken and has compiled this guidebook for you.

If you are a pastor or church lay leader, you will find this a useful handbook for leading individuals or small groups in a course on basic discipleship. Charlie Riggs has distilled practical teachings from a lifetime of teaching these biblical principles of Christian growth.

Lorne Sanny
Chairman of the Board,
The Navigators

P R E F A C E

Learning To Walk With God is essentially a book on discipleship. This has been my field of work for the past forty years. First with the Navigator Organization and now for several years with the Billy Graham Association. With both organizations, I have majored on helping individuals know and apply the Scriptures to everyday life—helping to equip the saints for the work of ministry (Ephesians 4:11,12).

This book, in a way, is a reflection of my own pilgrimage in the faith. Learning hard lessons through trial and error. Learning to do by doing, through on-the-job training in the trench warfare of real life. Learning to experience the Hand of God in and through my own life and ministry. Through my ups and downs, God has become very real to me. I would like Him to become very real to others.

There are no shortcuts to Christian maturity and usefulness. No easy paths or simple formulas. Discipline is the key to discipleship. There is no magic in this book. However, these twelve chapters are filled with Scriptures, personal illustrations, and practical instructions. If used properly, it could be a very practical help to new Christians, an excellent tool for the pastor in his discipleship training program and a provocative course book for any Bible study group.

Many have helped in the production of this book, but I owe a great debt of gratitude to one. Tom Phillips has added years to my life and ministry by his faithful service to me through the years. He encouraged me to write the book and provided all the quotations. May God enrich and multiply your ministry as you study and use this material.

Charlie Riggs

Tarpon Springs, Florida
September 1986

My hope is built
on nothing less
Than Jesus' blood
and righteousness;
I dare not trust
the sweetest frame,
But wholly lean
on Jesus' name.

(EDWARD MOTE)

A Solid Foundation

When you think of walking with God, it tends to blow your mind. To think that we mortals can not only know the Creator of Heaven and Earth, but can also enjoy an intimate relationship with Him. In fact, a daily walk. The Apostle Paul makes this very clear. "For ye are the temple of God; as God hath said, I will dwell in them and walk in them; and I will be their God, and they shall be my people."[1] God, by His Holy Spirit, does live in every believer. The potential for a fulfilling, productive life is there for every believer to develop.

The Bible says, "And Enoch walked with God: And he was not; for God took him."[2] Likewise, "Noah was a just man and perfect in his generations, and Noah walked with God."[3]

Was this walk, or way of life, the exclusive privilege of a select few? No, all of us can enjoy this same privilege and it begins with a personal relationship with Jesus Christ.

MY PILGRIMAGE

I was born the seventh child in a family of 8. My mother and father separated when I was 2 years old. I don't have any memories of a father at home. My mother was a godly, praying woman, and through her faith she kept a whole

---

[1]2 Corinthians 6:16, KJV   [2]Genesis 5:22, KJV   [3]Genesis 6:9

family together. Each of the older family members, in turn, found employment to help in the support of the family. My turn came at the age of 18 when I went to work in the Pennsylvania oil fields, where I labored for 7 years as a "roughneck" before my induction into the U.S. Army.

MY EARLY EXPOSURE TO THE FAITH

I attended Sunday school at a very early age, riding on the bars of my older brother's bicycle. My first teacher was a pretty girl, Peggy Dudley. I found I enjoyed beauty at the age of 4 or 5. I still have my lapel pin awarded me for perfect attendance my first year in Sunday school. I have another pin for memorizing Scripture from a small booklet which contained Scripture verses from A to Z. "All have sinned and come short of the glory of God."[4] "But God commendeth His love for us, in that, while we were yet sinners Christ died for us."[5] Many of the verses related to the death, burial and resurrection of Jesus Christ. I presume that the purpose of the booklet was to plant the good "SEED" in our hearts as we memorized these basic gospel and biblical truths. I lost the little booklet, but I can still remember some of the verses.

Our church was known as an evangelical church. One pastor I remember quite well was a good teacher and Bible expositor. Sunday after Sunday we were exposed to the truth. But as I look back now, I realize you can know a lot about a person without knowing that person personally. This is also true when it comes to knowing Jesus Christ. I was faithfully taught about Him, memorized many gospel verses, sang songs about Jesus, prayed to Him and gave offerings to Him, but did not know Him as my personal Savior. We often had revival meetings in our church and I can remember going to the altar rail many times with tears in my eyes, but nothing of any spiritual consequence took place. I am reminded that you can take a pig out of the pen, give him a bath, spray him with perfume and put a

[4]Romans 3:23   [5]Romans 5:8

ribbon around his neck—all of which will make him smell and look better. But, let him go and he heads straight back to the mud hole in the pigpen, because that is his nature. I realize now that my early trips to the altar were of no avail because no spiritual regeneration took place. Regeneration in the biblical sense and defined by Webster's dictionary indicates a new birth takes place. We are spiritually reborn. As the Bible says, "Therefore, if anyone is in Christ, he is a new creation; old things have passed away; behold, all things have become new."[6]

There are multitudes today who worship, pray, serve in the church, and believe that they are in God's family. But, they have never been regenerated, made new by the work of the Holy Spirit through personal faith in Jesus Christ.

HOW IT BEGAN WITH ME

I can remember the night. It was a Sunday night in 1932. I was 16 years old. My mother took me to the First Baptist Church in Olean, New York, where evangelist Dr. John R. Troy was holding special meetings. I sat out in a crowd of about 400 people and listened to Dr. Troy preach a message on "The Cross." For the first time in my 16 years, I realized that Jesus Christ died for me. He died to pay the penalty for my sins. I learned that I could be forgiven all my sins if I was willing to repent and receive Jesus Christ into my heart. When the appeal was given, I was one of the first to go forward with tears running down my cheeks. At 16, I didn't understand all that took place, but I am convinced that I was reborn that summer night long ago. That was the night that Jesus Christ came into my heart, and to this day lives in me through His Holy Spirit. It was the beginning, but it took a few years of wandering through the wilderness before I began to grow and appreciate my new life in Jesus Christ.

[6]2 Corinthians 5:17, KJV

4

A SOLID FOUNDATION

The title of this chapter is "A Solid Foundation." To walk with God and enjoy a growing and productive life, you must be born into His family. This new birth begins with a clear commitment to Jesus Christ. The ABC's of a clear commitment are as follows:

1. Acknowledging your sin and need of a Savior.
2. Believing that Jesus Christ died on the cross to atone for your sins.
3. Confessing Christ as your personal Lord and Savior.

ACKNOWLEDGE

The first step to salvation is acknowledging sin. The Bible states very clearly that all of us are sinners. "But the scripture has confined *ALL* under sin, that the promise, by faith in Jesus Christ might be given to them that *believe*."[7] The consequence of our sin is spiritual separation or alienation from God. The Bible says, "Behold, the Lord's hand is not shortened, that it cannot save; nor His ear heavy, that it cannot hear. But your iniquities have separated you from your God and your sins have hidden His face from you, so that He will not hear."[8]

Therefore, in our natural state, we are away from God, needing to be reconciled or brought back into harmony with God. Picture a deep chasm with you on one side and God on the other. A chasm so wide and deep that it cannot be bridged, humanly speaking, except by a loving act of God. The Bible says, "God is on one side and all the people on the other side, and Christ Jesus, Himself man, is between them to bring them together."[9] The cross is the bridge back to God, and it has been there for 2,000 years for all who will come to the cross and believe in Jesus Christ.

[7]Galatians 3:22, NKJ   [8]Isaiah 59:1,2, NKJ   [9]1 Timothy 2:5, TLB

BELIEVE

The second step to a clear commitment is to believe that Jesus Christ died on the cross to atone for your sins. In the old testament, worshipers had to offer a lamb as an atonement, or sacrifice for sin. The lamb had to be perfect, without blemish and without spot. The Bible identifies Jesus as the perfect lamb for our sacrifice; He was conceived by the Holy Spirit and born without a sinful nature. The Bible says, "God made Him [Jesus] who had no sin to be sin for us, so that in Him we might become the righteousness of God."[10] Christ was our atonement. He made it possible, by our trusting Christ, for us to satisfy God, to be right with God.

William Tyndale, who translated the New Testament into English, encountered difficulty in finding a word to convey the meaning of Christ's redeeming work. Finding no suitable word, he joined two simple words, "at" and "one" to make "atone." This gives, in the etymology of "atonement" a clue to the Bible's teaching of salvation by reconciliation. The Apostle Peter, a living witness to Christ's death, writes, "For you know that it was not with perishable things such as silver and gold that you were redeemed from the empty way of life handed down to you from your fathers, but with the precious blood of Christ, a lamb without blemish or defect."[11] "Jesus," John identifies, "was that perfect lamb who by His death took away the sins of the world."[12]

BELIEVING REQUIRES AN ACT OF FAITH

To believe requires an act of faith on your part. It connotes a commitment, in a spiritual sense, to Jesus Christ. To put your trust in the fact that through Christ's death and resurrection you can know the forgiveness of sins and the promise of everlasting life. When you truly believe in Christ you become a child of God—born into God's family. "But as many as received Him [Christ], to them He gave

[10]2 Corinthians 5:21   [11]1 Peter 1:18,19.   [12]John 1:29

the right to become the children of God, *even to those who believe in His name*: who were born, not of blood, nor of the will of the flesh, nor of the will of man, *but of God*."[13]

Many people today call themselves Christians but have never been born into God's family by the Holy Spirit. Nicodemus, for example, was a religious man—in fact, a religious leader. He was a Pharisee, keeping the law and all the rituals that are required. But he was not born again. In chapter 3 of John's gospel you have the story of Jesus and Nicodemus. In verse 3 Jesus told him, "Unless a man is born again, *he cannot see the Kingdom of God*." In verse 8, Jesus told him the new birth is wrought by the Holy Spirit. "The wind blows where it pleases," Jesus said. "You hear the sound, but you cannot tell where it comes from or where it is going. So is everyone who is born of the Spirit."[14] The true believer is born twice. First, into the natural family, a physical birth; and secondly, into God's family through the work of the Holy Spirit, a spiritual birth.

A father was attempting to explain this passage to his daughter. He wanted her to understand the work of the Holy Spirit and the new birth but he was having a difficult time making it clear. Then he stepped over to the window and opened it to allow a slight breeze to blow the curtain. He said to his daughter, "What's moving the curtain?" She replied, "The wind." Her father said, "How do you know, when you cannot see it?" She replied, "I can't see the wind, but I can see what it is doing." To observe the new birth take place is impossible, but the *evidence* of the new birth is observable. The Bible says, "Don't' you know that you are God's temple and that God's Spirit lives in you?"[15] Many Scriptures attest to the indwelling Holy Spirit and His ministry. His work in the believer can be clearly seen: "The fruit of the Spirit is love, joy, peace, patience, kindness, goodness, faithfulness, gentleness, and self-control."[16]

[13]John 1:12,13, NKJ   [14]John 3:8   [15]1 Corinthians 3:16   [16]Galatians 5:22,23

PERSONAL EXPERIENCE WITH MY DAD

I will never forget the night my dad received Christ as his Lord and Savior. I hardly remember my dad at home because he left when I was only 2 years of age. Yet our whole family loved him and prayed for him for many years. At age 78, a stroke brought my dad to the point of death. He immediately asked if I could come and see him. When I walked into his room, he broke into tears and said, "Son, I've lived a wicked life, but I want to go where mother is when I die."

My grandmother, his mother, was a devout Christian woman. Just before she died, she visited our home and impressed us to pray for our dad. She said, "He doesn't know the Lord." My dad knew that his mother was in heaven, and that's where he wanted to spend eternity.

After he had confessed to me that he had lived a wicked life, I shared Scripture with him, telling him that he had taken the first step by admitting his need. I turned to Revelation 3:20 and explained that Christ would come into his heart if he would invite Him in. He prayed and did ask Christ to come into his life. Then I turned to John 1:12,13 and we read the verses together. "Receiving Christ," I told him, "we become children of God. It is not another physical birth but a spiritual rebirth into the family of God." Having received Christ into his heart, he was now a child of God through faith in Jesus Christ. We looked carefully at John 1:13 about being born into God's family. "This verse is your spiritual birth certificate," I said, and I wrote in the margin of his Bible, "August 26, 1959." As I finished writing he looked over the top of his glasses and said, "Son, put down 9:30." New birth was that real to him. The next thing he did was to write out a check to take home to my mother, whom he hadn't seen for many years.

Shortly after dad received Christ my oldest sister walked into the room to ask if we wanted some refreshments. I said, "Dad, tell Esther what happened to you tonight." With quivering lips and moist eyes he made a clear confession of faith. He said, "I just asked Jesus to come into my heart and I became a child of God."

CONFESSING CHRIST

Having acknowledged your sin and need of a Savior, and believing that Jesus Christ died on a cross to make atonement for your sins, the third step in a clear commitment is to confess Christ as Lord and Savior. To confess means to declare openly by way of speaking out freely your deep conviction of facts. The Bible says, "The Word (God's message in Christ) is near you, on your lips and in your heart; that is, the Word—the message, the basis and object—of faith, which we preach. Because if you acknowledge *and* confess with your lips that Jesus is Lord and in your heart believe (adhere to, trust in and rely on the truth) that God raised Him from the dead, *YOU WILL BE SAVED.* For with the heart a person believes (adheres to, trusts in and relies on Christ) and so is justified (declared righteous, acceptable to God), and with the mouth he confesses—declares openly and speaks out freely his faith—and confirms [his] salvation."[17]

BEGINNING YOUR WALK

Every walk has its first step. Before you can walk with God you must be born into His family. You are ready to start your walk:

1. If your faith is anchored in Christ.
2. If you can make a clear confession that Jesus Christ is in your heart as Lord and Savior.
3. If you have received Christ you have been born into God's family. Now you have the indwelling Holy Spirit to help you in your walk.

The Christian life can be an exciting adventure as you live day by day in the power of the Holy Spirit. God has many wonderful things in store for you as you walk in obedience to His Word and live for His glory.

[17]Romans 10:8-10, TAB

STUDY QUESTIONS - LESSON ONE

A Solid Foundation

NOTE: For this and other studies in this book you may want to use another notebook to provide more space for answers. As you read each chapter, use a colored marker or hi-liter to mark or underline key words or phrases. This will aid you in your study.

1. Why is a solid foundation important to the Christian life?

2. Although the author knew the gospel message from an early age, what was missing from his life? (page 2)

3. Define spiritual regeneration. (page 3)

4. What happened when Jesus died on the cross? What does the cross provide for sinners? (pages 3, 4)

5. Define the word "believe." What does a person need to believe to become a Christian, a child of God? (page 5)

6. Explain the "new birth." (page 6)

7. Write out your confession of faith. Explain how you know you have been born into God's family. (pages 7, 8)

Memorize: Copy 2 Corinthians 5:17 on a 3 x 5 card. Memorize it and review it daily during this study course. (page 3)

Distinguished scientist Michael Faraday was asked by some of his students as he neared death, *"What are your speculations now?"* He immediately replied, *"Speculations? I have none. I'm resting on certainties."* Then he repeated slowly and deliberately, *". . . For I know whom I have believed, and am persuaded that he is able to keep that which I have committed unto him against that day"* (2 TIMOTHY 1:12 KJV)

2

Blessed Assurance

As Christians, we ought to be able to say, as Faraday did, that we are resting on certainties, not on chance. Jesus said, "Do not let your hearts be troubled. Trust in God, trust also in me. In my Father's house are many rooms; if it were not so, I would have told you. I am going there to prepare a place for you. And if I go and prepare a place for you, I will come back and take you to be with me that you also may be where I am."[1] Many passages assure us that Jesus is coming again. All five chapters of 1 Thessalonians emphasize the coming of our Lord Jesus Christ. The Apostle Paul closes out the fourth chapter of 1 Thessalonians with these words, "For the Lord Himself will come down from heaven, with a loud command, with the voice of the archangel and with the trumpet call of God, and the dead in Christ will rise first. After that, we who are still alive and are left will be caught up with them in the clouds to meet the Lord in the air. And so we will be with the Lord *forever.* Therefore, encourage each other with these words."[2]

Christ our Savior is coming again. We don't know the day or the hour, but He is coming to take us to be with Him *forever.* This is both a comfort, and a certainty that we can share with confidence. "Blessed Assurance"—the

[1]John 14:1-2 [2]1 Thessalonians 4:16-18

word "assurance" means "confidence, guarantee, presumption, certainty, a definite fact; fixed, settled, positive, without doubt." God wants us to be certain. The Bible says, "I write these things to you who believe in the name of the Son of God so that you may *know* that you have eternal life."[3]

God wants us to know for certain that we have eternal life, but for some reason many people doubt their salvation. They believe that the Bible is the Word of God. They believe that Jesus is God's Son, that He died on the cross and rose again. They simply are not sure that they have eternal life and will go to Heaven when they die.

Through my work with the Billy Graham Association, I have personally counseled many people with this problem, and have discovered several factors that lead to this problem.

1. *A person may not be truly "born again."* Many people today claim to be Christians. They go to church, read the Bible, pray, and say that they believe in God, but they have never been "born of the Spirit." They need to acknowledge their need of Christ and receive Him into their hearts by faith. Until they do, Jesus will never be real to them, and they will continue to have doubts.

2. *Satan will do everything in his power to cause doubts.* He hates to see people trust Christ and does everything he can to confuse God's children. Paul says:

> ". . . I promised you to one husband, to Christ, so
> that I might present you as a pure virgin to him.
> But I am afraid that just as Eve was deceived by
> the serpent's cunning, your minds may somehow
> be led astray from your sincere and pure devotion
> to Christ. For if someone comes to you and
> preaches a Jesus other than the Jesus we preached,
> or if you receive a different spirit from the one you

---

[3]1 John 5:13

received, or a different gospel from the one you accepted, you put up with it easily enough."[4]

Paul is saying to the Corinthians, "Keep it simple. Base your faith on Christ and Him alone. Don't let others come along and add anything to the Gospel." Then he says, "For such men are false apostles, deceitful workmen, masquerading as apostles of Christ. And no wonder, for Satan himself masquerades as an angel of light. It is not surprising, then, if his servants masquerade as servants of righteousness. Their end will be what their actions deserve."[5]

Since its inception, Christianity has been attacked by the evil one. False prophets have risen and Christians have been led astray through false teaching. Believers in Galatia were a prime example of false prophets at work. They had trusted Jesus Christ through the ministry of the Apostle Paul. Before long, however, they were led astray. The Bible says:

I am astonished that you are so quickly deserting the one who called you by the grace of Christ and are turning to a different gospel—which is really no gospel at all. Evidently some people are throwing you into confusion and are trying to pervert the gospel of Christ. But even if we or an angel from heaven should preach a gospel other than the one we preached to you, let him be eternally condemned! As we have already said, so now I say again: If anybody is preaching to you a gospel other than what you accepted, let him be eternally condemned."[6]

Remember, Satan never gives up. Don't let him cause you to doubt your salvation. It is by faith in Jesus Christ.

3. *People often confuse works and grace, or fact and feeling.* We are not saved by what we do. We may feel very unworthy because of something we have done and

---

[4]2 Corinthians 11:2-4   [5]2 Corinthians 11:13-14   [6]Galatians 1:6-9

think no Christian would behave like that. Some people apparently feel that Christians should be perfect and never think any unkind thoughts or do anything that would injure another individual. The Apostle Paul helps us clear up this problem by sharing his own testimony:

> *"I do not understand what I do. For what I want to do I do not do, but what I hate I do. And if I do what I do not want to do, I agree that the law is good. As it is, it is no longer I myself who do it, but it is sin living in me. I know that nothing good lives in me, that is, in my sinful nature. For I have the desire to do what is good, but I cannot carry it out. For what I do is not the good I want to do; no, the evil I do not want to do—this I keep on doing. Now if I do what I do not want to do, it is no longer I who do it, but it is sin living in me that does it. So I find this law at work: When I want to do good, evil is right there with me. For in my inner being I delight in God's law; but I see another law at work in the members of my body, waging war against the law of my mind and making me a prisoner of the law of sin at work within my members."*[7]

We must never forget that every believer has two natures—an old nature and a new nature. The old carnal nature with which we were born will never reform. It will go on lusting, giving us trouble until we die. Through the new nature we learn to say no to the old nature. There will be daily confrontation between the two natures. The Bible says, "So I say, live by the Spirit, and you will not gratify the desires of the sinful nature. For the sinful nature desires what is contrary to the Spirit, and the Spirit what is contrary to the sinful nature. They are in conflict with each other, so that you do not do what you want."[8]

As we grow, there will be times when we give in to the old nature and sin against God. I can remember many

[7]Romans 7:15-23   [8]Galatians 5:16-17

times when my old nature won the battle, and I fell into sin. But thank God He has made a provision for us when this happens. "If we claim to be without sin," 1 John 1 says, "we deceive ourselves, and the truth is not in us. If we confess our sins, he is faithful and just and will forgive us our sins and purify us from all unrighteousness. If we claim we have not sinned, we make him out to be a liar and his word has no place in our lives."[9]

Some people believe that they can live any way they want to: lie, cheat, steal, and be self-indulgent—as long as God forgives their sin. But God disciplines His wayward children:

> *"My son, do not make light of the Lord's discipline, and do not lose heart when he rebukes you, because the Lord disciplines those he loves, and he punishes everyone he accepts as a son. Endure hardship as discipline; God is treating you as sons. For what son is not disciplined by his father? If you are not disciplined (and everyone undergoes discipline), then you are illegitimate children and not true sons. Moreover, we have all had human fathers who disciplined us and we respected them for it. How much more should we submit to the Father of our spirits and live! Our fathers disciplined us for a little while as they thought best; but God disciplines us for our good, that we may share in his holiness."[10]*

New Christians can easily be confused concerning their faith and wonder about their salvation. During a follow-up telephone survey after a Billy Graham Crusade, I made a personal call to an inquirer to ask how he was spiritually and to offer further assistance. I called a pharmacist who had received Christ during the Crusade and asked if his commitment to Christ had made any difference in his life. He thought for a moment and replied, "Yes and no. I thought now that I'm a Christian the battle should be over,"

[9]1 John 1:8-10   [10]Hebrews 12:5-10

he said, "but I seem to be worse than ever." In reality, the battle is not over, it has just begun. Before receiving Christ, we have a green light to do whatever we please. We don't know any better. Of course, we shall suffer the consequences of our actions. When we receive Christ, God lives in us in the person of the Holy Spirit. The Spirit within is like a red light. We begin to have new convictions about activities and habits we never questioned before. We begin to see our lives as God sees them, and that is why we seem to be worse. *The closer we get to the Light, the more we see our imperfections.* This is a good sign that God is at work in us. Only one person ever lived a perfect life—Jesus Himself. We should not judge our saving relationship to Christ on the basis of behavior, whether good or bad.

Ephesians 2:8-10 puts faith and works in the proper perspective: "For it is by grace you have been saved, through faith—and this not from yourselves, it is the gift of God— not by works, so that no one can boast. For we are God's workmanship, created in Christ Jesus to do good works, which God prepared in advance for us to do." We are saved *for* good works, but not *by* our good works. Salvation is a free gift. We don't work for it, as demonstrated by the key word in this passage—grace. Grace means "unearned or unmerited favor from God." I cannot earn it, nor do I deserve it. I thank God every day for His willingness to look beyond my imperfections and see the potential in me that can be used for His glory. And as I recognize His grace, I can show my appreciation through service as I obediently yield daily to Him and allow Him to work in and through my life.

4. *People may be ignorant of the Scriptures or fail to take God at His Word.* Individuals who lack assurance of salvation seldom read the Bible. In fact, surveys indicate that most Christians don't average more than a few minutes a day reading the Bible and rarely do any in-depth study of the Scriptures. No wonder there is so much doubt among Christians today! The Bible is filled with passages that will

convince us of God's love and sovereign care. Until Jesus comes for us, His Word and the Holy Spirit's abiding presence are all we need to fill us with hope, joy, and peace. Paul says, "Now may the God of hope fill you with all joy and peace *in believing,* that you may abound in hope through the power of the Holy Spirit."[11] The God of hope wants to fill us with joy and peace. He wants us to abound in hope through the power of the Holy Spirit. "In believing," in taking God at His Word, we find hope and assurance.

PROMISES OF ASSURANCE

A number of Scripture passages assure us of eternal life and God's keeping power. The first promise is found in the first epistle of John:

> *"And this is the testimony: God* has given *us eternal life, and this life is in his Son. He who has the Son has life; he who does not have the Son of God does not have life. I write these things to you who believe in the name of the Son of God so that you may* know *that you have eternal life."*[12]

We don't have to wonder or guess about eternal life; we can be certain. Because many people never settle the issue of their salvation, they bobble like a cork at sea. They never grow in Christ. But we can nail it down once and for all: if I have Christ, I have life, and I can know it. God said so. I am taking Him at His Word.

A second promise, one that speaks with great certainty, is Philippians 1:6, "Being confident of this, that he who began a good work in you will carry it on to completion until the day of Christ Jesus." God began a work in us when we invited Christ into our lives. We can be confident, according to this passage, that He will continue His work until the task is complete and He comes to take us home with Him.

[11]Romans 15:13, NKJ   [12]1 John 5:11-13

A third promise, one that emphasizes God's keeping power is 1 Peter 1:3-5:

> *"Praise be to the God and Father of our Lord Jesus Christ! In his great mercy he has given us new birth into a living hope through the resurrection of Jesus Christ from the dead, and to an inheritance that can never perish, spoil, or fade—kept in heaven for you, who through faith are shielded by God's power until the coming of the salvation that is ready to be revealed in the last time."*

What a comfort! Through repentance of sin and faith in Christ, we have an indestructible home reserved for us in heaven. Until we go to occupy that home, we are *kept* by the power of God through faith. If we believe God, this can be an anchor for our faith.

The fourth promise deals with sin—a problem for many Christians, because our sin separated us from God and made it necessary for us to be redeemed. "In him [Christ]," Ephesians 1 says, "we have redemption through his blood, the forgiveness of sins, in accordance with the riches of God's grace."[13] Because of Christ's death, we are free from the penalty of sin which is death or separation from God for all eternity.

The fifth promise concerns the work of the Holy Spirit and His part in keeping us secure. "Having believed, you were marked in him with a seal, the promised Holy Spirit, who is a deposit guaranteeing our inheritance until the redemption of those who are God's possession—to the praise of his glory."[14] The Holy Spirit is our *seal,* an agreement that "confirms or ratifies or makes secure, a guarantee." A seal is irrevocable or indisputable. Verse 14 states that the Holy Spirit is the deposit of our inheritance. That means to bind a bargain, like making a down payment on a purchase. The Holy Spirit seals us: God has already purchased us, and He guarantees to *keep us* until Jesus comes for us.

[13]Ephesians 1:7　　[14]Ephesians 1:13-14

We can relax, rejoice and let the Holy Spirit assure us moment by moment. Paul says, "The Spirit Himself bears witness with our spirit that we are children of God."[15] The Holy Spirit helps us to understand the Scriptures, makes us more sensitive to what is right and wrong, puts a greater love on our hearts for others.

The sixth promise of assurance concerns the love of God:

> *"Who shall separate us from the love of Christ? Shall trouble or hardship or persecution or famine or nakedness or danger or sword? No, in all these things we are more than conquerors through him who loved us. For I am convinced that neither death nor life, neither angels nor demons, neither the present nor the future, nor any powers, neither height nor depth, nor anything else in all creation, will be able to separate us from the love of God that is in Christ Jesus our Lord."[16]*

In these days of turmoil, continual war, and bloodshed, nations filling their arsenals with most destructive weapons, evil seemingly on the ascendancy everywhere, a Christian needs to know that *nothing* can separate us from the love of God in Jesus Christ our Lord.

Write these promises out on 3" x 5" cards. Use them in your devotions for several days. I personally like to start the day with the Lord, and in addition to reading the Bible, I make it a habit to review several verses that I have copied on cards. In fact, I have gone over verses so many times that I know them by heart. The Holy Spirit can use these truths to minister to you and to me 24 hours a day. Why don't you try it? Write them out and review the blessed promises often. You can review them in a matter of minutes and God will minister to your heart continually.

To finish this chapter on assurance, look at some statements that Jesus made concerning eternal life.

[15]Romans 8:16, NKJ   [16]Romans 8:35,37-39

1. "Most assuredly, I say to you, he who hears My
   word and believes in Him who sent Me has everlasting life, and shall not come into judgment,
   but has passed from death into life."[17] Jesus
   makes it very clear we will not face judgment for
   our sin. We have eternal life now through faith in
   Christ.

2. "My sheep hear My voice, and I know them,
   and they follow Me. And I give them eternal life
   and they shall never perish; neither shall anyone
   snatch them out of My hand. My Father, who
   gave them to Me, is greater than all; and no one
   is able to snatch them out of My Father's hand."[18]
   Jesus makes several very clear statements here. I
   give unto them eternal life. They shall never perish. Neither shall any one snatch them out of my
   hand. No one is able to snatch them out of my
   Father's hand. Bev Shea often sings "He has the
   whole world in His hand. He has me and you,
   brother, in His hand." That's a safe place to be,
   in the hands of a loving God.

3. Speaking to Martha concerning the death of Lazarus, Jesus said, "I am the resurrection and the
   life. He who believes in Me, though he may die,
   he shall live. And whoever lives and believes in
   Me shall never die. Do you believe this?"[19] Eternal life is a present possession. It isn't something
   that we are going to get some day. One of these
   days Christ is coming for us and as the Scripture
   says, "So shall we ever be with the Lord."[20] We
   are told to comfort one another with these
   words.

[17]John 5:24, NKJ   [18]John 10:27-29, NKJ   [19]John 11:25-26, NKJ
[20]1 Thessalonians 4:17, KJV

STUDY QUESTIONS - LESSON TWO

Blessed Assurance

1. List several reassuring statements from the following Scriptures. (page 13)

   • John 14:1,2

   • 1 Thessalonians 4:16-18

2. Many Christians doubt their salvation. Of the four problems listed on pages 14-18, which one do you think is most prevalent today? (Please explain)

3. Reread Romans 7:15-23 on page 16. Circle key words and underline key thoughts. What is the most important lesson you learned from these verses?

4. Of the promises on pages 19-21, list one thought from each verse that is most assuring:

   • 1 John 5:11-13

   • Philippians 1:6

• 1 Peter 1:3-5

• Ephesians 1:7

• Ephesians 1:13, 14

• Romans 8:35-39

5. From these six thoughts, write a statement that describes your assurance.

6. On page 22, Jesus makes several statements relating to eternal life. In 20 words or less, summarize these statements.

Memorize: Write Philippians 1:6 (page 19) on a 3 x 5 card. Memorize and review it daily during this study course.

*The quality of a man's life
is in direct proportion
to his commitment to excellence,
regardless of his chosen field.*

(COACH VINCE LOMBARDI)

3

Practicing Lordship

The late Vince Lombardi was for many years coach of the Green Bay Packers of the National Football League. He was known as a strict disciplinarian, but his discipline paid off. He wanted his players to excel, to be the best—and they were, year after year. Football stars, tennis players, gymnasts, swimmers, and other athletes practice 8 to 10 hours a day to perfect their skills. And their dedication is reflected in trophies and medals.

What would happen if Christians had that same discipline and dedication? We would revolutionize the church— and that is exactly what Christ intended for us to do. Lordship means a total commitment to a sovereign Lord. A committed Christian is disciplined and dedicated to the cause of Christ.

As a committed Christian, what is the spiritual quality of my life? What is my purpose in life? What Christian goals am I pursuing? What steps in discipline am I taking to achieve these goals? How committed am I to the lordship of Jesus Christ?

In the first chapter, a strong emphasis was placed on a commitment to Jesus Christ as *Lord* and Savior. Becoming a Christian means much more than going through some ritual, repeating vows, praying to receive Christ or making a decision for Christ. It is more than joining a church and attending regularly. Becoming a Christian is a life-long commitment with obligations. A Christian is married to Christ. He is the bridgegroom and we, the church, are the bride. Christianity involves more than an hour's worship on Sunday. The true believer is committed to the lordship of Jesus Christ 24 hours a day, 7 days a week, for the rest of his life.

Most of us have a number of years ahead of us, and we want them to be fulfilling and productive years. We can, however, live for many years without purpose and fulfillment unless we are completely yielded to Christ and allowing Him full control of all of our activities day by day. This does not mean a drab, dull life of drudgery, with no thrills. Each new day with Christ in control is an exciting adventure. "You will show me the path of life," the Psalmist says; "in Your presence is fullness of joy; at Your right hand are pleasures forevermore."[1]

WHY SHOULD JESUS CHRIST BE LORD?

"Haven't you yet learned that your body is the home of the Holy Spirit God gave you, and that he lives within you? Your own body does not belong to you. For God has bought you with a great price. So use every part of your body to give glory back to God, because he owns it."[2] We have been bought with a great price. Christ gave His life to redeem us; now we are His servants, and we are to obey Him as Lord and Master. In some modern translations, the word "servant" appears as "slave." Because we are slaves to Christ, our sovereign master, we need to yield continually to His authority. When we do it, we will be amazed at what Christ will do for us. Our Master always has the best in store for us.

WHAT DOES PRACTICING LORDSHIP MEAN?

Acknowledging Jesus Christ as our Lord involves a total reorganization of our life's priorities. This new life-style of

[1]Psalm 16:11, NKJ   [2]1 Corinthians 6:19-20, TLB

submission and dependence involves a number of changes
in a new believer's life.

Lordship is a wholehearted way of life.

Pete Rose is a sports personality whose name has become a household word. In 1985 he set the all-time record
for the largest number of base hits in baseball. In his career
he has hit safely over 4,000 times. He has made famous the
head-first slide in running the bases. He is called "Mr. Hus-
tle," because he does everything with gusto even though
he is 44 years old! Rose is a winner because he has put his
whole heart into the game.

Similarly, Christians should be wholehearted in their service to God. King Hezekiah, in the history of Israel, was a
good king who had his heart turned toward God. "And in
every work that he began in the service of the house of
God, in the law and in the commandment, to seek his
God, he did it with all his heart. So he prospered."[3] In
chapters 29-32, Hezekiah honored God, restored worship,
brought renewal throughout the land, and God honored
him for his wholeheartedness.

The names of Joshua and Caleb stand out in biblical history for one reason: God singled them out as two men
who "wholly followed the Lord." These two men were
among the twelve spies who represented the twelve tribes
of Israel. They were sent to spy out the land which Israel
was to occupy. All brought back a negative report except
Caleb and Joshua. Ten men saw problems, fortress cities
and giants to overcome. They said it would be impossible
to invade the land, and they turned the hearts of the people. Two men saw the potential, "a land which flows with
milk and honey."[4] Only 2 of the original group which left
Egypt lived to enter the promised land. The others wandered in the wilderness for 40 years. "Because they have
not followed me wholeheartedly, not one of the men

twenty years old or more who came up out of Egypt will see the land I promised on oath to Abraham, Isaac and Jacob—not one except Caleb son of Jephunneh the Kenizzite and Joshua son of Nun, for they followed the Lord wholeheartedly."⁵ Many Christians today wander in the wilderness because they are not fully committed to Christ. But Joshua, whose life was committed, did lead a new generation of Israelites into the promised land and, through God, overcame all obstacles.

God sovereignly looks down from heaven and knows exactly what is going on in our hearts. David advised his son, "And you, my son Solomon, acknowledge the God of your father, and serve him with a wholehearted devotion and with a willing mind, for the Lord searches every heart and understands every motive behind the thoughts. If you seek him, he will be found by you; but if you forsake him, he will reject you forever."⁶ That advice was given by King David when Solomon, his son, was about to build the temple, and it is good advice for us today as well. We are to serve God with wholehearted devotion and a willing mind, because God is looking for such people: "The eyes of the Lord range throughout the earth to strengthen those whose hearts are fully committed to him."⁷

The challenge to us in these two passages is to be people with hearts fully committed to God, to serve Him wholeheartedly, not to be like the scribes and Pharisees who were religious but uncommitted. Jesus said of them, "These people honor me with their lips, but their hearts are far from me."⁸ Many of us spend a few minutes a day reading a Scripture and saying a prayer, but we are not locked in wholeheartedly to God. We are not sincerely seeking Him and preparing our hearts to walk uprightly through the day. Sunday after Sunday we worship, but it is simply a ritual. We open the song book to sing "Praise God From Whom All Blessings Flow," but our lips barely move. We are not singing from a heart that is overflowing with God's bless-

⁵Numbers 32:11-12   ⁶1 Chronicles 28:9   2 Chronicles 16:9   ⁸Matthew 15:8

ings through the week. We sing, "Crown Him Lord of All" with our lips, but not from a fully committed heart. We do draw near to God with our lips, but our hearts are far from Him. No wonder we have not come to know God intimately. Yet Jeremiah says, "You will seek me and find me when you seek me with all your heart."[9]

Lordship is a recognition of God's divine ownership and sovereign right to our lives.

"You are not your own; you were bought at a price," 1 Corinthians 6:19-20 says. Our lives belong to God; He is our master. We should seek His will for our lives, and bring glory to God by what we do.

Lordship is an attitude of reverential trust and respect for God.

"The fear of the Lord" is a concept found over and over in the Old Testament. It denotes an awe toward God, a reverential respect and trust—a trust so complete that we would commit our lives and everything that we possess to Him. One of the best illustrations of the fear of the Lord is found in the life of Abraham. God had promised Abraham a son and promised to bless and multiply his seed through this son. Abraham waited until he was nearly 100 years old before Isaac was born. Then, when Isaac was only 12 years old, God told Abraham to take him up to Mount Moriah and offer him as a sacrifice. Genesis tells us that Abraham, without question, obediently took his son and prepared for the sacrifice. As he raised the knife, the angel of the Lord said, "Do not lay a hand on the boy, . . . do not do anything to him. Now I know that you *fear God,* because you have not withheld from me your son, your only son."[10] In place of the son, God provided a ram.

The first verse of Genesis 22 reports that God was testing Abraham. Abraham passed the test, a vivid picture of one fully yielded to God and obedient. Abraham's act of obedience is later recorded in the book of Hebrews: "By faith Abraham, when God tested him, offered Isaac as a sacrifice. He who had received the promises, was about to sacrifice his one and only son, even though God had said to him, 'It is through Isaac that your offspring will be reckoned.' Abraham reasoned that God could raise the dead, and figuratively speaking, he did receive Isaac back from death."[11] Abraham obeyed God, and as a result, "The angel of the Lord called to Abraham from heaven a second time and said, 'I swear by myself,' declares the Lord, 'that because you have done this and have not withheld your son, your only son, I will surely bless you and make your descendants as numerous as the stars in the sky and as the sand on the seashore.'"[12] One moment Abraham thought he would be childless, and the next he is told that his seed will be multiplied like the stars. Walking in the fear of the Lord may cost us, but it pays great dividends.

Lordship is a surrender of our wills and a dedication of our lives to God as a living sacrifice.

The best way to demonstrate a reverential trust and acknowledge God's divine ownership, is to yield or surrender to Him. Surrender is a way of life; it may originally be a decisive action on our part at some specific time in life, but after that initial surrender, we must continually yield to His sovereign control. "Therefore I urge you, brothers," Paul exhorts, "in view of God's mercy, to offer your bodies as living sacrifices, holy and pleasing to God—which is your spiritual worship. Do not conform any longer to the pattern of this world, but be transformed by the renewing of your mind. Then you will be able to test and approve what God's will is—his good, pleasing and perfect will."[13] If we are to glorify God by our lives, we certainly must be transformed. If we are not being transformed, we will be conformed to this world's system.

[11]Hebrews 11:17-19   [12]Genesis 22:15-17   [13]Romans 12:1-2

Lordship is a love relationship expressed in obedience to God.

During His earthly ministry, Jesus had a confrontation with the Sadducees and the Pharisees over this question:

"Teacher, which is the greatest commandment in the Law?" Jesus replied, "'Love the Lord your God with all your heart and with all your soul and with all your mind.' This is the first and greatest commandment. And the second is like it: 'Love your neighbor as yourself.' All the Law and the Prophets hang on these two commandments."[14]

We can all too easily sing of our love for Christ or testify of our love for Him, without really loving Him. But we can demonstrate that we love Him, however, through obedience. John 14:21 says, "Whoever has my commands and obeys them, he is the one who loves me. He who loves me will be loved by my Father, and I too will love him and show myself to him." This passage is simple enough: "If you love me," the Lord says, "obey me." The dividends for loving and obeying God are outstanding—both God the Father and Jesus will love us in return, and Jesus will reveal Himself to us. We will get to know more about Him, and we will become more like Him.

Another passage that links love and obedience is found in Deuteronomy 6. God is speaking to Israel, but the passage applies to us as well: "Hear, O Israel: the Lord our God, the Lord is one. Love the Lord your God with all your heart and with all your soul and with all your strength. These commandments that I give you today are to be upon your hearts. Impress them on your children. Talk about them when you sit at home and when you walk along the road, when you lie down and when you get up."[15] If we love God, we will obey Him. We will take His words to heart, teach our children the Word, and have the Word on our lips throughout the day. Have you ever no-

[14]Matthew 22:36-40   [15]Deuteronomy 6:4-7

ticed that if God is not in the center of a person's life, you will rarely hear God's words repeated? The Bible is a closed book to many people. Is it because we don't love God with all our heart? A person can read the Bible, pray, give to the church, witness and serve the Lord in other ways, without demonstrating lordship. Obedience or surrender is the issue if we want to experience a genuine encounter with God day by day. There are no degrees in obedience—we either obey, or disobey. When we implicitly obey the Scriptures, Jesus can shape our lives and make us the people we ought to be. For example, the Bible says, "Wives, submit to your husbands, as is fitting in the Lord. Husbands, love your wives and do not be harsh with them. Children, obey your parents in everything, for this pleases the Lord. Fathers, do not embitter your children, for they will become discouraged."[16] If we, as Christians, could take that message, meditate on it, and apply it to our lives, wouldn't that do something for the Christian home to bring great glory to God? At the rate Christian homes are breaking up today, we need God's divine intervention. May God help us to be obedient Christians.

Lordship is a disciplined life with goals and priorities aimed at glorifying God.

Some time ago I applied some fresh concrete to the approach to my garage. I carefully smoothed a fresh layer of cement just before dark. The next morning I noticed a series of circles, each one a little larger and in the center was a bug. The bug had struggled going round and round in circles. Having reached the largest circle, about two inches in diameter, it crawled back to the center and expired. And I thought, as I considered that bug, that many people who call themselves Christians never seem to get anywhere in their spiritual lives.

Each of us has the same amount of time each day; how we use the time will determine how far we will go in our

[16]Colossians 3:18-21

Christian commitment. I am responsible for the depth of my life and ministry. God is responsible for the breadth of it. We must be disciplined, living with goals and priorities if we want God to use us. First Corinthians 10:31 (NKJ) makes our responsibility very clear: "Therefore, whether you eat or drink, or whatever you do, do all to the glory of God." Bricklayers, accountants, secretaries, physicians as well as clergy, all have the same responsibility—to give glory to God. We have the strange idea that some things are secular and some are sacred, but seven days a week, we all are responsible for glorifying God.

The most productive years of my life, in terms of personal evangelism, were the four years I spent in the U.S. Army. Before I entered the service, I prayed that God would make me a good soldier for Jesus Christ. I knew that if God answered my prayer, I would also be a good soldier for my country. I endeavored to give the Army my best. God honored my efforts, and what an opportunity I had for witnessing! I was living in a mission field. It was a "secular" job, but God made it sacred.

The Apostle Paul gives us an unequalled example of the practice of lordship. He lived a disciplined, goal-oriented life, desiring that "Christ will be magnified in my body, whether by life or by death. For to me, to live is Christ, and to die is gain."[17] We should have the same ambition as Paul—that Christ might be magnified in our lives.

Lordship is an abiding relationship with Jesus Christ.

Jesus said, "Abide in Me, and I in you. As the branch cannot bear fruit of itself, unless it abides in the vine, neither can you, unless you abide in Me. I am the vine, you are the branches. He who abides in Me, and I in him, bears much fruit; for without Me you can do nothing."[18] Without Christ we can do nothing. If we abide in Him, living in continuous union, fully recognizing our dependence upon Him, we will bear much fruit. Dr. C. I. Scofield defines

[17]Philippians 1:20-21, NKJ   [18]John 15:4-5, NKJ

"abiding" in this way: "No sin unconfessed or unjudged.
No life which Christ cannot share. No plans without Him."
If we are to bear fruit, we must continue in an abiding rela-
tionship with Jesus Christ.

REWARDS OF PRACTICING LORDSHIP

The Bible abounds with examples of the rewards of
practicing lordship. Joshua and Caleb were allowed to go
into the promised land because they wholly followed the
Lord. For Abraham's obedience, God blessed his seed and
multiplied it as the stars in the heavens. Because King Hezekiah gave wholehearted service to God, everything he did
prospered. Jesus promised that if we will abide in Him, we
shall bear much fruit. The Scripture also promises guidance
along the right paths, fullness of joy, and pleasures forever
more.[19]

  1. *Practicing lordship leads to success.* The exam-
     ple of Joshua demonstrates that God prospers
     those who honor Him. The Lord said to Joshua,
     'This day I will begin to magnify you in the sight
     of all Israel, that they may know that, as I was
     with Moses, so I will be with you.'"[20] Because
     Joshua wholly followed the Lord, God moved
     him up to Moses' place as General of the Army.
     Then, God provided the event that catapulted
     Joshua into the place of leadership and respect:
     "On that day the Lord magnified Joshua in the
     sight of all Israel; and they feared him, as they
     had feared Moses, all the days of his life."[21] Fi-
     nally, Joshua 6:27 summarizes the outcome of
     Joshua's submission to God: "So the Lord was
     with Joshua, and his fame was spread throughout
     all the country." One day Joshua was a foot sol-
     dier; the next day he became the Commander-in-
     Chief. He wholly followed the Lord!

[19]Psalm 16:11   [20]Joshua 3:7, NKJ   [21]Joshua 4:14, NKJ

2. ***Practicing lordship leads to fulfillment.*** "Delight yourself also in the Lord," Psalm 37:4-5 (NKJ) says, "and He shall give you the desires of your heart. Commit your way to the Lord, trust also in Him and He shall bring it to pass." The more committed we are to Christ and His ways, the more our desires conform to His will for our lives, and the more He fulfills our desires. God can give us a complete change of heart if we let Him. He gives us a distaste for things we once craved, and desire for things we once disliked, "For he satisfies the longing soul, and fills the hungry soul with goodness."[22]

3. ***Practicing lordship gives stability to life.*** In Luke 6:46-49 (NKJ), Jesus asks the startling question, "Why do you call Me 'Lord, Lord,' and do not do the things which I say?" He goes on, then, to stress obedience, and shows the result of obedience: "Whoever comes to Me and hears My sayings and does them . . . is like a man building a house, who dug deep and laid the foundation on the rock. And when the flood arose, the stream beat vehemently against that house, and could not shake it, for it was founded on the rock. But he who heard and did nothing is like a man who built a house on the earth without a foundation, against which the stream beat vehemently; and immediately it fell. And the ruin of the house was great." Storms, calamity, and adversity may come, but the believer whose life is built on the rock of obedience will be steadfast.

4. ***Practicing lordship leads to knowledge of God:*** For those who reverentially trust and respect God, "The secret of the Lord is with those who fear Him . . ."[23] The fear of the Lord is described

---

[22]Psalm 107:9, NKJ   [23]Psalm 25:14, NKJ

as "the beginning of knowledge" and "the beginning of wisdom."[24] Those who fear the Lord, those who are willing to reverently trust the Lord Jesus Christ, will come to know Him and will be blessed with "riches and honor and life."[25]

In addition to the Biblical rewards for practicing lordship, there is a practical and commonsense reason for letting Jesus Christ manage and control our lives. He knows what's down the road, over the hill and around the turn. He's been there, and can guide us safely along the way, saving us heartache, dead ends, wasted years and frustration. He sees life from a vantage point that we don't have. " 'For My thoughts are not your thoughts, nor are your ways My ways,' says the Lord. 'For as the heavens are higher than the earth, so are My ways higher than your ways, and My thoughts than your thoughts.' "[26]

My friend Jack once flew a small plane in his business. On one occasion he was flying between Indianapolis and St. Louis following a two-lane highway. The traffic was heavy in both directions, slowed down by a heavy concentration of semi-trailer trucks. He noticed a white passenger car following a big truck for miles, endeavoring repeatedly to pass. The driver of the car would edge out toward the center of the road to peer around the truck only to find traffic coming in the other direction which prevented his passing. As he watched the frustrated driver, Jack thought, "If only I had radio communication with him—then I could tell him when it was safe to pass." Jack could see from a higher perspective, while the frustrated driver was limited in his perspective; all he could see was the road directly in front of him.

Our lives will likewise be frustrated unless we allow Christ complete control. By practicing lordship, however, we can live life to the full with Jesus Christ in complete control. We can take a stand with Joshua who wholly fol-

---

[24]Proverbs 1:7, 9:10, NKJ   [25]Proverbs 22:4, NKJ   [26]Isaiah 55:8-9, NKJ

lowed the Lord: "Now fear the Lord and serve him with all faithfulness. . . . But if serving the Lord seems undesirable to you, then choose for yourselves this day whom you will serve. . . . But as for me and my household, we *will* serve the Lord."[27]

STUDY QUESTIONS - LESSON THREE

Practicing Lordship

1. What do you think Coach Lombardi is saying in his statement on page 26? Please explain.

2. Define commitment and state what you think it means to be totally committed to Jesus Christ as Lord and Savior. (page 28)

3. On pages 29-35, there are seven different facets of Lordship. From each facet, list one important truth which, if applied, could change your life.

Lordship is:

• A whole-hearted way of life. (page 29)

• A recognition of God's divine ownership. (page 31)

• An attitude of reverential trust. (page 31)

• A surrender of our wills to God. (page 32)

• A love relationship expressed in obedience. (page 33)

• A disciplined life with goals. (page 34)

• An abiding relationship with Jesus Christ. (page 35)

4. Now take your seven thoughts, and write a scriptural definition of what is involved in Lordship.

5. When does Jesus become Lord of your life? Please explain.

6. List several incentives for making Jesus Lord. (pages 36-39)

Memorize: Write Romans 12:1,2 on a 3 x 5 card. Memorize and review daily during this study course. (page 32)

One must be positively blind not to see the colossal role that evil plays in the world. Indeed, it took the intervention of God Himself to deliver humanity from the curse of evil, for without His intervention men would have been lost.

(CARL GUSTAV JUNG)

4

Spiritual Warfare

Once the Christian has begun to submit to the Lordship of Jesus Christ, he will soon discover the warfare that believers face daily. Jesus calls for total commitment as He builds the church, made up of the body of "called out ones." But Satan is taking Christians captive; the casualty list grows by the hour. All of us are targets on his hit list. We need to be aware of his wiles, lest we be caught in his web.

This spiritual warfare began when Satan, because of his pride, was cast out of heaven. Isaiah describes his fall:

"How you are fallen from heaven, Oh Lucifer, son of the morning! How you are cut down to the ground, you who weakened the nations! For you have said in your heart: I will ascend into heaven, I will exalt my throne above the stars of God; I will also sit on the mount of the congregation on the farthest side of the north; I will ascend above the heights of the clouds, I will be like the Most High. Yet you shall be brought down to Sheol, to the lowest depths of the Pit." [1]

After his fall, Satan caused Adam and Eve, created in God's image, to disobey God. Their sin brought the whole human race under sin's judgment.

[1] Isaiah 14:12-15, NKJ

What happened to Adam and Eve? They were placed in the midst of Paradise, in the Garden of Eden. They were told by God that they could eat of every tree but one. To eat from that tree meant death. But the evil one caused them to doubt the authority of God's Word and to take the fruit! "So when the woman saw that the tree was good for food, that it was pleasant to the eyes, and a tree desirable to make one wise, she took of its fruit and ate. She also gave to her husband with her and he ate."[2] They didn't die physically, but this act of disobedience resulted in original sin, the fall of man. Since that incident, every human being has been born away from God, in need of reconciliation. For their part in the fall, Adam and Eve were driven from the garden, but the evil one was also punished!

> *"So the Lord God said to the serpent: Because you have done this, you are cursed more than all the cattle, and more than every beast of the field; on your belly you shall go, and you shall eat dust all the days of your life. And I will put enmity between you and the woman, and between your seed and her Seed; He shall bruise your head and you shall bruise His heel."*[3]

Ever since that day, a battle has raged between God and the forces of evil, headed up by Satan, the god of this world. His mission is to keep people from trusting Christ. The Bible says, "If the Good News we preach is hidden to anyone, it is hidden from the one who is on the road to eternal death. Satan, who is the god of this evil world, has made him blind, unable to see the glorious light of the Gospel that is shining upon him, or to understand the amazing message we preach about the glory of Christ who is God."[4] If he cannot keep people from trusting Jesus Christ, Satan will do everything he can to frustrate those who do. "I am anxious for you with the deep concern of God himself," says Paul, "anxious that your love should be for Christ alone, just as a pure maiden saves her love for

---

[2]Genesis 3:6, NKJ   [3]Genesis 3:14-15, NKJ   [4]2 Corinthians 4:3-4, TLB

one man only, for the one who will be her husband. But I am frightened, fearing that in some way you will be led away from your pure and simple devotion to our Lord, just as Eve was deceived by Satan in the Garden of Eden."[5]

OUR ENEMY—THE WORLD

The battle is raging all around us, but the enemy doesn't have horns or carry a pitchfork. Our *enemy* is *"the world," "the flesh"* and *"the devil."* Everywhere you look, the attraction is there: on the magazine rack, television, billboards, in the movies. We are led to believe that the ultimate fulfillment is to be found in sex. Christians struggle to resist worldly appeal, for the enemy of our soul is the instigator, and he knows how to appeal to the lower nature. "For we are not fighting against people made of flesh and blood," Paul warns, "but against persons without bodies— the evil rulers of the unseen world, those mighty satanic beings and great evil princes of darkness who rule this world; and against huge numbers of wicked spirits in the spirit world."[6]

We are no match, humanly speaking, for the enemy. Unless we have God's supernatural power to undergird us, we will be drawn into the worldly system. Israel, God's own people, worshiped and served the living God, but they fell prey to temptation and were assimilated into a heathen culture. They were warned many times against fraternization, but didn't heed: "So the children of Israel dwelt among the Caananites, the Hittites, the Amorites, the Perizzites, the Hivites, and the Jebusites. And they took their daughters to be their wives, and gave their daughters to their sons; and they served their gods. So the children of Israel did evil in the sight of the Lord. They forgot the Lord their God, and served the Baals and Asherahs."[7] Their experience demonstrates a downward spiral:

1. They intermarried.
2. They did evil in the sight of God.

[5]2 Corinthians 11:2-3, TLB   [6]Ephesians 6:12, TLB   [7]Judges 3:5-7, NKJ

3. They forgot God.

4. They worshiped the heathen gods.

As believers, we cannot help being in the world, but we can resist letting the world squeeze us into its mold. Without scriptural convictions of right and wrong, we naturally conform. For nine years after my commitment to Christ, I continued to live like the people around me—and most of them not committed Christians. I adopted many of the bad habits of the men in the oil fields where I worked. On Sunday mornings, I didn't want anyone to ask me how I spent Saturday night. But the Scripture warns about the danger of worldly influences: "Do not be unequally yoked together with unbelievers. . . . For you are the temple of the living God."[8]

Within days of my induction into the Army at age 25, I became involved with the Navigators, a Christian organization that emphasizes Scripture memory, Bible study, and discipleship. I was challenged to memorize Scripture, and when I found 2 Corinthians 6:14-18, it gave me clear scriptural guidelines and convictions for living those four years among men who were worldly. With God's help, I was able to establish a Christian testimony, work up through the ranks and become an officer, and thus influence both officers and enlisted men. Living among men where profanity, drinking, gambling, and immorality were rampant was a severe test. But this is another memory verse that helped: "Lay hands suddenly on no man, neither be partaker of other men's sins: *Keep thyself pure.*"[9]

I prayed daily during my four years in the Army to be pure, and ask God to this day to keep me pure. We are all targets of the evil one. "Don't you realize that making friends with God's enemies—the evil pleasures of this world—makes you an enemy of God?" James 4:4 (TLB) says. Think about your life for a moment. Think about where you go, with whom you go, and what you do. If we are involved in worldly pleasures, this passage classifies

[8]2 Corinthians 6:14,16, NKJ   [9]1 Timothy 5:22, KJV

us as enemies of God. The Bible says, "For Demas has forsaken me, having loved this present world, and has departed for Thessalonica."[10] A sad statement, isn't it? Unfortunately, it can be said about a lot of us today. If we love God, we will keep His commandments. John gives us a clear test to discern our love for God: "Stop loving this evil world and all that it offers you, for when you love these things, you show that you do not really love God; for all these worldly things, these evil desires—the craze for sex, the ambition to buy everything that appeals to you, and the pride that comes from wealth and importance—these are not from God. They are from this evil world itself."[11] As believers we need to be committed to the lordship of Jesus Christ. We must determine to obey the Word of God and have our priorities clearly defined. Otherwise, the world can overpower us, and we will lose our Christian distinctive.

OUR ENEMY—THE FLESH

Walt Kelly's cartoon character, Pogo, said, "We have met the enemy, and he is us." We are our own worst enemy; we all live in a body of sin. According to Scripture, we all have deceitful hearts, capable of rationalizing and justifying even bizarre behavior at times. Our tongues can be a "world of iniquity" seemingly inspired by the fires of hell. The bitterness, envy, and strife found in most of our lives is earthly, sensual, and devilish. We are a cesspool of iniquity, and to our shame, we are not aware of our problem, or won't admit it. We are too proud.

The Apostle Paul has identified the problem for us in Romans: "I know that nothing good lives in me, that is in my sinful nature. For I have the desire to do what is good, but I cannot carry it out. For what I do is not the good I want to do; no, the evil I do not want to do—this I keep on doing."[12] This duality is a dilemma every Christian shares. The old carnal nature is a deadly enemy; we need to censor its

[10]2 Timothy 4:10, NKJ   [11]1 John 2:15-16, TLB   [12]Romans 7:18-19

behavior constantly. James asks, "What is causing the quarrels and fights among you? Isn't it because there is a whole army of evil desires within you? You want what you don't have so you kill to get it. You long for what others have, and can't afford it, so you start a fight to take it away from them. And yet the reason you don't have what you want is that you don't ask for it."[13]

King Saul is a good example of one whose life was torn by strife. He was anointed King of Israel. His position was secure, and yet he became a casualty through envy and jealousy. When the armies returned after David had killed the Philistine warrior Goliath, the women danced, and sang: "Saul has slain his thousands and David his tens of thousands." Saul was jealous of David's superiority, and after that time "kept a jealous eye on David."[14] Saul's jealousy led to insecurity. He could see his throne slipping away from him. Then his insecurity led to insanity. The next day Saul hurled his javelin at David, hoping to pin him to the wall and thus wipe out the opposition. His pride and jealousy caused him to live a tortured life and led him to an untimely death.

For years I worked with the Navigator organization, and now for many years I have been with the Billy Graham Association. Working alongside others brings the temptation to compare myself with them. I often find myself around others who outthink, outdo and outwork me. I have always been slow and inarticulate, so having to work alongside people I have considered to be more capable resulted in problems of inferiority and depression. But I have learned how to handle the problem: "We dare not [class] ourselves . . . or compare ourselves with some, who commend themselves. But they, measuring themselves by themselves, and comparing themselves among themselves are not wise."[15] A companion verse points out God's control in such circumstances, "But now God has set the members, each one of them, in the body just as it has pleased Him."[16]

[13]James 4:1-2, TLB   [14]1 Samuel 18:6-9   [15]2 Corinthians 10:12, NKJ
[16]1 Corinthians 12:18, NKJ

This latter passage teaches that God has placed the different members of the body as it pleased *Him*. The body of Christ has many different members, and each member has a different function. I no longer measure myself by the talents or gifts of others. I have found my place in the body and am developing the gifts which God has given to me. This helps me to avoid jealousy, rivalry and frustration.

The Lust Of The Flesh

Lust means "unhealthy" desire—any unhealthy desire, not only sex. It could be an intense desire for *possessions*, which leads to problems between husbands and wives or parents and children. It could be an unhealthy desire for *popularity*, so that we go along with a gang, just to find acceptance and become one of them. Or it could be an unhealthy desire for *position*, the compulsion to be number one. Lust can lead to ruin, as in the case of King David. He allowed sexual lust to lead him to commit adultery. He had an affair with Bathsheba while her husband was away fighting on the front lines for Israel.

Because of David's sin, many people suffered. Bathsheba's husband was killed. There were scars which never healed.

What a tragedy this was in the life of David! But could this happen to us? Yes, it is happening among Christians today—not only the sins of adultery and murder, but many other grievous sins. The fact is, no one is immune from the tempter's power; we need to be on guard constantly. Forgiveness is available with God, but scars remain.

Taming The Tongue

Another "problem of the flesh" we all face is the problem of controlling the tongue: "But the tongue can no man tame; it is an unruly evil, full of deadly poison."[17] The *tongue* can be caustic, critical, and complaining. The tongue can heal, and the tongue can hurt.

[17]James 3:8, KVJ

*"So also the tongue is a small thing, but what
enormous damage it can do. A great forest can be
set on fire by one tiny spark. And the tongue is a
flame of fire. It is full of wickedness and poisons
every part of the body. And the tongue is set on
fire by hell itself, and can turn our whole lives into
a blazing flame of destruction and disaster. Men
have trained, or can train, every kind of animal
or bird that lives and every kind of reptile and
fish, but no human being can tame the tongue. It
is always ready to pour out its deadly poison."* [18]

Nothing can be more damaging to the body of Christ
than the untamed tongue. Satan uses this little muscle to
slander, defame, and ruin the character of innocent people.
But Proverbs says, "There are six things the Lord hates,
seven that are detestable to him: haughty eyes, a lying
tongue, hands that shed innocent blood, a heart that devises wicked schemes, feet that are quick to rush into evil,
a false witness who pours out lies and a man who stirs up
dissension among brothers." [19] Because I have been guilty of
all these things that God hates, and my tongue has been
sharp, judgmental, caustic, critical and guilty of lying, I began an intensive study of the book of Proverbs, which
holds many references to the use of the tongue.

- *The healing tongue:* "Reckless words pierce like a
  sword, but the tongue of the wise brings healing." [20]

- *The cheerful tongue:* "An anxious heart weighs a
  man down, but a kind word cheers him up." [21]

- *The gentle tongue:* "A gentle answer turns away
  wrath, but a harsh word stirs up anger." [22]

- *The discerning tongue:* "A man of knowledge
  uses words with restraint, and a man of understanding is even-tempered. Even a fool is thought

[18]James 3:5-8, TLB   [19]Proverbs 6:16-19   [20]Proverbs 12:18   [21]Proverbs 12:25
[22]Proverbs 15:1

to be wise if he keeps silent, and discerning if he holds his tongue."[23]

* *The controlled tongue:* "When words are many, sin is not absent, but he who holds his tongue is wise."[24]

A Hungarian proverb states, "It takes a brilliant man to say more than the man who is silent." The more we talk, the more we show our ignorance; when we are silent, we are given credit for knowing more than we do.

"The devil starts many deliberate lies about God's servants that thousands of Christians grasp, believe, and pass along in ugly gossip," Billy Graham says. "Pray that God will help you to use your tongue to heal rather than hurt people." Under the control of the flesh, the tongue can only be a destructive instrument of the enemy. With the Spirit's control, it can be an agent of kindness, healing, and peace.

Bitterness And Unforgiveness

Christians who have been hurt often become very bitter and unforgiving, turning from their friends and, in many cases, even from God. They shut themselves off from the help they sorely need: the encouragement of praying friends and the healing touch from a loving God. And Satan rejoices, because he has separated a sheep from the flock and the care of the Good Shepherd. The Bible says, "Look after each other so that not one of you will fail to find God's best blessings. Watch out that no bitterness takes root among you, for as it springs up it causes deep trouble, hurting many in their spiritual lives."[25] Many divisions plague the body of Christ today because of bitterness and an unforgiving spirit. Satan fosters this division, so we must be gentle and ready to forgive, never holding grudges. The Lord forgave us, so we must forgive others.

---

[23]Proverbs 17:27-28   [24]Proverbs 10:19   [25]Hebrews 12:15, TLB

Man's Deceitful Heart

"The heart is deceitful above all things and desperately wicked; who can know it?" Jeremiah 17:9 says.

Many of the problems in my own life have been caused by my own deceitful heart. It has led to involvement in sinful activities. The Bible says, "Keep your heart with all diligence, for out of it spring the issues of life."[26]

Our deceitful hearts can lead us down the wrong paths in life. They will justify almost any kind of behavior, fantasize, and rationalize. Our hearts are unreliable and need to be checked.

OUR ENEMY—THE DEVIL

"That there is a devil is a thing doubted by none but such as are under the influence of the devil. For any to deny that being of a devil must be from ignorance or profaneness worse than diabolical" (Cotton Mather, American Congregational Minister, 1663-1728).

As Mather indicates, the devil is real; his influences can surface at a moment's notice. In the book of Job we see his reality, "Now there was a day when the sons of God came to present themselves before the Lord, and Satan also came among them. And the Lord said to Satan, 'From where do you come?' So Satan answered the Lord and said, 'From going to and fro on the earth, and from walking back and forth on it.'"[27] Job was a target of Satan; he was tested severely, but triumphed. Satan could go, however, only as far as God allowed, as verse 12 makes clear. Job was victorious in both attacks that Satan made on his life.

How does Satan work to undermine the Christian's relationship with God?

- He takes away the Word (Gospel) when it is sown in the heart.[28]

- He put it in the heart of Judas to betray Jesus.[29]

- He entered Judas' heart for the betrayal.[30]

[26]Proverbs 4:23, NKJ   [27]Job 1:6-7, NKJ   [28]Mark 4:15   [29]John 13:2   [30]John 13:27

- He tempted Jesus to sin.[31]
- He is deceiving the whole world.[32]
- He is the father of lies.[33]
- He is seeking people to devour.[34]
- He is blinding people's eyes so they can't believe.[35]
- He is transformed into an angel of light and works through false prophets today.[36]
- He filled the heart of Ananias and Sapphira and caused their death.[37]
- He was a thorn in the flesh to buffet the Apostle Paul.[38]
- He hindered Paul from ministering at Thessalonica.[39]
- He holds Christians captive.[40]

As we become aware of the tactics of our enemy, we can look to the Scripture for a warning concerning Satan: "Be careful—watch out for attacks from Satan, your great enemy. He prowls around like a hungry, roaring lion, looking for some victim to tear apart. Stand firm when he attacks. Trust the Lord; and remember that other Christians all around the world are going through these sufferings too."[41] The lion is at work; he stalks his prey, singling out one of the herd—a young, old, or weak animal. Then he cuts the animal from the herd and finishes the kill. Satan works in the same way among Christians today. Hugh Latimer, Bishop of the Church of England during the 15th century, said, "Who is the most diligent Bishop and Prelate in all of England? . . . it is the devil . . . He is never out of his diocese." Bishop Latimer was burned at the stake for heresy in 1485.

[31]Luke 4:3,6,9   [32]Revelation 12:9   [33]John 8:44   [34]1 Peter 5:8
[35]2 Corinthians 4:3-4   [36]2 Corinthians 11:14-15   [37]Acts 5:3-10
[38]2 Corinthians 12:7   [39]1 Thessalonians 2:18   [40]2 Timothy 2:26
[41]1 Peter 5:8, TLB

We are all in a battle today against "the world," "the flesh," and "the devil." Many have gone down in defeat and the battlefield is littered with casualties. But we can insure victory, staying in the battle for our Lord Jesus Christ, by using the resources God has provided for us.

RESOURCES FOR VICTORY

In 2 Chronicles 20, the kingdom of King Jehoshaphat was being invaded by the armies of Moab and Ammon. He called the nation to prayer and fasting; he reminded God of all of His promises to Israel. Then came the word of the Lord, "Listen, all you of Judah, and you inhabitants of Jerusalem, and you, King Jehoshaphat! Thus says the Lord to you: Do not be afraid nor dismayed because of this great multitude, for the battle is not yours, but God's. You will not need to fight in this battle. Position yourselves, stand still and see the salvation of the Lord, who is with you, O Judah and Jerusalem!"[42] And God, faithful to His word, delivered the children of Israel from the enemy.

Just as the Lord delivered Israel, He has promised to deliver us as well. "For though we live in the world," Paul says, "we do not wage war as the world does. The weapons we fight with are not the weapons of the world. On the contrary, they have divine power to demolish strongholds. We demolish arguments and every pretension that sets itself up against the knowledge of God, and we take captive every thought to make it obedient to Christ."[43]

God will help us fight our battles today, and has supplied us with an arsenal of mighty weapons:

1. *A Sovereign God.* Satan was defeated at Calvary when Christ shed His blood on the cross to redeem us from the bondage of sin. Satan designs to nullify what God has done, but Christ is our advocate. Charles Spurgeon, the great British preacher, used to tell of an old farmer who told him of a conversation he had with the devil.

[42]2 Chronicles 20:15, 17, NKJ   [43]2 Corinthians 10:3-5

"The other day, sir, the devil was tempting me and I tried to answer him; but I found he was an old lawyer, and understood the law a great deal better than I did, so I gave over, and would not argue with him anymore. I said to him, 'What do you trouble me for?' 'Why,' said he, 'about your soul.' 'Oh,' said I, 'that is no business of mine; I have given my soul over to the hand of Christ; I have transferred everything to Him; if you want an answer to your doubts and queries, you must apply to my advocate.'"

Jesus Christ is our advocate, according to 1 John 2:1-2, and He represents us daily at the throne.

The battle is not ours, but God's. The Bible says, "No temptation has seized you except what is common to man. *And God is faithful; he will not let you be tempted beyond what you can bear. But when you are tempted, he will also provide a way out so you can stand up under it.*"[44] God will find a way out for us, but He expects us to seek His help. "Submit yourselves, then, to God," James says. "Resist the devil and he will flee from you."[45]

2. *The Word of God.* One of the best illustrations of the power of the Word of God is found in the gospel of Luke. At the beginning of Luke 4, Jesus Christ was led by the Spirit into the wilderness to be tempted by Satan. Satan first asked Jesus to turn a stone into bread, then he offered Jesus the world if He would worship him. Satan offers the same today if we will but follow him. Finally Satan asked Jesus to put God to a foolish test by jumping off a high place, but Jesus refused. Neither should we put God to a test—doing foolish

---

[44]1 Corinthians 10:13   [45]James 4:7

things, expecting Him to take care of us, is both
provocative and presumptuous. Finally, Jesus returned in the power of the Holy Spirit into Gali-
lee. Jesus was in the custody of the Holy Spirit
all the time He was being tested.

Jesus used the Word of God every time Satan
asked Him to do something, quoting passages
from the book of Deuteronomy. The Word of
God gives us clear convictions to live by in times
of testing, helping us to take a stand on Jesus'
side. If we don't depend on the Word of God for
our convictions, we easily fall into conventional
living, doing what others to.

I can imagine what may have transpired after
Jesus' temptations. Satan convenes all his helpers
from all over the world. "I was sorely defeated
by Jesus Christ," he tells them. "Every time I
tempted Him to do something, He quoted Scripture to me. The Holy Spirit drove the Word of
God right into my heart; it was impossible to
stand against it. So, in the future here's what I
want you to do: keep the Word of God out of
the hands of people and confuse them about the
work of the Holy Spirit." The Word of God is a
mighty weapon against the enemy! "I write to
you, young men," John says, "because you are
strong, and the word of God lives in you, and
you have overcome the evil one."[46] The Psalmist
obviously found it was helpful to memorize the
Word of God. "How can a young man cleanse
his way? By taking heed according to Your
word. Your word I have hidden in my heart, that
I might not sin against You."[47] The Word of God,
hidden in the heart, does help us to prepare for
battle.

[46]1 John 2:14b   [47]Psalm 119:9,11, NKJ

A few years ago I spent several days in Los Angeles. At the motel I was served breakfast morning after morning by a pretty young girl named Goldie. She called me "honey" and "sweetheart" each day when she took my order. I enjoyed the attention and the flattery; my deceitful heart began to get the best of me! One day she told me how difficult it was for a young woman to take care of two little children without a husband. Long ago I memorized 1 Timothy 5:22, which ends with the warning, "Keep thyself pure." As I was reviewing this verse one particular morning, the word "pure" stood out to me. I went down to breakfast with one thought in mind. Before Goldie could take my order, I said, "Goldie, I work with Billy Graham; I'm a preacher; I'm a happily married man with three children." The word of God spoke to the situation, and the rest of my stay in Los Angeles was much more pleasant.

3. **Prayer.** "Watch and pray," Jesus told His disciples, "lest you enter into temptation. The spirit indeed is willing, but the flesh is weak."[48] By starting each day with a time of meditation and prayer, we can prepare ourselves for the battles we will face on a given day. Proverbs says, "A prudent man foresees evil and hides himself, the simple pass on and are punished."[49] The wise person foresees difficulties ahead and prepares for them. Through prayer and meditation at the beginning of each day we can actually project ourselves into the day and prepare ahead of time for the events that will take place. Many times we can avoid pitfalls.

4. **The Holy Spirit.** Before He began His public ministry, Jesus was led up by the Spirit into the

[48]Matthew 26:41, NKJ   [49]Proverbs 22:3, NKJ

wilderness to be tempted, and He returned in the power of the Spirit. Through the use of the Word of God and by the power of the Spirit of God, He soundly defeated Satan. "Walk in the Spirit, and you shall not fulfill the lust of the flesh," Paul says. "For the flesh lusts against the Spirit, and the Spirit against the flesh; and these are contrary to one another, so that you do not do the things that you wish."[50] Our responsibility is to practice walking in the Spirit so that we might overcome the flesh. In Luke 9:23, we are admonished to deny self. In Romans 13:14, we are instructed to say no to the old man. We are to put on Christ and make no provision for the flesh. "You are of God, little children, and have overcome them, because He who is in you is greater than he who is in the world."[51] The Holy Spirit indwells every believer and provides the power to overcome our enemy.

5. *Faith.* "For whatever is born of God overcomes the world. And this is the victory that has overcome the world—our faith."[52] The Hebrew children in Daniel 3 were not afraid of the burning fiery furnace. They said, "Our God is able." David said to Goliath, "You come to me with a sword and a spear and a shield, but I come to you in the name of the Lord of Hosts." He had faith in God. Ten of the spies who went up to spy out the promised land came back with horror stories and said, "We are not able." But Joshua and Caleb said, "We are able." They had faith in God. "Without faith it is impossible to please God," Hebrews 11:6 says, "because anyone who comes to him must believe that he exists and that he rewards those who earnestly seek him."

[50]Galatians 5:16-17, NKJ   [51]1 John 4:4, NKJ   [52]1 John 5:4, NKJ

A good soldier will become well acquainted with his weapons because he needs them in the battle. The Christian soldier ought to be well acquainted with his weapons of warfare, too. We need to know the Word of God, memorize it, and use it in the battle. We must learn to use the weapon of prayer, through prayer to call down power from heaven. Finally, we need to learn to walk in the Spirit. What a power the Holy Spirit affords us! Using all the weapons God has provided, we can meet the enemy on his own ground and win the battle.

STUDY QUESTIONS - LESSON FOUR

Spiritual Warfare

1. I think you will agree with Dr. Jung (page 42), that evil plays a colossal role in the world today. List several current incidents that support this fact.

2. Where did evil originate? What do you think was the root cause? (pages 43, 44)

3. What caused the falling away of the Israelites and how can we avoid having this happen to us today? (pages 45, 46) Also, see 2 Corinthians 6:14-16.

4. Why are we our own worst enemy? (page 47)

5. What caused both King Saul and King David to go down in defeat? List one tragic result in each case. (pages 48, 49)

   • King Saul

   • King David

6. Why is tongue control so important to the believer? (pages 50, 51)

7. List two practical steps you can take to control your tongue.

8. What is the most important lesson you can learn about the devil? (pages 52, 53)

9. Study the rewards for victory on pages 54-59. By each resource below list one truth that can help you in the battle.

   • A sovereign God

   • The Word of God

   • Prayer

   • The Holy Spirit

   • Faith

10. Take your 5 key thoughts and write a paragraph stating your battle strategy that will lead to victory.

Memorize: Write 1 Peter 5:8 on a 3 x 5 card. Memorize and review daily during this course (page 53).

I am of the opinion that the chief dangers which confront the coming century [twentieth] will be religion without the Holy Spirit, Christianity without Christ, forgiveness without repentance, salvation without regeneration, politics without God, and heaven without hell.

(WILLIAM BOOTH, FOUNDER, SALVATION ARMY)

Walking in the Spirit

Today we can go into many churches without hearing much about the Holy Spirit or seeing much evidence of His work in the lives of the congregation. There seems to be little life and hardly any vitality. Today Satan does everything in his power to keep people from reading the Bible and discovering the full power of the Holy Spirit in their lives. But if we wish to live fruitful, productive lives and be equipped for ministry to others, we must understand and apply the work of the Holy Spirit in our own lives.

HIS INDWELLING

The Holy Spirit lives in every born-again believer. The Apostle Paul makes this indwelling very clear: "You, however, are controlled not by the sinful nature but by the Spirit, if the Spirit of God lives in you. And if anyone does not have the Spirit of Christ, he does not belong to Christ."[1] If I believe in Jesus Christ, then I have the Holy Spirit dwelling within me. Paul speaks of the indwelling Spirit in 1 Cor. 6:19-20: "Do you not know that your body is a temple of the Holy Spirit, who is in you, whom you have received from God? You are not your own; you were bought at a price. Therefore honor God with your body."

[1]Romans 8:9

There may be little evidence of His indwelling, but His power lies dormant within every believer. He is eager to release His power and demonstrate it in many different ways.

HIS WORKS

Jesus lived on the earth 33½ years. The last few years of His life were spent training His disciples. They watched Him feed the multitudes, calm the seas, heal the blind, and do many other miracles. They were fearful when they learned that He would be crucified and leave them alone here on earth. But He gave them this promise: "I will pray the Father, and He will give you another Helper, that He may abide with you forever."[2] We have that same Helper living in us today, standing by to assist us at every turn, and can seek His help daily.

In addition to being our Helper, the Holy Spirit is our Teacher. The Bible is a closed book to those who are without Christ—even believers sometimes find it hard to understand. The Holy Spirit makes the truth real to us. Jesus promised, "The Helper, the Holy Spirit, whom the Father will send in My name, He will teach you all things, and bring to your remembrance all things that I have said to you."[3] In the Holy Spirit the Christian has a special private tutor. Each time we open the Bible, our Teacher is ready to instruct us. Although we may find the Word a little hard to understand at the beginning, the more we read the more the Spirit enlightens us.

The Holy Spirit, Jesus said, is also our Guide. He has been down the road before us and knows all the turns, and He can save us from a lot of dead-ends and wasted time. He is able to help us interpret God's will for our lives and make wise decisions. He will help us in our work, if we will commit that to Him. Proverbs 16:3 says, "Commit your works to the Lord, and your thoughts will be established." Many times I have felt very muddled in my thinking. Having a lot to do, I just haven't known how to get

²John 14:16, NKJ   ³John 14:26, NKJ

things organized. I have found repeatedly, however, that spending a little time in prayer to seek God's guidance has made me able to lay out my priorities in order. As we seek God's face often, and ask for His guidance often, the Holy Spirit stands ready to guide.

In addition to helping, teaching, and guiding us, the Holy Spirit also *prays* **for us:** "Likewise the Spirit also helps in our weaknesses. For we do not know what we should pray for as we ought, but the Spirit Himself makes intercession for us with groanings which cannot be uttered. [And] He who searches the hearts knows what the mind of the Spirit is, because He makes intercession for the saints according to the will of God."[4] I pray every day, but sometimes I have a difficult time expressing to God what I really have on my heart. God searches our hearts and knows the deep longings that we have. What I am unable to articulate clearly to God, the Holy Spirit does for me. While we are at prayer, the Holy Spirit is helping us—a strong incentive for us to pray.

The Holy Spirit also *seals* **us in Christ:** "In Him you also trusted, after you heard the word of truth, the gospel of your salvation; in whom also, having believed, you were sealed with the Holy Spirit of promise, who is the guarantee of our inheritance until the redemption of the purchased possession, to the praise of His glory."[5] In everyday language, God assures us that until Jesus Christ comes to take us to be with Him forever, the Holy Spirit is keeping us. He is God's guarantee that Jesus will positively return.

The Holy Spirit seals us, and He *empowers* **us as well.** His power transforms weak, defeated Christians into dynamic witnesses for Jesus Christ. At the trial of Jesus, when he was accused by a maid of being the Lord's follower, Peter denied Him and said, "I don't know the man."[6] Yet, after Pentecost, Peter, filled with the Holy Spirit, boldly witnessed to the Jewish High Priest and other religious leaders. Acts 3 records Peter healing a lame man. In the fourth

---

[4]Romans 8:26-27, NKJ   [5]Ephesians 1:13-14, NKJ   [6]Matthew 26:72

chapter Peter is arrested and brought before the Sanhedrin
for questioning.

"And when they had set them in the midst, they asked,
'By what power or by what name have you done this?'
Then Peter, filled with the Holy Spirit, said to them, 'Rulers
of the people and elders of Israel: If we this day are judged
for a good deed done to the helpless man, by what means
he has been made well, let it be known to you all, and to
all the people of Israel, that by the name of Jesus Christ of
Nazareth, whom you crucified, whom God raised from the
dead, by Him this man stands here before you whole.'
Now when they saw the boldness of Peter and John, and
perceived that they were uneducated and untrained men,
they marveled. And they realized that they had been with
Jesus. And seeing the man who had been healed standing
with them, they could say nothing against it."[7]

Peter and John were uneducated and untrained men and
yet they spoke with boldness as the Holy Spirit gave them
power. Jesus promised, "You will receive power when the
Holy Spirit has come upon you; and you will be witnesses
to Me in Jerusalem, and in all Judea and Samaria, and to the
end of the earth."[8] The Holy Spirit gives us a dynamic for
living, a supernatural power to be witnesses for Jesus
Christ. We need to surrender daily to that power.

The Holy Spirit not only empowers, He gives *gifts:*
"There are different kinds of gifts, but the same Spirit.
There are different kinds of service, but the same Lord.
There are different kinds of working, but the same God
works all of them in all men. Now to each one the mani-
festation of the Spirit is given for the common good."[9]

The Holy Spirit gives different gifts to different people,
and these gifts are usually discovered when they begin to
be used within the life of the local church. As we get involved in the church's training and outreach, and as we
grow and develop in Christ, others may recognize our gifts
before we do and press us into the service of the church.

[7]Acts 4:7-10, 13-14, NKJ   [8]Acts 1:8, NKJ   [9]1 Corinthians 12:4-7

The Apostle Paul makes some very important observations at the end of chapter 12. There are many members in this body, he says, but their *gifts differ.* Because one member has the gift of teaching does not mean that I should teach. God may have an entirely different calling for me. We should not compare ourselves to others, but rather surrender moment by moment to the Holy Spirit, the giver of gifts, and let Him equip us as He will.

HIS LOVE

Paul closes chapter 12 with a most practical and needy challenge: "But eagerly desire the greater gifts. And now I will show you the most excellent way."[10] More important than all these gifts is love. We can speak with tongues, prophesy, be full of knowledge, have faith to move mountains, give all we have to the poor, and even give our lives to be burned, but if we don't have love it is all for nothing.[11]

The world is hungering for love. Our wives, our husbands, our children are starving for love. Love could revolutionize the cause of Christ, change families, set churches aglow, and unite believers in Christ. Our adversary knows this all too well, and so he occupies us with other issues.

For years after my discharge from the United States Army I was involved in the Navigator ministry. As a Navigator Director, I taught Scripture memory, led in Bible Studies, directed many conferences, and worked in a discipling ministry. I knew many Scripture verses by memory, and had a fair knowledge of the Bible through study, but it was mostly in my head and didn't show in my life. I lived for the most part by the letter of the law. Like the Pharisees, I was very legalistic, long on obedience to the Scripture, but short on compassion, understanding, mercy, forgiveness, and love.

And legalism is deadly. I was dogmatic, demanding, domineering, and demeaning. I was never satisfied. My wife

[10]1 Corinthians 12:31   [11]1 Corinthians 13:1-3

could do nine things right and one wrong, and I would always find fault with her failures, but rarely praised her for any good thing. I played God and majored on minors, not realizing how poorly I was coming across to people. I was insensitive to the feelings of others and filled with the pride God hates.

At last, God in His faithfulness stepped in to show me the error of my ways. My faithful wife LaRue put up with me long enough; then one day she let me have it. "You are impossible to live with," she said. "I can never measure up to your demands. I ought to leave you now."

That encounter with my wife made me miserable, but I refused to take responsibility for our problems. Then I faced another jolt—this time by the Navigator staff and leadership. They confronted me in love, but were very straightforward about my lack of spiritual leadership. I was put on probation, and the discipline drove me to my knees and to my wife. Through these two harsh encounters, God was able to get my attention and do some new things in my life. I began to see how legalistic I was, and how sorely I needed the love of God in my life. As I began to meditate on 1 Corinthians 13, wonderful changes began to occur in my life and my relationships with others.

Jesus was very firm in His insistence that we love one another. He said, "A new commandment I give to you, that you love one another; as I have loved you, that you also love one another."[12] But Jesus knew that we would have trouble loving one another. We are selfish and self-centered people; we can never generate love. To enable us to carry out His command to love one another, He gives us His Holy Spirit: "And hope does not disappoint us, because God has poured out his love into our hearts by the Holy Spirit, whom he has given us."[13]

HIS CONTROL

Concerning the control of the Holy Spirit in our lives, Paul says, "Do not get drunk on wine, which leads to de-

[12]John 13:34, NKJ   [13]Romans 5:5

bauchery. Instead, be filled with the Spirit."[14] In order for Him to control our lives, we need to yield continually to this control. Surrender to Him is not once-for-all, but a moment by moment, day by day yielding to His control. And such surrender is not an option, but a command. Every believer should be Spirit-filled.

When an individual is Spirit-filled, the results will be very evident in his life:

1. *Victory.* "This I say then: Walk in the Spirit, and you shall not fulfill the lust of the flesh."[15] One of the biggest battles that we face as Christians is the temptation to give in to our lustful nature. A Spirit-led, Spirit-controlled Christian will demonstrate consistency in his life. He will learn to say no to the "old man" and say yes to the "new man." He will learn to deny self and walk consistently in the Spirit.

2. *Power.* "But you will receive power when the Holy Spirit has come upon you; and you will be witnesses to Me in Jerusalem, and in all Judea and Samaria, and to the end of the earth."[16] We will have power, boldness, unembarrassed freedom of speech when we walk in the Spirit. This supernatural dynamic, sooner or later, should be evidenced in the believer's life.

3. *Quality.* "But when the Holy Spirit controls our lives he will produce this kind of fruit in us: love, joy, peace, patience, kindness, goodness, faithfulness, gentleness and self-control; and here there is no conflict with Jewish laws."[17] One of the greatest evidences of the Spirit-filled and controlled life is love. When the Holy Spirit is not in control, one's life will be very unattractive, as Galatians 5:19-21 demonstrates. But the person who habitually allows the Spirit of God to con-

---

[14]Ephesians 5:18   [15]Galatians 5:16, NKJ   [16]Acts 1:8, NKJ   [17]Galatians 5:22-23, TLB

trol him will have a Christ-like quality of life: "We all, with unveiled face, beholding as in a mirror the glory of the Lord, are being transformed into the same image from glory to glory, just as by the Spirit of the Lord."[18]

Every day, as I give my life back to God as a living sacrifice, I surrender my life afresh and anew to the Holy Spirit's control. I have lived too much of my life in the energy of the flesh, and I know the frustration of such a life. I pray to God that the rest of my life might be lived in the Spirit, truly manifesting the love of God.

Walking in obedience and walking in the Spirit are not something we do naturally. Surrender to the Spirit demands yieldedness and discipline. There's a price to be paid. But we can enter into the Spirit-controlled life through:

1. *Confession,* 1 John 1:9. Confess all known sin.

2. *Obedience,* Ephesians 5:18. Keep on being filled.

3. *Practice,* Galatians 5:16. Learn to walk in the Spirit.

Learning to live the Christian life is like learning to walk. There will be many ups and downs, especially in the beginning. As the Psalmist points out, "The Lord delights in the way of the man whose steps he has made firm; though he stumble, he will not fall, for the Lord upholds him with his hand."[19]

When my children were learning to walk, they often fell down—but they didn't stay down. They reached out to the hands their mother and I extended to them, and got back on their feet. Similarly, we learn to walk one step at a time in the Spirit. When we fall by sinning against God, we can reach out to Him through prayer, accepting His merciful helping hand.

We are admonished in the Bible not to quench the Holy Spirit and not to grieve Him. Little is said in the Bible about what it means to quench and grieve the Spirit; how-

[18]2 Corinthians 3:18, NKJ   [19]Psalm 37:23-24

ever most Bible scholars will agree that when we sin, we grieve or quench Him. His power becomes nullified in our life, and fellowship with our Heavenly Father is broken. When we confess our sins, God forgives us and cleanses us. Thus, we are restored into fellowship. We surrender afresh to the Holy Spirit so that He can control our lives. We are put back on our feet again by the help of a loving Heavenly Father's hand. Like the child who grows to adulthood, as we mature we will stay on our feet more consistently, walking in the Spirit and giving glory to God through our obedience.

Paul, in the book of Acts, states, "And herein do I exercise myself, to have always a conscience void of offence toward God, and toward men."[20] In that way you can go to bed tonight at peace, clean. The "clear conscience" principle is a good one by which to live.

---

[20]Acts 24:16, KJV

STUDY QUESTIONS - LESSON FIVE

Walking in the Spirit

1. Respond to William Booth's statement on page 62. What evidence do you see today that confirms his prophetic word? (Give a word of explanation.)

2. On pages 64-66 several truths concerning the works of the Spirit are found. Review the works and for each work list one helpful truth, which if applied, could enrich your life.

   • Helper

   • Teacher

   • Guide

   • Prays

   • Seals

   • Empowers

   • Gifts

3. Circle key words and underline key thoughts concerning the need for love. (pages 67, 68)

4. From the key words and thoughts, what lessons can you learn concerning the need for expressing love to others? (List several)

5. From pages 69 and 70, what can you learn about the Spirit-filled-and-controlled life, and why is it so important to be Spirit-controlled?

   a. What can I learn?

   b. Why is it so important?

6. What practical steps can you take to learn to walk in the Spirit? (pages 70-71)

Memorize: Write Galatians 5:16 on a 3 x 5 card. Memorize and review daily during this study course. (page 69)

M*an's hatred of the Bible has been of the most persistent, determined, relentless, and bitter character. It has led to 18 centuries of repeated attempts to undermine faith in the Bible, and to consign the Bible itself to oblivion. . . . Every engine of destruction that human philosophy, human science, human reason, human art, human cunning, human force, and human brutality could bring to bear against the book has been brought to bear against this Book, and yet the Bible stands absolutely unshaken today. At times almost all the wise and great of the earth have been pitted against the Bible, and only an obscure few for it. Yet, it has stood.*

(DR. R. A. TORREY)

6

Applying the Scriptures

The Bible has stood through the ages because it is the Word of God. "The grass withers, the flower fades, but the word of our God stands forever."[1]

Recognizing the power of the Word, accepting the promises in the Word, making practical applications to the Word, and practicing time alone in the Word deepen our relationship with Christ.

THE POWER OF THE WORD OF GOD

Man may try to eradicate the Word, and Satan may attempt to choke out the seed, but the Bible will stand. The fact that the Bible is alive and life-giving gives it both power and longevity.

"The word of God is living and active. Sharper than any double-edged sword, it penetrates even to dividing soul and spirit, joints and marrow; it judges the thoughts and attitudes of the heart."[2]

More than a collection of words on pages, the Bible is "God-breathed." God's authority and power are present in every word and can penetrate into the deepest parts of our

[1]Isaiah 40:8, NKJ   [2]Hebrews 4:12

being. God describes His Word as a "seed" and as a "sword," a "hammer" and "fire." Multitudes through the ages, from kings to peasants, have had their lives radically changed through the Word, because through it the living God speaks to us through the power of His irresistible Holy Spirit.

PROMISES IN THE WORD OF GOD

The Bible is filled with promises, many that relate to blessings which come as we study and apply the Scriptures to our lives. One such promise appears in 2 Timothy 3:16-17: "All Scripture is God-breathed and is useful for teaching, rebuking, correcting and training in righteousness, so that the man of God may be thoroughly equipped for every good work."

This passage promises growth, productiveness, and maturity through application of the Word of God. Paul says that study of the Word and obedience to it will result in four important developments in our lives:

1. *A solid foundation in the basic doctrines of the Bible.* We need to have a clear understanding of what the Bible teaches about salvation, the Holy Spirit, baptism, santification, and the second coming. What we believe affects our behavior and the course of our lives.

2. *Rebuke from the Scripture.* The Holy Spirit uses the Scriptures to point out any behavior that is displeasing to God—perhaps the company we keep, cheating, lying, an immoral act or any disobedience. Through the conviction of the Word, God shapes our lives and conforms us to the image of Jesus Christ.

3. *Correction in the direction of our lives.* As we study the Bible, God will give us a new perspective for living. We begin to see the value of living according to His plan and purpose. Beyond the

censoring of rebuke, God speaks through His
Word the positive aspects of correction—we are
turned *from* our sin *toward* a whole new life-
style of pleasing God.

4. *Instruction in righteousness.* Not only will God
   censor our behavior and give us a new direction
   for our lives, He will "lead us in paths of righteousness." He promises to be our Instructor: "I
   will instruct you . . . and guide you along the
   best pathway for your life; I will advise you and
   watch your progress."[3]

As we study and apply God's Word, He leads us down
the pathway to purity, honesty, humility, holiness of life,
and victory over the world, the flesh and the devil. As we
progress along these scriptural paths, we mature and become equipped for every branch of service.

A second promise concerning the blessings of obedience
to the Word appears in Psalm 1:1-3:

*"Oh, the joys of those who do not follow evil men's
advice, who do not hang around with sinners,
scoffing at the things of God. But they delight in
doing everything God wants them to, and day and
night are always meditating on his laws and
thinking about ways to follow him more closely.
They are like trees along a river bank bearing lus-
cious fruit each season without fail. Their leaves
shall never wither, and all they do shall prosper."*

For years we lived in a home which had a creek in the
back yard. Huge trees lined the bank of this creek throughout our neighborhood. The roots of the trees reached
down into the unending moisture supply. Sometimes during the heat of summer the creek became almost dry, but
the trees never lacked water to sustain their growth. Their
lofty branches and well-nourished leaves provided a cool
shaded area where the children played. In the fall these

[3]Psalm 32:8, TLB

huge maples and oaks added brilliance to the landscape
with their red, yellow, orange and golden hues.

As Christians, we are like these trees planted along a
riverbank. God is our unending source of energy, power,
and divine moisture. His Word supplies all the nutrients for
healthy growth. But one condition is required for growth
and fruitfulness. We *must* give God's Word a prominent
place in our lives. To meditate day and night doesn't mean
carrying the open Bible everywhere we go—school, the office, the shop, or the factory. Rather, we carry the Bible in
our hearts and thoughts. The Word can shape our thinking
and our behavior. According to this passage in Psalms,
when we do give a high priority to the Bible in our lives,
several observable results begin to appear:

1. *Pleasure* or happiness will result from aligning
   our lives with the Word of God instead of the
   negative thinking of the world.

2. *Productivity* and progress continue regardless of
   circumstance.

3. *Prosperity* will be the norm. God's touch on our
   lives will be evidenced in all that we do. Material
   wealth might or might not be our lot. But the
   more important values—peace, fellowship with
   God, a fruitful ministry—are assured to those
   who sink their roots into His Word. The Bible
   says, "As sorrowful, yet always rejoicing; as poor,
   yet making many rich; as having nothing, and
   yet possessing all things."[4]

When our lives are deeply rooted in Christ we are spiritually rich regardless of circumstances. We are "heirs of
God, and joint-heirs with Christ."[5] We may not be rich in
this world's goods, but we can share the imperishable
riches of Christ with others.

A third promise from Scripture, like the second, promises prosperity and success. "Do not let this Book of the

[4]2 Corinthians 6:10, NKJ   [5]Romans 8:17, KJV

Law depart from your mouth," God commanded Joshua. "Meditate on it day and night, so that you may be careful to do everything written in it. Then you will be prosperous and successful."[6] Obedience is the main principle taught in this passage—obedience to God by following His law, commandments, precepts, testimonies, or statutes. Again we are admonished to meditate day and night. We are to look at the Scripture over and over until we get a clear picture of what it says. What is God asking us to do? How does this compare to our present behavior?

The Psalmist approached the Scripture in the same way: "I thought about my ways, and turned my feet to Your testimonies. I made haste, and did not delay to keep Your commandments."[7] The Psalmist meditated on the Word, looking at the Word and then at his own life. Where he saw discrepancies, he corrected them according to the teaching of the Word. He lived in conformity to the truth.

The life of obedience brings about many additional benefits. Psalm 119 lists a number of results that come from hearing and obeying the Word:

- A clean life (v. 9).
- Victory (v. 11).
- Answers for the critics (v. 42).
- A deeper understanding of life (v. 104).
- Light for our pathway (v. 105).
- Peace (v. 165).

God wants His people to enjoy a productive, fulfilling, victorious, and holy Christian life. He has made every provision for such a life, but many Christians never discover God's plan or tap into His resources. They stop short of the promised land; they get off God's pathway.

The writer of Hebrews discovered this problem: "Though by this time you ought to be teachers, you need someone to teach you . . . all over again."[8] Many Christians

---

[6]Joshua 1:8   [7]Psalm 119:59-60, NKJ   [8]Hebrews 5:12

have for years been taught by the best Bible expositors, read scores of good Christian books, listened to dozens of tapes, but are still spiritual babies whose immaturity can be triggered by the slightest test or temptation. Unfortunately, this illustrates many of us today—many years in Christ, but little spiritual growth to show for it.

The Apostle Paul dealt with the same problem in Corinth. In 1 Corinthians 3:1-4, he calls the believers there "infants in Christ"—babies who could not be fed with the "meat" of the Word but had to be bottle-fed with the "milk" of basic teaching. Their lives were characterized by jealousy, quarreling, and factions; the church was divided, and the believers' individual growth was stagnant.

But God gave us His Word not only to increase our knowledge, but to change our lives. The Pharisees knew the law and kept it religiously, but their behavior was terrible. Jesus called them hypocrites; He might well level the same charge at us today. We take an academic approach to the Bible, gaining a theoretical knowledge, but fail to apply the truth of the Bible to life. I can know, for example, that God is holy and that I am exhorted to a life of holiness, yet live immorally. I can know that the Bible teaches honesty and yet be dishonest. We need to work the scriptural principles into our life-style as described by James:

> *"Don't, I beg you, only hear the message, but put it into practice; otherwise you are merely deluding yourselves. The man who simply hears and does nothing about it is like a man catching the reflection of his own face in a mirror. He sees himself, it is true, but he goes on with whatever he was doing without the slightest recollection of what sort of person he saw in the mirror. But the man who looks into the perfect mirror of God's law, the law of liberty, and makes a habit of so doing, is not the man who sees and forgets. He puts that law into practice and he wins true happiness.*[9]

'James 1:22-25, Phillips

The Bible is a mirror. When we look intently into the mirror of the Word, we see ourselves as God and others see us. The mirror exposes the filth, dirt, and grime that need the Spirit's cleansing so that our lives become "a vessel for honor, sanctified and useful for the Master."[10]

PRACTICAL APPLICATION OF THE WORD OF GOD

Making the Bible part of our lives should be uppermost in our thoughts if we desire to please God and live productive lives.

1. *Gaining knowledge and understanding.* Proverbs 2 uses strong verbs in describing the believer's attitude toward God's Word: "My son, if you *receive* my words, and *treasure* my commands within you, so that you *incline* your ear to wisdom, and *apply* your heart to understanding; yes, if you *cry out* for discernment, and *lift up* your voice for understanding, if you *seek* her as silver, and *search* for her as for hidden treasures; then you will understand the fear of the Lord, and find the knowledge of God. For the Lord gives wisdom; from His mouth come knowledge and understanding."[11] We will never get to know the deep things of God by reading a little devotional thought each day; we must seriously discipline our minds if we want to profit from our Bible study. If I truly want to know God more intimately and enjoy His wisdom and understanding, I will have to seek His face through earnest prayer, dig deeply into the Word as if I were mining for gold in order to treasure the nuggets of His Word in my heart. We need discipline if we are to know God more intimately.

[10]2 Timothy 2:21, NKJ   [11]Proverbs 2:1-6, NKJ

2. *Gaining a grasp of Scripture.* The "hand illustration" used by the Navigators illustrates how to
get a firm grasp of Scripture. Each finger and the
thumb represents a definite method of intake or
retention.

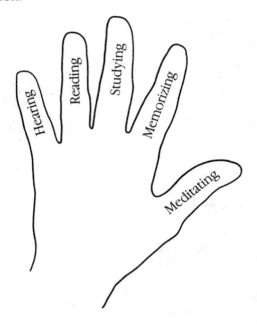

We forget 90 percent of what we hear. If we
want to retain knowledge of the Bible, therefore,
we must do more than just listen. Scripture
memory pays the greatest dividends in Bible
knowledge (100 percent), but meditation is necessary to make the Bible a part of one's life. Meditation, giving attention to truth with the intention of doing something about it, is the key to
application and assimilation of the Scriptures.

The digestive process provides a good illustration of scriptural intake. I put in the food: bread,

meat, vegetables—all the various things I eat. My digestive system turns the food into physical energy that keeps me alive and well. It creates new cells in my body and moves life-giving power through the bloodstream.

We can "digest" the Bible and assimilate its truths into our lives the same way. Jeremiah 15:16 says, "Your words were found, and I ate them, and Your word was to me the joy and rejoicing of my heart; for I am called by Your name, O Lord God of hosts." The prophet Jeremiah didn't place a page of Holy Writ in his mouth, chew on it, and swallow. He "chewed" on the Word of God as a cow chews the cud in order to extract nourishment. Jeremiah ruminated on the Word and thus assimilated it into his life.

3. *Gaining right thought patterns.* Some time ago, at the Ocean Grove Conference Center in New Jersey, I found this inscription over the speaker's platform:

SOW . . .	REAP . . .
a thought	an act
an act	a habit
a habit	a character
a character	a destiny.

The "sowing and reaping" illustration shows how the Word of God becomes a part of our lives. If I sow a scriptural thought on honesty, I reap an act of honesty. If I sow repeatedly the act of honesty in my daily life, I reap the habit of honesty. If I sow the habit of honesty, I reap an honest character. I become known as an honest man; a man whose word can be believed. Six months from now I will be living an honest life because I have put myself on God's scriptural pathway to honesty. If I am pulled off the path

by an act of dishonesty, I will recognize it immediately. The Holy Spirit uses the Scripture to con-
vict me. I confess my sin, making amends where
I need to, and get back on the pathway again.
Living by the Scripture is a way of life.

Where we are six months or a year from now
in our spiritual pilgrimage will depend largely on
what we are feeding into our minds today. "Garbage in = garbage out." On the contrary, if we
sow scriptural thoughts daily, those thoughts will
become acts, habits, and character.

PRACTICING TIME ALONE WITH GOD

Some time ago I was teaching counseling classes in San
Francisco, emphasizing the Quiet Time, or time alone with
God. After the class a Naval officer came to me with an experience that illustrated the importance of starting the day
with God. "We keep our ships on course," he told me, "by
what is known as the 'Celestial Fix.' With our instruments
fixed on the stars, we can tell exactly where we are on the
trackless ocean, and whether or not we need to correct
our course."

Believers need a "Celestial Fix" on God for daily guidance. Proverbs 15:3 says, "The eyes of the Lord are in
every place, keeping watch on the evil and the good." His
eyes scan like a surveillance camera. He knows where we
are at any given moment. When we tune in daily with
open hearts, desiring direction, He will show us where we
are and guide us back on course if we have drifted. Psalm
143:8 (NKJ) says, "Cause me to hear Your lovingkindness in
the *morning*, for in You do I trust; cause me to know the
way in which I should walk, for I lift up my soul to You."

Just before I entered the Army in 1942, my pastor came
to visit and encourage me. "How's your Quiet Time, Charlie?" he asked. I had none. But God was beginning a new
work in my life after many years of wandering in the wilderness, and my pastor's query about my devotional habits

challenged me to start each day with the Lord. I began the next day, and have maintained that practice for 43 years, missing very few days in all those years. Every day I have felt responsible to God. The Holy Spirit has gone with me everywhere, holding me responsible for all my actions. Paul reminds us, "We are the temple of the living God. As God has said: 'I will live with them and walk among them, and I will be their God, and they will be my people.'"[12]

The realization that the all-knowing, all-powerful, ever-present God lives within us makes a great difference in our conduct. God dwells in me, walks in me, and goes everywhere I go. As I learn to empty myself of self, God occupies a larger place in my life. My hope and prayer is to be "filled with all the fullness of God," as the Apostle Paul prayed,[13] to "know the love of Christ which passes knowledge."

For years I had the goal of never missing church. I was faithful in weekly worship. But now, in addition, I enjoy a daily relationship with God—and what a difference it has made! My daily walk enhances the weekly worship and makes it much more meaningful. As I sing, "Praise God From Whom All Blessings Flow," I think of all that God has done during the past week as I have walked daily with Him. Each day, after spending time devotionally, I should say, "Okay, God, let's go. What exciting things do you have in store for me today?" Enoch and Noah walked with God. Brother Lawrence, a 17th Century Carmelite monk, practiced the presence of God throughout each day. We can add our names to the list of those who walked with God by daily fellowship with Him in the Word.

If I were invited to have breakfast at the White House with the President, I would certainly be excited. Anyone, Democrat or Republican, would count it a great privilege to meet with our Head of State. But every day we can have breakfast with the King of kings, the Lord of lords, the Creator of the universe, the all-wise and all-powerful God. Ac-

[12]2 Corinthians 6:16   [13]Ephesians 3:19, NKJ

cording to John 4:24, God seeks for us to worship Him.
He has extended a special invitation to all of us to come to
breakfast. For years now, I have accepted that daily invitation. With my open Bible I sit at the table with the living
God. When He speaks, His pure eyes penetrate me, especially if I have been willful in my attitude. But His love,
mercy, and compassion lift and encourage me, and prepare
me for our walk together. What a difference it makes
throughout each day!

*Time alone with God is the most important time of
every day.* If we start each day with a "Celestial Fix" and
plug into God's "guidance system" for the day, we can develop a deep root system in the Word.

1. *Set a time.* Most of the successful Christians I
   know start their day with the Lord when the
   mind is fresh and rested. If we start the day with
   the Lord and walk with Him through the day,
   we can practice the presence of God.

2. *Find a quiet place.* In the Army I found it difficult to be alone. But I sat on my footlocker and
   read the Bible while 39 other occupants of the
   barracks came and went to breakfast. After reading my Bible, I would walk and pray—as I do to
   this day—to get my blood circulating and lift my
   voice to God. Psalm 46:10 says, "Be still and
   know that I am God." If I am in a quiet place, it
   doesn't take long to "lock in" to God and to
   have Him chart my course for the day.

3. *Make it a daily habit.* A person's devotional
   time can take many different forms. I often read
   the Bible in a modern translation and, with a
   colored highlighter, mark key words or verses.
   Many times I will write out the key verses on 3"
   by 5" cards and commit them to memory. In addition, I usually review a number of these verses
   as a part of my devotional time. Whatever
   method may be used, the consistency of a per-

son's devotional life is the key to growth. If we get into the habit of a daily Quiet Time, we will begin to see new light in the Word. Before long, Bible truth will begin to stand out like mountain peaks. Without searching for it, we will be able to mentally visualize a page and remember some prominent truths. Chapter after chapter will open like a flower with all its fragrance. We will discover truths which, through application, can change our lives and we will be equipped to share with confidence what God has revealed to us.

Although many have tried to destroy or suppress its truth, the Bible has stood for centuries as a beacon of God's light to those who look to Him. The Word is "God-breathed," alive, powerful, able to change, purify, and conform us to the image of Jesus Christ. As we learn to assimilate the Scriptures our lives begin to reflect the glory, the power, and the promise of the God who has spoken to His people.

STUDY QUESTIONS - LESSON SIX

Applying the Scriptures

1. What do you learn about the Bible on pages 74, 75? (Including Dr. R.A. Torrey's statement)

2. In your own words, what does 2 Timothy 3:16, 17 say about your progressing as a Christian? (pages 76,77)

3. What do you think it means to meditate? List several fruits resulting from meditation. (pages 77,78)

4. If the promises on pages 76-80 are true, why are we not seeing more mature, fully equipped, productive Christians?

5. Under "Gaining Knowledge and Understanding" on page 81, circle key words and underline key thoughts. What can you learn from these verses that will help you grow as a Christian?

6. In your mind, what is the most important lesson you can learn from the "Hand" illustration? (pages 82, 83)

7. How can the "Sow-Reap" illustration help you in your daily walk? (pages 83, 84)

8. Circle key words and underline key thoughts related to practicing time alone with God. (pages 84-87) List several practical suggestions that relate to the Quiet Time.

9. In a few words, why is the Quiet Time or Time Alone With God important? Share briefly your plan for daily devotions.

Memorize: Copy Joshua 1:8 on a 3 x 5 card. Memorize and review daily during this study course. (pages 78, 79)

The spectacle of a nation praying is more awe-inspiring than the explosion of an atomic bomb. The force of prayer is greater than any possible combination of man-controlled powers, because prayer is man's greatest means of tapping the infinite resources of God.

(J. EDGAR HOOVER)

Practicing Prayer

Most of my adult life I have been out of my league socially, educationally and spiritually. My work has put demands on me that have stretched me to the limit and beyond. In other words, I have been over my head. I've been doing things that are not natural for me to do, and it has been good for me. I have had to spend a lot of time on my knees, looking up to a sovereign God who has been a constant helper.

I have learned that prayer is more of an attitude than a posture or a form of expression. An attitude of dependence on God. A realization that I am not sufficient and need help. I can't do it but God can help me do it. As the song says, "I need thee every hour," or "Learning to Lean." Our whole life, when it is lived to the glory of God, can be a form of prayer. We learn to lean on Jesus throughout every day for help to live a supernatural life in a tough, worldly environment. It is like "praying without ceasing."[1]

HOW IT STARTED WITH ME

This absolute dependence on God started for me as a result of a traumatic experience when I was 19 years old. I had barely finished high school and my church brotherhood elected me to be president. My older brother, Jim,

[1]cf., 1 Thessalonians 5:17, KJV

thought it was a good idea to put a younger man in office who might influence other young men to become active in the brotherhood. Shortly after the election a dinner was held for the men in the brotherhood organization and their wives. About 60 people turned out for the occasion. As I arrived at the dinner, I was asked to give a speech which I was in no way prepared to do. As I mentioned, in the first chapter, we were a family of eight with no father at home, and all of us had to work at an early age. I had no interest in books, social activities, choral groups, debate clubs, drama or other activities that would have enriched my high school years. Instead, I went home from school for a bite to eat and then to the bowling alley at 5:00 to set up pins. I did this for all four years of high school.

As you can imagine, my speech went over like a "lead balloon." All I said was, "Ladies and Gentlemen," and I blacked out. My tongue was tied, I couldn't think of a thing to say. My pride was crushed. I was embarrassed and right then I determined that would never happen again. I never officiated at one brotherhood meeting. First, I enrolled in a night course that kept me busy on the nights the brotherhood met. Then I concocted all kinds of reasons for not being available. For the seven years following, I worked in the Pennsylvania oil fields and like Jonah, I ran from the Lord. I avoided any responsibility of leadership and I paid dearly for it. Tie your arm to your side for six months and without use it atrophies. The muscle deteriorates and it takes therapy and exercise to restore its use. The tongue is a muscle and for seven years I didn't make proper use of it. Many a day I worked all alone pumping oil. I worked with men of little education and all their language, much of the time, was not fit to repeat. After a few years, without a normal social life, interaction with other sharp Christians, reading books and developing my mind, my tongue atrophied. I found it difficult to express myself. Words would not come to mind. I developed a slight speech impediment and at times ended sentences in the middle for lack of words. The worse it became, the more I withdrew.

But God had something in mind for me, and turned my life around at 25 years of age. Whether it was my mother's prayers or my older brother, I don't know. I started to take an interest in spiritual things. I became involved with other young people in Bible study at the church. At one point we went as a group to a "Singspiration Rally" where I can remember being challenged. The speaker closed by saying, "Let God have your life to develop the innate potential that is resident in every believer." One day shortly after that, I was on one end of a six-foot crosscut saw felling a tree. The thought came back to me, "Let God have your life." Right then, I said, "God, I don't have much to offer, but I want you to use me." It was a feeble prayer but from the heart. It wasn't long before I was inducted in the U.S. Army, and God began to answer that prayer.

A NEW START

Within weeks I was instructed to report to my induction station. I'll never forget the scene in the living room of our little home in Olean, New York. I hugged my little mother with tears streaming down my cheeks. I had been the breadwinner for several years, and now the government allotment check would have to take over. I knew that God would not let her down.

I prayed all the way to the induction center at Ft. Niagara. Many of my buddies wanted me to sign up for the Army "Ski Troopers." I was a member of the local cross-country ski team. Somehow, I had enough sense to seek God's will and let Him make the assignment. Within three days, I was on a troop train that carried me from Niagara Falls, New York, to the San Francisco Bay area. It seemed I prayed all the way.

DEVELOPING THE INNATE POTENTIAL

For the next four years I was in the army, where I was out of my league and over my head most of the time, but

God went with me. In the previous Chapter, I related how my pastor had introduced me to the Quiet Time and the importance of starting the day with the Lord. Additionally, my brother gave me a "Daily Guide" with a verse, a thought, and a prayer for each day; and I used it daily.

I felt impelled to memorize the verses each day. The first verse was a promise that God made to Jacob, "And, behold, I am with you, and will keep you wherever you go."[2] What a promise to claim as I was starting a new career miles away from my family.

At this first base in San Francisco, I met The Navigators and was introduced to their Scripture memory program. God had it all planned and that is the advantage of seeking His will and letting Him have His way. Within days, I was on a train again and this time to the Los Angeles port of embarkation, which was to become my base for the best part of the next 22 months.

OFF TO SCHOOL

Before I was inducted in the army, I prayed that God would make me a good solder for Jesus Christ. That, I thought, would make me a good soldier for my country. Within two weeks at the Los Angeles port, I was singled out to go to an ordinance school for three months in Stockton, California. God knew I needed training and developing. There I was trained in automotive ordinance; but, more important, I became involved in a very active group in a local church. Every Saturday night they held street meetings on a corner downtown, and I stood with them to sing and share my witness. As I met God daily to pray and read the Bible, God used those three months to develop some of that innate potential.

BACK TO BASE

Within six months after my return to the Los Angeles base, I was given three stripes and promoted to "Buck Ser-

[2]Genesis 28:15, RSV

geant." Now I had to babysit a barracks full of guys who wanted nothing but out. They were for the most part men from Brooklyn, Bronx, and Upstate New York. They were like David's band of men. "And everyone that was in distress and everyone that was in debt, and everyone that was discontented, gathered themselves unto him; and he became a captain over them."[3] For the next several months I had to ride herd on this band of men. My job was to drill, train, and supervise their work at the base automotive shop. You know that that took a lot of prayer. Each morning I would sit on my foot locker and read my devotional book. But I would take a walk to pray, because of all the noise from the men shouting to one another, dressing, making beds, and getting ready for the day. I was living in a mission field and God opened many opportunities for me to share Christ and take men to the base chapel. The Bible says, "For thou, Lord, wilt bless the righteous; with favor wilt thou compass him as with a shield."[4]

Having built up my body in the oil fields, I was able to compete athletically with most of them, and did. This gave them some respect for me as a regular guy, and God did the rest. It wasn't long before they were calling me Padre and coming to me for counsel and help. Being a good soldier for Jesus Christ does make one a good soldier for his country. Within months, I was sent to Officers' Training School for a 17-week course. God knew I needed the training and a new responsibility would make me more dependent upon Him.

OFFICERS' TRAINING

I barely passed the entrance exam. Ninety was the lowest score allowed and I passed with a 91. Most of the men in my class were college grads and with some professional training. It was a grueling 17-week course made up of hours of classroom, rigorous training, field exercises, and forced marches. I was way over my head once again and

[3]1 Samuel 22:2, KJV   [4]Psalm 5:12, KJV

prayed my way through the 17 weeks. What sustained me was the many verses I knew by heart and could meditate on during the day. Another verse from the "Daily Guide" that I learned and often used was "Fear thou not; for I am with thee: be not dismayed; for I am thy God: I will strengthen thee; yea, I will help thee; yea, I will uphold thee with the right hand of my righteousness."[5] God did all of that and more, and prepared me for more responsibility.

After my graduation I was assigned to the Seattle port of embarkation and made Property Officer for all the materials handling equipment in the port. Millions of dollars worth of equipment and a large number of personnel were my responsibility for the next 22 months until my discharge.

The best thing that happened to me during that 22-month period was meeting Lorne Sanny, Director of The Navigators work for the northwest area. For the best part of that time I attended a weekly Bible study in a Navigator home. God was answering prayer and filling a great void in my life. I became very active in the Navigators ministry and when discharged from the army in November 1946, Lorne Sanny asked me to join his staff in Seattle, Washington. I did. And after Christmas in 1946, I moved into the Navigators home to be discipled by Lorne Sanny. I was looking forward to learning from this man of God who was later to become President of The Navigators. Lorne was a person who led by example, and I learned so much from just watching him from day to day. He lived the Scriptures and taught me the value of personal application of its truth.

GOD CONTINUES TO WORK

Being taught by Lorne was short lived. By the end of summer in 1947, Lorne was moved back to California for a new assignment; and I was appointed Director of The Navigators for the northwest area. I marvel at the way God works in and through our lives to develop that innate potential. The Bible says, "For it is God who works in you to

[5]Isaiah 41:10, KJV

will and to act according to his good purpose."[6]

Now I was responsible for a ministry for which I had very little training or experience. To add to this responsibility, I was married in the summer of 1947 and started back to school in September. At this point, I was only six years out of the oilfields and, like Moses who said to the Lord, "O, my Lord, I am not eloquent, neither heretofore, nor since thou has spoken unto thy servant: but I am *slow of speech* and of a slow tongue."[7] I struggled through four years of army, with God's help. Now I was faced with marriage, school and The Navigators ministry. Realizing my inadequacy, I did like Paul and sought the Lord—not three times, but continuously and to this day. Paul had an infirmity which he asked God to remove. "Three times I pleaded with God to take it away from me. But he said to me, 'My grace is sufficient for you, for my power is made perfect in weakness.' Therefore I will boast all the more gladly about my weaknesses, so that Christ's power may rest on me. That is why, for Christ's sake, I delight in weaknesses, in insults, in hardships, in persecutions, in difficulties. *For when I am weak, then I am strong.*"[8]

What helped me most in the fall of 1947 was the realization that God could use my weakness and make me strong in Him. I learned to pray about everything and learned to lean on Him continually. School and my work with The Navigators helped further to develop that innate potential, and led me to even greater responsibilities.

BILLY GRAHAM CRUSADES

In 1951 Mr. Graham asked Dawson Trotman, founder of The Navigators, to help with Crusade counseling and follow-up. Lorne Sanny was one of The Navigators staff assigned to train counselors for the Billy Graham Crusades. In May of 1952, Lorne invited me to assist him in Houston, Texas, which I did and for several Crusades to follow. In London, England, in 1954, one of Lorne's classes had an

[6]Philippians 2:13   [7]Exodus 4:10, KJV   [8]2 Corinthians 12:8-12

overflow into another church hall. I was the only other BGEA staff member present, so they asked me to teach the overflow crowd. I would give anything to know what I taught that night. I did know a large number of Scripture verses by heart and had heard Lorne teach many times; but I had never taught before, and for obvious reasons. In a recent message, recorded in The Navigators Discipleship Journal, Lorne Sanny made this statement, "Before I met Charlie Riggs, he worked for seven years as a roughneck in the oilfields of Pennsylvania. The social graces weren't particularly prominent in his life. He could hardly talk without stuttering. If you asked a personnel board to consider him as a trainer for, of all things, a Billy Graham Crusade, he would have been last on the list. But God picked him."

When Jerry Beavan, the London Crusade Director, saw the interest in the counseling classes he decided to schedule additional classes for me to teach. Classes in Ilford, Ealing, and Watford—all towns at the very end of the London subway where I could practice without being too obvious. God was good in launching me into the teaching ministry. The Navigators and Crusade staff would not have naturally thought of me as a teacher because I was not articulate, but God saw something that they missed. As the Scripture says, "For the Lord seeth not as man seeth; for man looketh on the outward appearance, but the Lord looketh on the heart."[9]

The next year in Glasgow, Scotland, Lorne Sanny started the classes on a Monday night; and halfway through the first class he developed a voice problem and had to stop. He could not teach for the next two weeks. I took over all his classes while he was recuperating. I could tell many stories of how God sovereignly prepared me for what I am doing today. Let me share just one more.

NEW YORK CITY 1957

Mr. Graham held a Crusade in New York in 1957. It was

[9]1 Samuel 16:7, KJV

held in Madison Square Garden as a four-week Crusade and continued for 16½ weeks. This was his longest Crusade in the history of the Billy Graham Association. I went up to New York in the fall of 1956 to assist the Crusade Director and became heavily involved in the preparation of the Crusade. I was once again way over my head. Among other things, I taught counseling classes attended by corporate executives and pastors of very large churches. On Monday night I taught a class in Stamford, Connecticut. The Chairman of the Crusade was the late Roger Hull. He was President of Mutual of New York (MONY). He lived in Darien, Connecticut. I would ride up to Darien with Mr. Hull on Monday night, teach the class in nearby Stamford, and stay overnight at the Hulls. Mr. Hull and his wife Rosalie attended the classes. The Lord knit our hearts together during the several weeks of training. This was in preparation for the next big event in my life. God is good to us and He does answer our prayers.

DIRECTING THE NEW YORK CRUSADE

In early 1957 the Crusade Director took a sabbatical, making it necessary for a new Director to be appointed. The Executive Committee told Mr. Graham that I was their choice. Mr. Graham made this remark to the Executive and has repeated it often since. "What! Charlie Riggs? All he can do is quote Scripture and pray." I did a lot of praying during those days. It was not only the longest Crusade in the history of our organization but also the costliest. We were on television every Saturday night for several weeks.

It was during the New York Crusade that I was appointed Director of Counseling and Follow-up for the Billy Graham Association. After Mr. Trotman's death in 1956, Lorne Sanny was made President of The Navigators. His duties made it impossible for him to continue working with the Billy Graham Association. Mr. Graham graciously gave me the responsibility that Mr. Sanny carried for several years.

POWER IN WEAKNESS

For the past 32 years, I have been doing what is most difficult for me to do—and it has kept me on my knees. Whenever I speak or teach, I find myself praying over every verse and note, asking God to bring the message or lesson to life. I have taught counseling classes now for over 30 years and still follow the same practice day after day. I like to pray over every verse and note. And I have noted how God brings out a new freshness of thought, illustration, or other Scripture verses.

As I look back on the past 40 years since leaving the oilfields, I thank God for the way He works through weak vessels. "For [simply] consider your own call, brethren; not many [of you were considered to be] wise, according to human estimates and standards; not many influential and powerful; not many of high and noble birth. [No,] for God selected—deliberately chose—what in the world is foolish to put the wise to shame, and what the world calls weak to put the strong to shame. And God also selected—deliberately chose—[what] in the world [is] low born and insignificant, and branded and treated with contempt, even the things that are nothing, that He might depose and bring to nothing the things that are; so that no mortal man should [have pretense for glorying and] boast in the presence of God."[10]

PRACTICING PRAYER

Lorne Sanny said, "I don't need another book on prayer. I know enough about prayer. I simply must take time to pray. We will never find time, we must take time."

At the start of every new day I like to do two things. Give my life back to God as a living sacrifice (Romans 12:1). If we are growing, we should be giving our life back at a deeper level every day. Secondly, I surrender afresh and anew to the control of the Holy Spirit, and ask

[10]1 Corinthians 1:26-29, The Amplified Bible

God to help me walk in the Spirit. For years, it has been my habit to start the day with the Lord. After I have spent time in the Scriptures I like to walk and pray. Walking is good exercise and it keeps me alert. Meeting God in the morning is simply the beginning of the daily walk. I am learning, as Brother Lawrence did, to practice the presence of God. He lives in me and goes with me wherever I go. I am learning to lean on Him throughout the day for guidance, wisdom and strength. What a difference He makes in my day. "Those who wait on the Lord shall renew their strength; they shall mount up with wings like eagles, they shall run and not be weary, they shall walk and not faint."[11]

Let me encourage you to give your life back to God at a deeper level—a level beyond your own capability, where you must seek God's help to fulfill your responsibility. If you are equal, humanly speaking, to your responsibility, you don't need God. Commit yourself more deeply to the Lord, to where you have to pray for His help and begin to experience His good helping hand daily.

[11]Isaiah 40:31, NKJ

STUDY QUESTIONS - LESSON SEVEN

Practicing Prayer

1. Read and reread this short chapter on prayer. Underline key truths on each page that teach valuable lessons related to prayer and walking with God. List one or more truths from each page listed below.

- 91

- 92

- 93

- 94

- 95

- 96

- 97

- 98

- 99

- 100

- 101

2. From the truths you have listed, what do you learn about God's sovereignty? (How He works in our lives.)

3. What do you learn from the following verses that should help your prayer life and walk with God?

   • Isaiah 41:10 (page 96)

   • 2 Corinthians 12:8-12 (page 97)

   • 1 Samuel 16:7 (page 98)

   • 1 Corinthians 1:26-29 (page 100)

   • Isaiah 40:31 (page 101)

4. In your mind, why do Christians spend so little time in prayer?

5. What has helped you most in your own prayer life? Explain in a few words.

Memorize: Copy Isaiah 40:31 on a 3 x 5 card. Memorize and review daily during this study course. (page 101)

If we confess our sins,
he is faithful and just
and will forgive us our sins
and purify us
from all unrighteousness.

(1 John 1:9)

8

The Discipline of Confession

King Saul is one of the prominent figures in the Old Testament. Standing head and shoulders above everyone else as the first King of Israel, he exemplified how sin can spoil a relationship with God, destroy a career and ruin a life. Saul, the mighty warrior for God, didn't last long.

In 1 Samuel, we see the rise and fall of King Saul. In chapter ten the Spirit of God was promised to him so that he might become a new person. Subsequently, God gave Saul another heart, a new mind-set, a new purpose in life, and a new motivation. Then in chapter 13, Saul committed an act of disobedience (v. 13). As a result, he was told that he would be replaced by another person of God's choosing. One act of disobedience leads to another and yet another, as it did in the case of Saul.

In chapter 15, however, Saul seems to have had a reprieve, another chance. He is sent on a mission with specific instructions (vv. 1-3), but again, he disobeys God (verses 8-11). Then, as is common to all of us, he attempts to put the blame on others (vv. 20, 21). But each of us *must* take the responsibility for our actions. If not, we will go through life always blaming others. Samuel didn't accept Saul's excuses; he reminded the king, "Obedience is better than sacrifice; rebellion is as the sin of witchcraft, and stubbornness is as iniquity and idolatry." Samuel again foretells that Saul will lose his throne through disobedience (vv. 22, 23).

Soon after, a new king is anointed to replace Saul.[1] The Spirit of the Lord departs from Saul. From that moment on, disaster followed disaster. I have witnessed Christians lose the anointing of God in their lives as a result of sin. The Holy Spirit doesn't actually leave them, but they nullify His power and operate in the flesh; then, almost anything can happen.

In chapter 18, Saul, insanely jealous over the fact that David received more acclaim than he (vv. 6-9), did what many of us would do against people who receive more attention than we. He tried to destroy David (v. 10). From that moment on, Saul lived with one consuming desire: to eliminate David. He ended up a pathetic individual, no longer in communion with God, even stooping to the use of a medium in order to get some guidance from Samuel.

> "Now Samuel said to Saul, 'Why have you disturbed me by bringing me up?' And Saul answered, 'I am deeply distressed; for the Philistines make war against me, and God has departed from me and does not answer me anymore, neither by prophets nor by dreams. Therefore I have called you, that you may reveal to me what I should do.' Then Samuel said: 'Why then do you ask me, seeing the Lord has departed from you and has become your enemy?'"[2]

Doesn't your heart go out to Saul from whom God had departed, who no longer received answers from God? How would you like to be in that condition? Have you ever been there? Do you happen to be in that place now, completely cut off from God? What a lonely place to be!

---

[1]1 Samuel 16:13-14   [2]1 Samuel 28:15-16, NKJ

WHAT IS SIN?

Because of sin, many Christians today are in Saul's condition. But we face another problem—our poor definition of sin. The eminent psychiatrist, Dr. Carl Menninger, asks this probing question in his book, *Whatever Became of Sin?* Few of us want to face sin, the root cause of many of our problems. We rationalize, blaming the environment, blaming others, blaming God; but we will not admit, personally, that we are guilty of any wrongdoing. Our pride won't permit it. I have Christian friends, a husband and wife, who cannot live together. Although they say they love each other, they have to bear the cost of separate dwellings, professional counseling services, and loneliness. They bear the consequences of their sin, while a loving God stands ready and willing to pardon and to heal. Like this couple, we too, suffer the dreadful consequences of our pride and stubbornness.

Sin is described as "any thought, word, action, omission, or desire, contrary to the law of God." The Scriptures give us a clear picture of sin:

- 1 John 3:4—Sin is a transgression of the law.
- 1 John 5:17—All unrighteousness is sin.
- James 2:9—Showing partiality is sin.
- James 4:17—Knowing to do good, but not doing it is sin.

The Westminster catechism describes sin as "any want of conformity unto, or transgression of, the law of God." To transgress means passing over or a violation of the law, rebellion or disobedience. Sin is missing the mark, wandering from a marked-out path of uprightness and honor, doing or going wrong. Iniquity means crookedness as opposed to straightness and uprightness; wrong as opposed to right.

How clearly we can see the shortcomings in the lives of others while remaining completely blind or insensitive to our own! We can be absolute bores and not know it because we are so self-centered and egotistical. We can strut around as if we were God's gift to humanity, ignorant that people laugh behind our backs because we are so pompous. Out of touch with reality, when we think of sin we think only of adultery, robbery or murder. Yet, in God's sight, we are guilty of things far worse.

WHAT GOD HATES

Our disobedience grieves God. He hates some of the things we do: "These six things the Lord hates, yes, seven are an abomination to Him: a proud look, a lying tongue, hands that shed innocent blood, a heart that devises wicked plans, feet that are swift in running to evil, a false witness who speaks lies, and one who sows discord among the brethren."[3]

A Proud Look

A proud look or haughtiness leads the list of the things God hates. Pride led to Lucifer's fall and the beginning of evil in the world. As recorded in Isaiah, Lucifer used the personal pronoun *I* five separate times. "I will ascend into heaven. . . . I will exalt my throne above the stars. . . . I will also sit on the mount of the congregation. . . . I will ascend above the heights of the clouds. . . . I will be like the Most High."[4]

All our problems today stem from that proud disobedience. No wonder God hates pride; no wonder He judges it harshly! Furthermore, the Word offers the following passages concerning pride:

- Pride, arrogance and the perverse mouth do I hate.[5]

- When pride comes, then comes shame; but with the humble is wisdom.[6]

- By pride comes only contention.[7]

[3]Proverbs 6:16-17, NKJ   [4]Isaiah 14:13-14, NKJ   [5]Proverbs 8:13, NKJ
[6]Proverbs 11:2, NKJ   [7]Proverbs 13:10, NKJ

- Pride goes before destruction and a haughty spirit before a fall.[8]
- A man's pride will bring him low, but the humble in spirit will retain honor.[9]
- Those who walk in pride, He [God] is able to abase.[10]
- God resists the proud, but gives grace to the humble.[11]

The folly of pride and the blessing of humbling ourselves before God become clear through a study of the words *pride, proud, humble* and *humility* as they are used in the Scriptures. We need to examine our hearts and judge the sin of pride in our lives. Just the fact that "God resists the proud" should make a Christian want to humble himself. Life is hard enough without God's putting roadblocks in the way.

One testing by God helped me to see more clearly the subtlety and folly of pride. We were preparing for a crusade in Philadelphia, and one of our pre-crusade ministers' meetings was held at a theological seminary. At a morning meeting with some 250 area pastors and several seminary faculty members, I had the privilege of challenging those present to become fully involved in the Crusade. I was introduced as the man who had trained more people to be counselors than anyone else in the world. Being human, I thoroughly enjoyed all the good things that were said about me. Success went to my head.

On that particular morning God helped me speak far beyond my normal ability. The Holy Spirit brought to my mind many illustrations and Scriptures which gave authority to the message. After the meeting we met with the area church leaders and faculty members to discuss the possibility of having a counseling class at the seminary. We decided on a Wednesday afternoon class at 2:00 to allow not only area ministers to attend, but also faculty and students. At

[8]Proverbs 16:18, NKJ   [9]Proverbs 29:23, NKJ   [10]Daniel 4:37, NKJ
[11]James 4:6, NKJ

that time, Lyman Coleman, my assistant, made all the arrangements and decided to tape the classes so that they could be used to train counselors in several regions around Philadelphia.

The following Wednesday, about 150 crowded into a classroom for the first session. Never in my life have I had so much difficulty in speaking and expressing myself! For an hour, I struggled through my notes, perspiring profusely. Bells rang; professors looked at their watches and left. I could imagine what was going on in their minds: "Where did Billy Graham get this instructor? I wonder if he has ever taught a class before?" Awkwardly, I struggled on and finished the class.

Within seconds, Lyman Coleman came bounding down from the recording room and said, "Charlie, I have never heard you speak so poorly! We are going to have to record this lesson again." Since Lyman lived in Huntington Valley, about 40 miles from downtown Philadelphia, he immediately called his pastor to ask if we could attempt the first class again at the prayer meeting that night to do another recording. I was willing to be led around like a dog on a leash because my pride was so crushed.

That night when we took over the prayer meeting at the church, the class and the recording couldn't have gone better. We decided to continue the training, inviting two small neighboring churches to participate as well. Week two went very well. However, I was in trouble again in the third week. Not finding liberty to speak, I cut the class short after ten minutes and turned it into a prayer meeting.

God led me to share an experience in my own life. For years, I told them, I had daily reviewed Philippians 2:5— "Let this mind be in you, which was also in Christ Jesus." If I had the mind of Christ, I thought, I would have His wisdom, love, and compassion. I would be more like Him. Then one day I looked at verse 7—Jesus made Himself of no reputation and took upon Himself the form of a servant. Modern translations don't use the word *reputation*, but at that time, the word *reputation* and *servant* stood out to me. God said to me, "If you want to be like Christ, you must be willing to be without reputation, to be a servant." I asked God at the time to help me accept that challenge. I had been tested severely by God during that week, and I learned the subtlety and folly of pride.

After I shared my testimony, we went to prayer. And what a prayer meeting it was! At the close, the pastor invited to the parsonage any who wanted to sit through another recording. On the way out of the church, the pastor of a neighboring church came to me in tears. He had been so moved by God he could hardly speak. "God really spoke to me tonight," he mumbled. Ironically, I didn't give a lesson: *I was the lesson!* The experience helped me to get a better perspective of how God works in and through our lives.

Because we seek greatness, some of us will never be great. We take pride in our position of authority. Jesus said about servanthood, "For who is greater, he who sits at the table, or he that serves? Is it not he who sits at the table? Yet I am among you as the One who serves."[12]

From childhood, many of us have learned to avoid carrying the load, either for ourselves or for others. We are *being a burden* instead of helping with the burden. We enjoy being waited on. Jesus said, "You know that those who are considered rulers over the Gentiles lord it over them, and their great ones exercise authority over them. Yet it shall not be so among you; but whoever desires to become great among you shall be your *servant*. And whoever of you desires to be first shall be *slave* of all. For even the Son of Man did not come to be served, but to serve, and to give His life a ransom for many."[13]

If we want to be great, we must realize that *the way up is down.* As John the Baptist said, "He must increase, but I must decrease." God hates pride. Now, let us look at something else He hates.

[12]Luke 22:27, NKJ   [13]Mark 10:42-45, NKJ

A Lying Tongue

A few years ago a certain prominent politician used television a great deal. He was not always truthful, but it was said of him that one could easily detect when he was lying or telling the truth. While he stroked his chin, adjusted his glasses, or rubbed his nose, he was telling the truth. But when he opened his mouth, he was lying. Some people have an answer for everything, but it may not be right. As Christians we need to be trustworthy. Honesty is the foundation stone in building Christian character and credibility. Honesty affects every relationship in life, especially our relationship to God.

During one final examination in college, I struggled over an answer to a question and finally received help from the paper of the student sitting next to me. I rationalized my dishonesty by saying to myself that I knew the answer but didn't understand the question. A few months later, in July, I attended a Navigators summer conference. The first speaker's opening remarks were, "Let's face reality, some of you need to go back to a teacher and confess that you cheated on an examination." That troubled my conscience all summer. In August, Billy Graham was holding his first Crusade in Seattle, Washington, where I was serving with the Navigators. My college teacher was a crusade counselor supervisor. On the second night of the crusade, I found my teacher in the counseling area and confessed that I had cheated. The confession didn't make any difference in my grade, but it certainly helped my peace of mind.

An Unruly Tongue

Looking back on my own life and ministry, the tongue is near the top of the list as the cause of many of my problems. Constantly, my tongue needs to be guarded. Solomon said, "He who guards his mouth and his tongue keeps himself from calamity."[14] Often, one's tongue gets the person

¹⁴Proverbs 21:23

into trouble. Lying, scolding, provoking, complaining, criticizing, defaming, hurt in many ways. Rarely do people consider anything said as sinful, nor seek God's forgiveness, nor apologize to someone they have hurt. I would like to recommend a study on the tongue. Go through the books of Proverbs and Psalms and mark the verses that deal with *speak, mouth, lips, answer, words* and *tongue.* You will be amazed at what you find. This study has helped me become more aware of my unruly tongue and take practical steps to control it.

A Complaining Tongue

Most of us are guilty of complaining. We are never satisfied. We fuss about our homes, school, or work. We are always treated unfairly, passed over at promotion time, and underpaid. We don't like the food service at the hotel, nor the room we have been assigned. The complaint may be legitimate, but *God may be trying to teach us something.* Knowing what is best for us, God is attempting to shape our characters into Christ-likeness. When we complain, we react against God, telling Him that He doesn't know what is best for us. Paul says, "Do everything without *complaining* or *arguing* so that you may become blameless and pure, children of God without fault in a crooked and depraved generation, in which you shine like stars in the universe."[15]

A Critical Tongue

Daily, all around the world, Christians sit in court sessions judging fellow believers. Some seem to delight in criticizing others. We may feel that we are God's "fruit inspectors," but God has never commissioned us to examine others, and God despises any disparaging remarks about His children. Psalm 15 says, "Lord, who may dwell in your sanctuary? Who may live on your holy hill? He whose

[15]Philippians 2:14-15

walk is blameless and who does what is righteous, who speaks the truth from his heart and has *no slander on his tongue,* who does his neighbor no wrong and *casts no slur on his fellow man.*"[16]

To slander is to utter, in another's hearing, a false statement or statements damaging to the third person's character or reputation. To slur is to disparage or discredit, to cast aspersions—any remark or action that harms someone's reputation. We are all guilty of talking behind other people's backs, but it is a cowardly thing to do. The mature Christian way of handling a problem with a brother or sister is to go and lovingly confront: "Debate your case with your neighbor himself, and do not disclose the secret to another."[17]

JUDGING IS GOD'S PREROGATIVE

In college, I had a friend named George. We had all the answers. We were proud of the fact that we knew so much Scripture. No one seemed to measure up to our stature. We criticized our professors, fellow students, and chapel speakers alike. One day, through Scripture, God opened my eyes to my sin. To help me out of the rut, I decided on two practical responses: 1) to pray as I went into the chapel, and to pray for the speaker and to say nothing if I didn't have a good word to say after the meeting; and 2) to go to George and share my burden and what God was saying to me about my critical tongue. I looked George straight in the eye and asked him to cut off any critical remarks in the future. I began to enjoy the chapel services, and George and I were on our guard when we met together. To this day, I ask God to make me miserable if I cut down another Christian. If I have a problem with someone, I ask God to give me the grace and humility to talk directly to him.

The Bible has a lot to say about judging. "Judge not, that you be not judged," Jesus said. "For with what judgment you judge, you will be judged; and with the same measure

16Psalm 15:1-3   17Proverbs 25:9, NKJ

you use, it will be measured back to you."[18] If we take Jesus at His word, this passage should make us think twice before we say another unkind word about anybody.

The Apostle Paul, too, has a lot to say about judging others. He was often the target of the critical tongue. Yet he said:

"I care very little if I am judged by you or any human court; indeed, I do not even judge myself. My conscience is clear, but that does not make me innocent. It is the Lord who judges me. Therefore, judge nothing before the appointed time; wait until the Lord comes. He will bring to light what is hidden in darkness and will expose the motives of men's hearts. At that time each will receive his praise from God."[19]

Since God is my judge, I am responsible for pleasing Him. He alone knows my heart and my motives. Others may easily misjudge my motives and disagree with what I am doing. They have the privilege to come to me and question something about my life or actions. They might help me to see where I have been insensitive or ignorant of some misgiving. But judging is God's prerogative.

The Bible says, "You have no right to criticize your brother or look down on him . . . Remember, each of us will stand personally before the Judgment Seat of God. . . . So don't criticize each other any more."[20]

DISCIPLINE OF CONFESSION

We all face sin in our lives that must be confronted and confessed. David's sexual lust led him to murder. Lust for riches caused Achan to sin and affected the whole nation of Israel. Envy and jealousy caused Joseph's brothers to sell him into slavery. King Saul fell so low in his life that he appealed to a medium to get answers. But the Bible says, "I cried out to him with my mouth; his praise was on my tongue. If I had cherished sin in my heart, the Lord would

[18]Matthew 7:1-2, NKJ   [19]1 Corinthians 4:3-5   [20]Romans 14:10-13, TLB

not have listened; but God has surely listened and heard my voice in prayer. Praise be to God, who has not rejected my prayer or withheld his love from me!"[21] God knows your heart and my heart. He knows everything about you and me. He hasn't missed a thing since we were converted. The Bible says:

> "*And there is no creature hidden from his sight, but all things are naked and open to the eyes of Him to whom we must give account. . . . Let us therefore come boldly to the throne of grace, that we may obtain mercy and find grace to help in time of need.*"[22]

Sin affects our relationship with God and hinders prayer. As the Psalmist points out, God will listen and not reject our prayers if we are not harboring sin in our lives. If we want our prayers answered we must be honest and open with God:

> "*If our consciences are clear, we can come to the Lord with perfect assurance and trust, and get whatever we ask for because we are obeying him and doing the things that please him.*"[23]

RESULTS OF CONFESSION

King David sinned grievously against God and tried to hide his sin. He felt, as we probably do, that it would "all go away." God had to send Nathan, the prophet, to get David's attention. David finally accepted responsibility for his behavior and confessed his sin to God. Then in Psalm 32 he responds to his experience of forgiveness. "Blessed is he whose transgressions are forgiven, whose sins are covered. Blessed is the man whose sin the Lord does not count against him and in whose spirit is no deceit. *When I kept silent,* my bones wasted away through my groaning all day long. For *day and night your hand was heavy upon me;* my strength was sapped as in the heat of sum-

[21]Psalm 66:17-20   [22]Hebrews 4:13-16, NKJ   [23]1 John 3:20-22, TLB

mer. Then I acknowledged my sin to you and did not cover up my iniquity. I said, 'I will confess my transgressions to the Lord and you forgave the guilt of my sin.'[24]

In David's prayer of confession, several truths stand out:

1. Happiness in forgiveness. (v. 1 & 2).
2. Misery in unforgiveness. (v. 3 & 4).
3. Proper order for confession (v. 5).
   - I acknowledge my sin.
   - No attempt to cover up.
   - I confess my sin.
   - God forgives my sin.

WALKING GOD'S PATHWAY

In one of our Christian Life and Witness Classes we use a graphic illustration called "Walking God's Pathway." The illustration has four parts:

1. God's promise: Fulfillment and joy.
2. Man's problem: Sinful, selfish desires.
3. God's provision: Forgiveness and restoration.
4. Man's practice: A pre-determined course.

Walking in the Spirit, in obedience to the Word, we can expect to grow and become useful Christians. But Satan will do everything in his power to impede our progress and pull us off the path. He works through our carnal nature and causes us to walk in the flesh. Through sinful, selfish desires, we give in. We lose, momentarily, the peace and joy and find ourselves guilt-ridden, alienated, frustrated, and lonely. However, God in His love has made provision for sidetracked Christians to be restored to the pathway and once again enjoy His presence and blessing— confession of sin. "If we confess our sins, he is faithful and just and will forgive us our sins and purify us from all unrighteousness."[25]

---

[24]Psalm 32:1-5   [25]1 John 1:9

To me, 1 John 1:9, is one of the most important verses in the Bible. Every believer should memorize this verse and use it daily to maintain an abiding relationship with Jesus Christ. When we get pulled off God's pathway, and all of us will, we can quickly return through confession of sin.

To stay consistently on God's pathway, we should have a pre-determined course that we follow. We should know why we are here. We should live daily with the purpose of glorifying God. When Jesus was tempted by Satan, He quoted Scripture, and the Holy Spirit used the Word as a mighty weapon to give Jesus victory over Satan.[26] We, too, should live by the convictions that come to us through Scripture. We need to start every day with the Lord and give our lives back as a living sacrifice. When we surrender to the control of the Holy Spirit, the Word of God becomes our road map to guide us along God's pathway to blessing and usefulness. Then, when we sin and get pulled off God's pathway, we can confess our sin immediately and be restored to fellowship and a personal walk with God.

[26]Luke 4:1-14

STUDY QUESTIONS - LESSON EIGHT

The Discipline of Confession

1. On pages 105 and 106 you read of King Saul's downfall.

   a. What resulted from his disobedience? (List several facts)

   b. In your mind, what is the primary lesson you can learn from Saul's experience?

2. Write out your own personal definition of sin. (page 107)

3. Of the seven things God hates which one do you think causes a Christian the most problems, and why? (page 108)

4. What lessons can you learn about pride from pages 108-111? List several.

5. From pages 112-114, record what you think is the most important truth concerning the tongue.

6. What do you learn about judging others from pages 114 and 115?

7. Why should we practice the discipline of confession? (pages 115-118) List several reasons.

Memorize: Copy 1 John 1:9 on a 3 x 5 card. Memorize it and review it daily during this study course. (page 117)

*S*ometimes God sends His love letters in black-edged envelopes. He allows us to taste the bitterness of want and the desolation of bereavement. If you have lived many years, you have passed through the narrows. We have all been there. It looks as if things have got out of hand, and somehow or other we have been forgotten. When there is no one at hand to say it to you, say it to yourself, "God is faithful, Who will not suffer the pain to exceed the measurement of my endurance."

(C. H. SPURGEON)

9

Adversity Builds Character and Christlikeness

Visibility on the two-lane Florida highway grew dim as evening approached. The headlights shone ineffectually into the gathering dusk, and the asphalt absorbed the last of the twilight. I never saw the man until I struck him, throwing his limp body up over the hood of the car onto the windshield in front of me.

I slammed on the brakes and jumped from my car, terrified at the scene before me.

"Get help!" I shouted to the man who had pulled up behind me on the road. "I've hit him!"

But it was too late for human help. The man was dead on the side of the road, his briefcase lodged in the front grill of my car. And I had killed him.

The coroner's inquest brought the facts to light. The man, a Seventh-Day Adventist teacher, habitually crossed the highway at this point every Friday evening. After work he would get off his bus at the edge of town and run across this highway to teach a Bible class in a private home. When they pried his battered briefcase out of the grill of my car, they found his Bible, full of underlined

Scripture references.

"If only I had been going a mile an hour slower—or faster!" I moaned. "I never would have been there to hit him. Or if I had stayed at the cafe for one more cup of coffee—it never would have happened."

But it did happen. I accidentally killed a man with my car. And although I tried to understand it and rationalize it logically, I could not make the pieces fit. I kept coming back to the tormenting question, "Why?"

THE PERSISTENCE OF ADVERSITY

We live in a fallen world, a world plagued by sin, sickness, tragedy, death—in short, a world filled with adversity. We may seek to avoid adverse circumstances, but we will end up facing them nevertheless. Bad things, as the popular title informs us, *do* happen to good people—and to bad people as well. Like it or not, we live with distress, with trouble, with affliction, with calamity, with suffering. And we must, if we are to remain sane and sound, learn how to deal with adversity from a biblical perspective.

Biblical history, from Genesis to Revelation, offers multiplied accounts of God testing His people—or allowing them to be tested. Submission to God has never provided an easy escape from adversity, even for God's own Son. On the contrary, as Billy Graham asserts, "Christians are called to suffer. God does not promise Christians an easy pathway to heaven. . . ."

Every believer suffers adversities. Often, the most godly men and women seem to suffer the greatest trials and afflictions. The Apostle Paul, for example, suffered with a "thorn in the flesh"—perhaps a physical infirmity. Three times he prayed for God to remove it, but God's response was, "My grace is sufficient for you, for my power is made perfect in weakness." Paul accepts God's answer, and concludes:

> *Therefore, I will boast all the more gladly about my weaknesses, so that Christ's power may rest on*

me. That is why, for Christ's sake, I delight in weakness, in insults, in hardships, in persecutions, in difficulties. For when I am weak then I am strong.[1]

In addition to his "thorn," Paul also suffered from beatings, imprisonment, shipwreck, robbers, and other dangers.[2] We cannot escape the truth that similar persecutions are being endured by Christians around the world today—as Paul himself testifies: "For it has been granted to you on behalf of Christ not only to believe on him, but also to suffer for him."[3]

In the Old Testament, Job provides another example of a godly person who suffered greatly. Job lost his family, his possessions—even his health. Recognizing the place of adversity in the believer's life, Job declared, "Shall we accept good from God and not trouble?"[4]

Job was a man "blameless before God," yet he came to a startling conclusion about his adversity. "My ears had heard of you," he says to the Lord, "but now my eyes have seen you. Therefore I despise myself and repent in dust and ashes."[5] Through days and weeks of testing, trial, and tribulation, Job began to see himself as God saw him, and the struggle resulted in the purifying of his life before God.

THE PURPOSES OF ADVERSITY

If the Bible is filled with examples of godly, righteous people who endured great suffering, it is also filled with evidence of a righteous, loving Father who desires the best for His children. As an earthly father I know that sometimes the "best" for my children includes actions and decisions that they cannot understand at the time. The Christian's acknowledgement of God as Father includes trust in His character, and recognition that even suffering and adversity can serve His purposes in our lives.

The purposes of suffering are not always easy to discern.

[1]2 Corinthians 12:8-10   [2]2 Corinthians 11:23-27   [3]Philippians 1:29
[4]Job 2:10   [5]Job 42:5-6

Christians often pray, "God, make me more Christ-like. Help me to be a better Christian, to be more obedient and kind." But when God answers those prayers, perhaps through some experience of adversity designed to conform us to the image of Christ, we resist. We want Him to flood our lives with love and goodness, but we don't want Him to confront us with ourselves. We prefer instant holiness to the process of developing a disciplined, holy life.

God has, in fact, made provision for us to become like Christ. The Holy Spirit indwells every believer, and He will—if allowed to work freely in our lives—change us dramatically. We, "with unveiled faces all reflect the Lord's glory," and are "transformed into his likeness with ever-increasing glory, which comes from the Lord, who is the Spirit."[6]

But it doesn't happen overnight. Life, with all its experiences, is the Christian's proving ground. Adversity is the crucible of our transformation.

Before our experiences can be used in refining us, however, we must understand the general purposes of affliction. I learned some important lessons about refining when I was directing the Billy Graham Crusade in Pittsburgh. On that particular occasion, I found out why Pittsburgh is known as the "Iron City." Everything that could go wrong did, and I found myself frustrated to the point of despair. Then I picked up a Christian magazine and saw an article entitled, "What's Happening?" Believe me, I wanted to know! In the course of the article the author related Newton's discovery of the law of gravity—as tradition tells it, through an apple falling on his head. When the apple fell, Newton looked beyond the event, the falling fruit, and realized the existence of a governing principle more significant than the event itself.

Similarly, as believers in Christ, we need to learn to discern "what's happening." When experiences come our way, good or bad, we need to ask, "What is the governing prin-

ciple here? What is God doing through this experience?
What is He wanting me to learn to make me more mature
and Christ-like? Christ Himself "learned obedience from
what he suffered."[7] We, as His disciples, can also grow
through experiencing life's adversity.

Discipline

Adversity and affliction can be a form of discipline that
God uses in our lives when we need correction. In Psalm
119:67, 71, 75, David testifies that God afflicts us because
of His faithfulness, to get our attention and bring us back
to obedience.

As I look at my right hand today, I realize the truth of
David's words. Several years ago I was part of a bowling
team with four others, none of whom were Christians. I
could have used the situation as an opportunity to demonstrate my faith in Christ, but instead I began to be influenced by their life-styles, learning bad habits and being carried further from the Lord. I struggled with convictions of
my wrongdoing, but I took no action to correct my behavior. One day my bowling hand was caught in some ma-
chinery, and the crippling of four of my fingers ended my
bowling career.

Was the crippling of my fingers "just an accident," or
was the Lord using that circumstance to deal with me? Hebrews 12:5-10 gave me a clear answer:

My son, do not make light of the Lord's discipline,
and do not lose heart when he rebukes you, be-
cause the Lord disciplines those he loves, and he
punishes everyone he accepts as a son. Endure
hardship as discipline; God is treating you as sons.
For what son is not disciplined by his father? If
you are not disciplined (and everyone undergoes
discipline), then you are illegitimate children and
not true sons. Moreover, we have all had human
fathers who disciplined us and we respected them

Hebrews 5:8

for it. How much more should we submit to the Father of our spirits and live? Our fathers disciplined us for a little while as they thought best; but God disciplines us for our good, that we may share in his holiness.

In these verses I discovered five important principles concerning the Lord's discipline through adversity:

1. I must not make light of the Lord's discipline; on the contrary, I must take it seriously and learn from it.

2. I must not lose heart, but accept the discipline with the right attitude.

3. Every Christian can expect discipline.

4. God disciplines me because He loves me.

5. God wants me to share in His holiness.

Because of my tendency to wander and disobey, God has had to deal harshly with me. I have many scars to remind me of God's firm, but loving, hand of discipline. Not all adversity is God's discipline for sin, of course, but discipline is one of His purposes for suffering. If we are guilty of sin, we need to make confession and learn from our error, so that we may "share in his holiness."

Depth

In addition to discipline, a second result of adversity in our lives is increased depth in our relationship with God. The trials we experience can deepen and develop our faith. But if we view them incorrectly, our experiences of adversity may discourage and depress us and become stumbling blocks to an understanding of His will.

Psychologists affirm that our attitudes toward the daily experiences of life have a greater effect upon us than the experiences themselves. Proverbs 17:22 observes, "A cheerful heart is good medicine, but a crushed spirit dries up the bones." Modern life confirms God's diagnosis: negative attitudes literally kill us—through anxiety, neuroses, and mental illness. A positive outlook does not change the circumstances, but it does change our response to the circumstances, setting us free from anxiety, bitterness, frustration, and neuroses.

My mother, a devout Christian woman, mother of eight, was abandoned by my father when I was two years old. She worked tirelessly to raise her children in a Christian environment and give them an example of godly living. When I was grown and in the Army, I helped to support her, as each of the older children had done. The home we rented, where she had lived and raised her children, was suddenly sold. All her memories and her security were threatened. Faced with the loss of her home and the dread of moving, my mother had a nervous breakdown and was committed to a mental hospital.

When, three thousand miles away, I received the terse telegram informing me of her condition, I was tempted to storm the gates of heaven with my desperate plea: "Why?"

Some of my family of eight did respond that way. "Why, God?" they asked. "How could God allow this to happen to a godly mother who kept the family together all these years?"

But I was memorizing a passage from Job at the time: "But he knows the way that I take; when he has tested me, I will come forth as gold."⁸ I did not understand all the "whys" of my mother's illness, but I did know that I wanted to "come forth as gold" through the difficulties.

After five shock treatments, God restored my mother to live normally for several more years. What *seemed* to have transpired was that my mother had had a breakdown and was hospitalized. But what *really* happened was that God became more real to all of us through the ordeal. When I saw the principle behind the experience, I was able to understand that even my mother's breakdown could be used by God to deepen me and my family in our relationship with Him.

Most of us, when we face adversity, have trouble seeing beyond the falling apple to the governing principle of gravity—that is, we miss the deeper spiritual developments that may be taking place as we endure the difficulty. We see only the circumstances rather than looking to the loving character of God to put those circumstances into perspective. As Billy Graham says, we ask:

"Why does God allow fear to grip the hearts of men in this enlightened age? Where is God's power? Why doesn't He stop all this misery and cruelty with which this age has been cursed? If God is good and merciful, why are men and women crushed by agonies almost beyond their endurance?"

Such questions, Graham continues, are raised not only by atheists and enemies of religion, but also by bewildered Christians who, staggering under the burden of anguish, cry out, "Why must I bear this misery?"

And yet, if we have eyes to see and ears to hear, we realize that "Christians suffer in order that they might glorify God in their lives."

Demonstration

Suffering glorifies God in the believer's life, not only through discipline and depth, but also through demonstration—through the believer's example of faith to those who see his or her response to adversity.

Viktor Frankl, a Viennese psychiatrist, spent years in a Nazi concentration camp during World War II. He was subjected to inhumane treatment, starvation, exposure, indignity. A mere skeleton when released, Frankl explained his secret for survival: "If you can give people the *why* of existence, they will put up with almost any *how.*"

The early disciples, subjected to persecution by religious as well as governmental leadership, were motivated to endure affliction because of their *why*—the "living hope" in Christ Jesus:

> *In his great mercy he has given us new birth into a living hope through the resurrection of Jesus Christ from the dead. . . . In this you greatly rejoice, though now for a little while you may have had to suffer grief in all kinds of trials. These have come so that your faith—of greater worth than gold, which perishes even though refined by fire—may be proved genuine and may result in praise, glory and honor when Jesus Christ is revealed.*[9]

The disciples had that living hope, that "why" of existence that motivated them to endure even the most severe of persecutions. They knew that the trial of their faith not only resulted in a deeper personal relationship with God, but served as a demonstration of the validity of that faith to those around them—comrade and captor alike.

The Old Testament account of Daniel's three friends in the fiery furnace provides a fascinating example of God's purposes for demonstration of His power and glory through adversity. The three young men refused to bow down to the idolatrous image of Nebuchadnezzar and were condemned to death by fire in the King's furnace. They continued to trust in God, even though their death seemed certain. But when the moment of truth came and the flames engulfed them, only the cords that bound them were burned away.

Similarly, God uses the fiery trials of our lives to burn away the cords that tie us to the world. As we put our faith in Him, He protects and strengthens us. We emerge from the flames purified in our service to Him, an example of His power and love to those who have seen our struggles.

THE PARADOXES OF ADVERSITY

Even when we are able to recognize and acknowledge the purposes of adversity, we are still faced with the appar-

[9]1 Peter 1:3-7

ent paradoxes of suffering. God the Father, who loved us
so much that He gave His Son to die for us, still allows us
to experience heartbreak and tragedy as part of the process
of maturing in the image of Jesus Christ. "Sometimes," as
the great preacher C. H. Spurgeon said, "God sends his
love letters in black-edged envelopes."

If we desire to respond positively, constructively, to the
adversities that befall us, we can learn from Scripture how
to grow through suffering, recognizing our difficulties as
"love letters" from a Father who wants the best for us.

Lay Out the Welcome Mat

The Bible clearly teaches that, although we often try to
escape trouble and adversity, God intends to use the difficult times in our lives to teach and change us. Confrontation is good for us. It results in health. It brings out the
best—or the worst—in us, and ultimately works to build
character.

James, therefore, gives Christians some positive, but para-
doxical, advice in dealing with adversity:

> When all kinds of trials and temptations crowd
> into your lives, my brothers, don't resent them as
> intruders, but welcome them as friends! Realize
> that they come to test your faith and to produce in
> you the quality of endurance. But let the process
> go on until that endurance is fully developed, and
> you will find you have become men of mature
> character, men of integrity with no weak spots.[10]

How often, despite James' advice, do Christians bar the
door of their lives against trials and temptations, rather than
putting out the welcome mat and greeting them "as
friends"? Yet difficulties can serve as "friends" to us—as opportunities to learn to trust God, to develop endurance, to
mature in character and integrity. If we welcome them, we
look beyond the immediate circumstances to the growth
inherent in the struggle.

[10]James 1:2-4, Phillips

Rejoice!

Paul describes a second paradox of adversity in the book of Romans—the importance of rejoicing in suffering. Many Christians can understand that adversity must be *endured,* but how can we rejoice in it?

> . . . *We also rejoice in our sufferings, because we know that suffering produces perseverance; perseverance, character; and character, hope. And hope does not disappoint us, because God has poured out his love into our hearts by the Holy Spirit, whom he has given us.*[11]

The ability to rejoice in adversity depends, in large part, on our perspective of suffering. Paul looks at adversity from the vantage of God's ultimate purposes in our lives. Rather than focus upon the immediate gratification of personal peace and transitory happiness, he calls the Christian's attention to several important long-range results of adversity:

> 1. *Suffering, if perceived from God's perspective, results in perseverance, the ability to continue in spite of difficulties or opposition, to be steadfast in purpose. With this attitude, the Christian becomes a winner, an overcomer, a living demonstration of God's supernatural power at work.*
>
> 2. *Perseverance results in Christlike character. The believer becomes stable, deeply rooted in Jesus Christ.*
>
> 3. *Character builds hope—both dependence upon God in the present, and assurance of Christ's future return.*

Francis Bacon, the sixteenth-century English philosopher, succinctly stated, "The virtue of adversity is fortitude." As the winds along a coastline buffet the trees until they grow

[11]Romans 5:3-5

sinewy and strong, so adversity builds strength into the Christian's life.

Conform to Christ's Image

In addition to admonishing Christians to welcome trials and rejoice in their sufferings, the Bible presents a third paradox of adversity: the assertion that through trials—not victories—we are conformed to the image of Christ. Paul writes in Romans 8:

> And we know that in all things God works for the good of those who love him, who have been called according to his purpose. For those God foreknew he also predestined to be conformed to the likeness of his Son, that he might be the firstborn among many brothers. [12]

Many Christians have struggled over this passage, trying to understand logically how "all things work together for good," as the King James Version translates verse 28. How can the death of a man on a desolate stretch of Florida highway be "good"? How can an elderly Christian woman's nervous breakdown be "good"?

Suffering, adversity, tragedy in themselves, apart from the higher purposes of God are not good, of course. But if we believe in God's control, if we acknowledge His lordship and His wisdom, we can affirm—as the NIV translates— "in all things God works."

God worked in my accident on that Florida highway; God worked in my family during my mother's breakdown; God worked through the crippling of my fingers. He taught me important lessons, disciplined me, drew me and others into a deeper relationship with Himself. And as He worked in and through the difficult experiences of my life, His purpose was to develop Christlike character, to conform me to the image of His Son.

The Scripture abounds with examples of God using ad-

---

[12]Romans 8:28-29

versity for the higher purpose of conforming His people to His image. Joseph, in Genesis 37-50, was a mere lad of seventeen when his brothers, jealous of his relationship with his father, sold him to a band of Ishmaelite traders. Taken to Egypt and sold as a slave, Joseph proved his integrity in the service of an official named Potiphar, only to be wrongfully accused of seduction by Potiphar's wife and confined to prison for two years.

Throughout his unjust imprisonment, Joseph remained faithful to God and entrusted himself to God's care. The Lord honored his faithfulness and raised him to a position in Egypt second only to the Pharaoh himself. A famine in the land brought Joseph's brothers to Egypt to obtain food, and when they found Joseph in command of all Egypt, they feared for their lives.

Joseph, however, recognized God's purposes even in his brothers' evil actions. "It was not you who sent me here," he declared, "but God."[13] *In all things,* even Joseph's slavery and imprisonment, *God worked.* "You intended to harm me," Joseph concluded, "but God intended it for good to accomplish what is now being done, the saving of many lives."[14]

Joseph endured the paradox of his adversity, willing to trust that God had a greater plan for him than slavery and imprisonment. And God did work—both for Joseph's good and for the good of the nation.

"In all things God works," Romans 8:28 declares, "for the good of those who love him, who have been called according to his purpose." But what is God's purpose? Clearly, the ultimate purpose of God is revealed in the following verse, "to be conformed to the image of his Son."

If God's primary purpose for us is to become like Jesus Christ in character and in obedience, and if Jesus learned obedience through suffering,[15] how much more should we, as His disciples, look upon adversity as an avenue of maturity? According to our desire to be like Jesus, to bring glory

[13]Genesis 45:8   [14]Genesis 50:20   [15]Hebrews 5:8

to God through our lives, God puts us through His refining process, using adversity to purge and mold us, conforming us to the likeness of His Son. That end result—the image of Christ reflected in us—confirms God's ability to work in all things for our good, and for His glory.

Give Thanks

In 1 Thessalonians 5, Paul identifies a fourth paradox in dealing with adversity: "Be joyful always; pray continually; give thanks in all circumstances, for this is God's will for you in Christ Jesus."[16] To be joyful always is, at best, "unnatural." To pray continually is difficult. But to give thanks in everything is totally unreasonable! No one can be that good!

Yet our mental attitudes determine how we accept life day by day—the "why" of existence helps us cope with the "how." Dr. Hans Selye, a scientist who specialized in the field of stress, says, "Attitude determines whether we perceive any experience as pleasant or unpleasant; and adopting the right attitude can convert a negative stress into a positive one."

Adversity, in a general sense, is "negative stress." But as we come to realize the higher principle, the gravity behind the falling apple, we can begin to convert that negative stress into a positive affirmation of God's control, wisdom, and love.

At the age of seventeen, an athletic young woman with a bright future ahead of her dived into the murky waters of Chesapeake Bay. She struck her head and floated to the surface a quadriplegic, her spinal cord severed. Through the months that followed, she struggled with God and her faith was tested to its limits. Then God, through His Word, brought her to an emotional and spiritual victory as she realized that her Father had purposes for her life that she could not yet conceive.

Today that same woman, Joni Eareckson Tada, heads a

---

[16]1 Thessalonians 5:16-18

nationwide organization, Joni and Friends, which touches multitudes with life and hope. Her films and radio program reach millions around the world with the Bible's message of God's purposes. Her paintings, accomplished with a brush held between her teeth, enrich many lives with their beauty, and strengthen many more with the hope of a productive life.

The Scripture passage that is the foundation of Joni's ministry demonstrates the truth of Paul's evaluation of his own suffering:

> *We are hard pressed on every side, but not crushed; perplexed, but not in despair; persecuted, but not abandoned; struck down, but not destroyed. We always carry around in our body the death of Jesus, so that the life of Jesus may also be revealed in our body. For we who are alive are always being given over to death for Jesus' sake, so that his life may be revealed in our mortal body. So then, death is at work in us, but life in you.*
>
> *Therefore we do not lose heart. Though outwardly we are wasting away, yet inwardly we are being renewed day by day. For our light and momentary troubles are achieving for us an eternal glory that far outweighs them all. So we fix our eyes not on what is seen, but on what is unseen. For what is seen is temporary, but what is unseen is eternal.*[17]

In this passage Paul summarizes the essential principles by which a Christian can understand and grow in adversity:

1. Life is filled with problems that are meant to deepen our faith but not destroy us.
2. Through testing, Christ can be made real and magnified in and through our lives.

[17] 2 Corinthians 4:8-12, 16-18

3. Testing chips away at the old nature, and facili-
   tates the development of the new life of Christ
   in the Spirit.

4. Through trials, God can help us perceive life
   from His perspective and thus enjoy more of His
   presence and power.

Adversity, discipline, suffering, and trials inevitably come
to all believers in Jesus Christ. Christ did not exempt Himself from suffering; rather, He embraced it, learned obedience to the Father through it, and used it fruitfully for our
salvation.

In the midst of our own sufferings and difficulties, we
can be comforted with the realization that God never
leaves us to ourselves. As a concerned and loving Father,
interested in our maturity, He oversees the challenges His
children face.

If we, as imitators of the Master, learn to welcome the trials that come our way, to rejoice in suffering, to give
thanks for the Father's work in our lives, we will see the
positive results of that adversity. We will grow in discipline
and in obedience; we will deepen in our faith; we will be a
demonstration of the love and grace of God to those
around us.

A master sculptor, chipping away delicately at an enormous slab of marble, was asked by a curious observer,
"What are you making?"

"A horse," the sculptor replied.

"How can you make a horse out of that?" the onlooker
asked skeptically.

"Well," mused the artist, "I simply take away everything
that's not a horse."

Similarly, as we grow in the likeness of the Lord we
serve, the Father lovingly uses the adversities of our lives as
hammer and chisel to chip away all that does not enhance
His image. We suffer wounds and carry scars—some of
them painful, deep, and penetrating. But the end product is
Christlikeness.

Adversity Builds Character and Christlikeness

1. Analyze the statement made by Mr. Spurgeon on page 122. In your own words, what is he saying to you?

2. On pages 123-131, you will find several divisions or headings. Circle key words and underline key truths under each heading. List one or more truths under each heading that helps you understand more clearly how God works through adversity.

   • Persistence of adversity (page 124)

   • The purpose of adversity (page 125)

   • Discipline (page 127)

   • Depth (page 128)

   • Demonstration (pages 130-131)

3. On pages 131-136, you will find four paradoxes of adversity. Analyze the paradoxes and record what in your mind is the most important truth or lesson to be learned from each one.

• Lay out the welcome mat (page 132)

• Rejoice (page 133)

• Conform to Christ's image (page 134)

• Give thanks (page 136)

4. What stands out in Joni Eareckson Tada's experience that should encourage all Christians? (pages 136, 137)

5. Write a summary statement. How does adversity build character?

Memorize: Copy Romans 8:28 on a 3 x 5 card. Memorize it and review it daily during this study course. (page 134)

Tell me what you think about money, and I can tell you what you think about God, for these two are closely related. A man's heart is closer to his wallet than almost anything else.

(BILLY GRAHAM)

10

Giving Liberally

Of all the promises in the Bible, none are more specific than the passages regarding giving. "Each man should give what he has decided in his heart," says Paul, "not reluctantly or under compulsion, for God loves a cheerful giver."[1] When we give gladly, willingly, or cheerfully, we demonstrate an unselfish attitude, an attitude of appreciation for what God has done for us by giving us new life and hope through Jesus Christ. The result of such giving is highly motivating. God loves a cheerful giver. To be loved by God gives us inner security, joy, and a peace of mind.

In spite of the promised blessings and periodic teaching on giving, most Christians fail to give back to God what is required and rightfully belongs to Him. Lack of giving could be the result of biblical ignorance on our part, but most likely it is due to lack of obedience to the admonitions in Scripture. It could be selfishness on our part and unwillingness to share what we possess. Someone has said, "Jesus Christ must be Lord of all or not at all"—including, of course, our purse or wallet.

The pity is that God's work suffers due to shortage of funds, and Christians suffer because they withhold. Billy Graham notes: "If every Christian were giving 'as he purpo-

[1] 2 Corinthians 9:7

143

seth in his heart, not grudgingly, or of necessity,'—but
cheerfully as God has prospered him—there would be
more than enough to advance the kingdom of God in this
most critical period of human history." Proverbs 11:24 says,
"One man gives freely, yet gains even more; another withholds unduly, but comes to poverty." This passage speaks
mainly about spiritual poverty or shallowness, but miserli-
ness could also lead to economic ruin.

MISCONCEPTIONS ABOUT GIVING OR TITHING

"Tithing" comes from a Hebrew word meaning "one
tenth." People argue today that tithing is an Old Testament
teaching, or they say, "It's not important how much I give,
it's my attitude in giving." Yet 2 Timothy 3:16-17 indicates
that *all* Scripture is profitable and should be applied to our
lives, *all* Scripture comes from God, and its purpose is to
teach us how to live. Paul says in Romans, "For everything
that was written in the past was written to teach us, so that
through endurance and the encouragement of the Scriptures we might have hope."[2] Everything that was written in
the past was to teach us; some of our most valuable lessons
and truths come from the Old Testament.

Early in biblical history we learn about Jacob promising
to give back a tenth of all that God gave him. Jacob was
just leaving his family and beginning his pilgrimage with
God. His first night away from home he slept under the
stars. God came to him in a dream, promising him great
blessings for the future. In response, Jacob made a vow,
saying, "If God will be with me and will watch over me on
this journey I am taking and will give me food to eat and
clothes to wear so that I return safely to my father's house,
then the Lord will be my God. This stone that I have set
up as a pillar will be God's house, and of all that you give
me I will give you a tenth."[3] In the account of Jacob's life,
we find that God did richly bless Jacob.

The word "tithe" appears many times in the Bible. In

[2]Romans 15:4   [3]Genesis 28:20-22

Leviticus we read, "A tithe of everything from the land, whether grain from the soil or fruit from the trees, belongs to the Lord; *it is holy to the Lord.* The entire tithe of the herd and flock—every tenth animal that passes under the shepherd's rod—will be holy to the Lord. . . . These are the commands the Lord gave Moses on Mount Sinai for the Israelites."[4]

God has a purpose in everything He asks us to do. The tithe is important to the one who gives—as an obedient response to God's command, as an event in our lives which frees us from self-centeredness, and as an opportunity for God to bless in return. But it is also God's way of equitably financing His work: spreading the good news, caring for the needy, and building His church.

USE AND ABUSE OF MONEY

Greed is one of the seven deadly sins, and we are all guilty of it. Greed can lead to a form of idolatry when money or possessions replace God as first in the Christian's life. Paul says, "But godliness with contentment is great gain. For we brought nothing into this world, and we can take nothing out of it. But if we have food and clothing, we will be content with that. People who want to get rich fall into temptation and a trap and into many foolish and harmful desires that plunge men into ruin and destruction. For the love of money is a root of all kinds of evil. Some people, eager for money, have wandered from the faith and pierced themselves with many griefs."[5] This passage paints a vivid picture of the danger of greed.

A good example of the result of greed is demonstrated in a story from one of Aesop's fables:

> "Once upon a time a dog was crossing a bridge over a small river and carrying a piece of meat in his mouth. Seeing his own reflection in the water, he thought that he saw another dog with a bigger

[4]Leviticus 27:30-34   [5]1 Timothy 6:6-10

piece of meat. In an attempt to snatch the bigger piece of meat away from the other dog he opened his mouth and dropped the piece of meat that he already had.

"The result was that he had nothing. He couldn't get the other piece of meat because it didn't exist; and his own piece of meat, which fell out of his mouth, was swept down the stream by the swift current."

Another admonition concerning money comes from the book of Hebrews, "Keep your lives free from the love of money and be content with what you have, because God has said, 'Never will I leave you; never will I forsake you.'"[6] This passage exemplifies the problem of discontentment. We seem never to be satisfied. God says to us, "Don't let the love of money ruin your life. Be content with what I have given you. Don't depend on 'things' for fulfillment. Find your joy and happiness in me. I will never leave you nor forsake you." The Apostle Paul drives home the same message: "I know what it is to be in need, and I know what it is to have plenty. I have learned the secret of being content in any and every situation, whether well fed or hungry, whether living in plenty or in want. I can do everything through him who gives me strength."[7]

JESUS' ADVICE REGARDING MONEY

In Matthew, Jesus said, "Do not store up for yourselves treasures on earth, where moth and rust destroy, and where thieves break in and steal. But store up for yourselves treasures in heaven, where moth and rust do not destroy, and where thieves do not break in and steal. For where your treasure is, there your heart will be also."[8] I have had my home broken into twice, and I can identify with this passage. We did not have a lot of goods that thieves can market easily; therefore our loss was minimal.

[6]Hebrews 13:5   [7]Philippians 4:12-13   [8]Matthew 6:19-21

But the experience has given my wife and me a better perspective on life and personal possessions. Our real home is in heaven, not here on earth—the lesson Jesus teaches in this passage. He is not against savings accounts. He is against our getting preoccupied with money and things. He wants us to have the right priority in the use of our time and our money. "Where your treasure is, there your heart will be also." Greed can cause us to be so preoccupied with secular pursuits we forget why we are here. We are to "lay up treasures in heaven." The more we give to God of our money and service, the more treasure we are laying up in heaven. For our investment, God offers great dividends to us here in this life.

Greed, self-centered priorities, and lack of commitment to God's work have been problems through the ages. The prophet Haggai was faced with this problem in his day. Jerusalem had been sacked, God's people had been taken into captivity, and God's house lay in ruins. God stirred Cyrus, King of Persia, and commissioned him to rebuild the temple in Jerusalem. Ezra, the scribe, led a large remnant back to rebuild God's house, but they became complacent. Haggai's rebuke to the remnant of the people regarding priorities applies to us today:

> "This is what the Lord Almighty says: 'These people say, the time has not yet come for the Lord's house to be built.' Then the word of the Lord came through the prophet Haggai: 'Is it time for you yourselves to be living in your paneled houses, while this house remains a ruin?' Now this is what the Lord Almighty says: 'Give careful thought to your ways. You have planted much, but have harvested little. You eat, but never have enough. You drink, but never have your fill. You put on clothes, but are not warm. You earn wages, only to put them in a purse with holes in it.' This is what the Lord Almighty says: 'Give careful thought to your ways. Go up into the mountains and bring down

timber and build the house, so that I may take pleasure in it and be honored,' says the Lord. 'You expected much, but see, it turned out to be little.
What you brought home, I blew away. Why?' declares the Lord Almighty. 'Because of my house,
which remains a ruin, while each of you is busy
with his own house. Therefore, because of you the
heavens have withheld their dew and the earth its
crops.'"[9]

Are we not similarly guilty? We often lack fulfillment because of self-centered goals. Our lives are fruitless and bar-
ren; God has withheld His blessing. Twice in this passage
we are admonished to consider our ways. How much are
we contributing to the work of God?

A few years ago I was asked to speak at my home
church. The emphasis of the day was on stewardship—it
was the time of the year to pledge toward the budget, and
the pastor wanted a strong message on tithing. After the
evening service, I was sitting in my home when a couple
from our church knocked on our door. The wife entered
with tears in her eyes, followed by her husband who had a
troubled look on his face. They had been discussing tithing
and had had a violent disagreement. She had come from a
tithing family and was committed to the tithe, but her husband said they couldn't afford to tithe. They wanted me to
settle their problem. But his mind was made up.

Within a matter of days a misfortune struck that family
which cost them hundreds of dollars. Today, many years
later, they have a troubled relationship in their marriage.
Perhaps their problems are not a result of the husband's attitude toward tithing, but it certainly pays to give liberally
to God's work. If we don't give back to God that which is
rightfully His, much of what we have simply is lost or
wasted. Billy Graham says, "You cannot get around it, the
Scripture promises material and spiritual benefits to the

'Haggai 1:2-10

man who gives to God. You cannot out-give God. I challenge you to try it and see."

Tithing with the wrong motive, however, does not guarantee automatic blessing. In fact, Jesus leveled an indictment against the Pharisees who majored in tithing: "Woe to you, teachers of the law and Pharisees, you hypocrites! You give a tenth of your spices—mint, dill and cummin. But you have neglected the more important matters of the law—justice, mercy, and faithfulness. You should have practiced the latter, without neglecting the former."[10] When we tithe as a ritual or to gain returns we are guilty of wrong motivation. We should give liberally to God because of obedience, out of commitment to the lordship of Jesus Christ.

Many Christians don't understand why they should be concerned about giving to God. They work hard day after day to earn a living. Shouldn't their money be theirs to do with as they please? What right does God have to a tenth? After all, who provides our income? These questions no doubt plague many Christians. But the Scripture offers an important reminder:

> *"Be careful that you do not forget the Lord your God, failing to observe his commands, his laws and his decrees that I am giving you this day. Otherwise, when you eat and are satisfied, when you build fine houses and settle down, and when your herds and flocks grow large and your silver and gold increase and all you have is multiplied, then your heart will become proud and you will forget the Lord your God, who brought you out of Egypt, out of the land of slavery . . . You may say to yourself, "My power and the strength of my hands have produced this wealth for me." But remember the Lord your God, for it is he who gives you the ability to produce wealth . . ."[11]*

---

[10]Matthew 23:23   [11]Deuteronomy 8:11-18

Several truths are evident in this passage:

1. *Increase* (vv. 12 and 13). God has a wonderful way of enriching our lives.

2. *Ingratitude* (v. 14). We forget easily what God has done for us.

3. *Indebtedness* (v. 14). We belong to God. We have been brought out of bondage—not out of Egypt, but out of the bondage of sin.

4. *Insolence* (v. 17). I did it, not God.

5. *Insight* (v. 18). God gives us ability to produce wealth. He provides our income. God is the source of life. We owe everything to Him and the sooner we realize it, the better. The Apostle Paul makes this point very clear. "And he is not served by human hands, as if he needed anything, because he himself gives all men life and breath and everything else."[12]

Another Old Testament passage reinforces the truth that God is our source. King David asked his people for an offering to build the Tabernacle of God. They responded by bringing silver and gold in abundance. Overwhelmed by their spirit of giving and generosity, he offered this prayer of praise and thanksgiving to God: "Wealth and honor come from you; you are the ruler of all things. In your hands are strength and power to exalt and give strength to all. Now, our God, we give you thanks, and praise your glorious name. But who am I and who are my people, that we should be able to give as generously as this? Everything comes from you, and we have given you only what comes from your hand."[13] King David certainly understood the source of life and wealth. We are not giving anything that is our own—it all comes from God. If we can accept this truth, we will be motivated to give cheerfully and liberally.

[12]Acts 17:25   [13]1 Chronicles 29:12-14

BLESSINGS THAT RESULT FROM GENEROSITY

Jesus promises in Luke: "Give, and it will be given to you. A good measure, pressed down, shaken together and running over, will be poured into your lap. For with the measure you use, it will be measured to you."[14] This passage offers three principles about giving selflessly:

1. We must give to get a return.
2. The return will be bountiful.
3. The size of the return will be determined by the size of the gift.

A man once contributed the money to build a church. Later he lost all his property. "If you had the money you put into that church," someone said to him, "you could start again." But the good man wisely replied, "That is the only money I have saved. If I had not given it to the Lord it would have gone with the rest. Now it will always be mine."

A second promise appears in the book of Proverbs. "One man gives freely, yet gains even more; another withholds unduly, but it comes to poverty. A generous man will prosper; he who refreshes others will himself be refreshed."[15] We gain by giving. We lose by withholding.

Another promise is found in the book of Malachi, one of the most familiar regarding the tithe. It carries both an indictment and a promise:

> *"Will a man rob God? Yet you rob me. But you ask, 'How do we rob you?' "In tithes and offerings. You are under a curse—the whole nation of you—because you are robbing me. Bring the whole tithe into the storehouse, that there may be food in my house. Test me in this," says the Lord Almighty, "and see if I will not throw open the floodgates of heaven and pour out so much blessing that you will not have room enough for it."*[16]

---

[14]Luke 6:38   [15]Proverbs 11:24-25   [16]Malachi 3:8-10

Three words stand out in this passage:

1. *Rob.* We can actually rob God by withholding what is rightfully His.

2. *Prove.* The Christian life is a walk of faith. We need to take God at His Word and give with a right attitude out of a heart of obedience.

3. *Blessing.* God will open the storehouse of heaven and flood us with His abundance.

In the fourth century, Augustine, in a harvest sermon, said: "Our forefathers abounded in plenty because they gave God the tithe and to Caesar tribute. But now, because our devotion has receded, the imposition of taxes has advanced. We are unwilling to share with God, giving Him the tenth, and now, behold . . . a taxgatherer takes from us that which God receives not."

PRINCIPLES FOR GIVING

The Bible gives clear instructions for the believer who wants to develop a godly perspective on giving:

"Remember this: Whoever sows sparingly will also reap sparingly, and whoever sows generously will also reap generously. Each man should give what he has decided in his heart to give, not reluctantly or under compulsion, for God loves a cheerful giver. And God is able to make all grace abound to you, so that in all things at all times, having all that you need, you will abound in every good work."[1]

Several principles stand out in this passage:

1. *The law of sowing and reaping.* We get out what we put in.

2. *Commitment to giving.* We must decide what we will give, settle it once and for all. All our

[1] 2 Corinthians 9:6-8

wealth belongs to God, and we need to give back a portion of what He has given to us.

3. *Attitude.* We give freely. When we love God and want to obey Him, we acknowledge that we owe God our very life. All that we have is His. When we give, we help to further His work. When we give with the right attitude and motive, His grace abounds toward us by supplying everything that we need, and more.

In 1 Corinthians 16:2, Paul gives a good formula for consistent giving. On the *first day of every week,* each one of you should *set aside a sum of money in keeping with his income,* saving it up, so that when I come no collections will have to be made." If we want to be obedient to give back to God what He has given us, we should give:

a. *Regularly:* "On the first day of the week."

b. *Specifically:* "Set aside a sum of money."

c. *Proportionately:* "In keeping with his income."

d. *Cheerfully:* "God loves a cheerful giver."

The late R.G. LeTourneau was a successful businessman who built earth moving equipment. Instead of giving 10 percent as a tithe, he decided to give God 90 percent and live on the tithe. God bountifully blessed this man and used his inventive genius and money to touch people all over the world. If we give "in proportion to the way the Lord your God has blessed," we will give the tithe—and more. When we "seek first His kingdom and His righteousness," as Jesus said, everything else shall be ours as well.

STUDY QUESTIONS - LESSON TEN

Giving Liberally

1. Analyze Mr. Graham's statement on page 142. In your mind, what did he mean by "a man's heart is closer to his wallet than almost anything else"?

2. Why do many Christians fail to give back to God what is rightfully His? (page 143)

3. In your mind, what is the chief misconception about giving? (page 144)

4. Use a dictionary and write out a good definition for greed.

5. Study 1 Timothy 6:6-10 on page 145. In your mind, what is the most important lesson to be learned from this passage?

6. On pages 146-150 you will find several principles concerning wealth—its source and misuse. List two or three that speak to you personally today.

7. In your mind, what is the main blessing resulting from giving? (page 151, 152)

8. Why should every believer give at least a tithe back to the Lord?

Memorize: Copy 2 Corinthians 9:6-8 on a 3 x 5 card. Memorize and review this verse daily during this study course. (page 152)

T*he evangelistic harvest is always urgent. The destiny of men and of nations is always being decided. Every generation is strategic. We are not responsible for the past generation, and we cannot bear the full responsibility for the next one; but we do have our generation. God will hold us responsible as to how well we fulfill our responsibilities to this age and take advantage of our opportunities.*

(BILLY GRAHAM)

11

Witnessing

To "witness" is to attest to a personal knowledge of facts, to have seen and to give a firsthand account. No one living today saw Jesus Christ die on the cross; knowing Him as personal Lord and Savior, however, we can witness to His reality. As the Apostle Peter wrote, "Whom having not seen you love. Though now you do not see Him, yet believing, you rejoice with joy unspeakable and full of glory."[1] Rejecting the testimony of a man born blind, whom Jesus had healed, the critical Pharisees "again called the man who was blind, and said to him, 'Give God the praise! We know that this Man is a sinner.' He answered and said, 'Whether He is a sinner or not I do not know. One thing I know: that though I was blind, now I see.'"[2]

True witnesses may know little about the Bible, but all who know Christ can say, like that once-blind man, "Now I see." We have something to share—life transformed by Jesus Christ is difficult to ignore. As Christ works in us, we can then share with others what we learn of Him. Sharing Christ, in fact, is both the responsibility and privilege of every believer.

Two of the early witnesses were ordinary fishermen. When Jesus called the two, Simon Peter and his brother, Andrew, He said, "Come, follow me and I will make you

[1] 1 Peter 1:8, NKJ   [2] John 9:24-25, NKJ

157

fishers of men."[3] That promise still applies to all who put their faith in Jesus Christ—He reaches the lost today through faithful witnesses. The Apostle Paul said, "Therefore, if anyone is in Christ, he is a new creation; the old has gone, the new has come! All this is from God, who reconciled us to himself through Christ and gave us the ministry of reconciliation: that God was reconciling the world to himself in Christ, not counting men's sins against them. And he has committed to us the message of reconciliation. We are therefore Christ's ambassadors."[4] The word "reconcile" means to bring into harmony. Our work today as ambassadors is to bring people, who are separated from God by sin, back into harmony through faith in Jesus Christ.

Only a few people have the gift of evangelism, but every believer can be a planter of the good seed, the Word of God. Paul called himself a planter: "I have planted, Apollos watered, but God gave the increase."[5] Whether we know it or not, we plant seeds in others' lives by the way we live. Our lives are "living epistles, known and read of all men."[6] We can plant by our lips, as God gives us opportunity of sharing a word of testimony. We can plant the seed of the Word through a letter that we might write, or through giving Scripture portions to others; and as we plant, God sovereignly works in and through our lives, by the Holy Spirit, through the Word of God. He is responsible for the results.

GOD'S SOVEREIGNTY IN WITNESSING

We don't become Christians by keeping the commandments, doing the best we can, joining a church or any other human effort on our part. A Christian will live by the commandments, love and serve others, and become active in a church. But those responses come subsequent to the new birth. Regeneration is an act of God; the Holy Spirit

[3]Matthew 4:19   [4]2 Corinthians 5:17-20   [5]1 Corinthians 3:6, NKJ
[6]2 Corinthians 3:2

places us into the family of God. God does the wooing, drawing, and regenerating,[7] and those who respond to His call experience the "new birth."

A beautiful picture of personal evangelism is found in the book of Acts, where our sovereign Heavenly Father works through a cleansed life, by His Holy Spirit, using His Word. Philip's life was a witness;[8] he has been called one of the first deacons. In Acts 8:1, the church is being persecuted and the believers are scattered throughout all the regions. Philip goes to Samaria and is having a fruitful ministry when an angel instructs him to go to Gaza where he is to meet an Ethiopian official who needs the Savior. This official had journeyed hundreds of miles to Jerusalem to worship God. Now he is returning home, but without Christ. Sovereignly, God places in his hands Isaiah 53. "He was led as a sheep to the slaughter; and like a lamb silent before its shearer, so He opened not His mouth. In His humiliation His justice was taken away. And who will declare His generation? For His life is taken from the earth" (Acts 8:32-33).

The Ethiopian, hungering for righteousness, holds in his hand the Seed of the Word. When Philip arrives on the scene, the Holy Spirit instructs him to join the Ethiopian. Philip hears the man reading the Scriptures and asks him if he understands what he is reading. The Ethiopian invites Philip to sit down and help him. Philip, using the same passage of Scripture, tells him about Jesus and leads him to the Savior.

What a privilege for Philip to explain that Jesus was the sacrificial lamb of God who gave His life for the sins of the world! The Holy Spirit opens the understanding of the Ethiopian. He confesses, "I believe that Jesus Christ is the Son of God."

Christians today have the same privilege of introducing people to Jesus Christ. God will help us by His Holy Spirit if we will be faithful in planting the seed.

John 6:44   [8]Acts 6:3

PLANS FOR SHARING

To plant that seed, there has to be soil. The Gospel needs a human heart, but where do we find that heart? A tried and proven plan, called "Operation Andrew" might help you to start. Andrew met Jesus one day and brought his brother to Jesus.[9] Similarly, in "Operation Woman of Samaria," the woman met Jesus at the well and brought many others to Jesus.[10]

OPERATION ANDREW

1. Think of several people you know who are unchurched and in spiritual need. Put them on a list and pray regularly that God will open doors for you to witness and gain favor with them. They can be neighbors, people at work or school; or people you see on a regular basis like the barber, hairdresser, or service station operator.

2. Develop a friendly, genuine interest in these people. Do things for them and with them to show them care. Provide a meal in time of need, offer transportation when given opportunity. Help them mend a fence, play tennis, or go fishing—anything to show interest. Build good bridges by being available over a period of time.

3. Invite them to a film showing, a breakfast or luncheon, a rally or a Bible study fellowship, where they can be exposed—in a positive way—to the Gospel.

4. Lead them to a place of commitment. They may be ready after the first exposure to the Gospel, or they might need many. At the proper time and place, find out where they are in their relationship to Christ. Ask questions such as:

- What did you think of the meeting, speaker, film or Bible study?
- Have you ever received Jesus Christ as your personal Savior, or are you thinking about it?

[9]John 1:41   [10]John 4:29-39

- What do you believe about life after death?
- Do you believe there is a heaven and a hell?
- Where do you think you will spend eternity?
- What determines whether you go to heaven or hell?
- If you were to die today, would you go to heaven?
- Why should God accept you in His heaven?

Any one of these questions will help you to find out where the individual is spiritually. Is he trusting in Christ? If not, would he like to trust in Him? If you sense interest, share your own testimony of how Jesus Christ came into your life. Use Scriptures you know and any graphic illustrations with which you are familiar.

THE BRIDGE TO LIFE

The "Bridge to Life" illustration is a graphic approach which anyone can use to present the "good news" of Jesus Christ. The Navigators have used this illustration for years, all around the world, with great success.

God's Plan—Peace and Life

When God breathed life into man, He made him an eternal being, to live forever. The Scriptures clearly speak of both heaven and hell. Eternity is forever, and every thinking person should be concerned about where he or she will spend it. God in His great love for the world has made eternity with Him possible for all who believe in His Son, Jesus Christ. John 3:16 says, "For God so loved the world that he gave his only begotten Son, that whoever believes in him should not perish but have everlasting life." God had made eternal life possible, but it is not automatic.

Man's Problem—Separation

God created man in His own image[11] and placed him in Paradise, in a beautiful garden, with but one regulation. He could eat of the fruit of every tree but one. To eat of that tree meant spiritual death or separation from God. Genesis 2:16-17 says, "And the Lord God commanded the man, saying, 'Of every tree of the garden you may freely eat; but of the tree of the knowledge of good and evil you shall not eat, for in the day that you eat of it you shall surely die.'" God did not make man like a robot to automatically love and obey, but gave him a will and a freedom of choice. One day he chose to disobey God, and disobedience resulted in separation from God: "So when the woman saw that the tree was good for food, that it was pleasant to the eyes, and a tree desirable to make one wise, she took of its fruit and ate. She also gave to her husband with her, and he ate."[12] Adam and Eve did not die physically, but they were separated from God. This separation exists today for all who are without Christ as Lord and Savior.

Picture in your mind a chasm with God on one side and man on the other side separated by SIN. All of mankind since Adam has been born away from God in need of reconciliation. Paul says, "Sin entered the world through one man, and death through sin, and in this way death came to all men, because all sinned."[13] As a result of man's original sin, a chasm or gulf became fixed between God and man, as illustrated in the story of Lazarus.[14] Man through the ages has tried to bridge this chasm in many different ways, but without success. Religion is man's attempt to get to God. Many modern cults and sects are trying to build bridges back to God through religious ritual, good works, morality and philosophy. But there is only one remedy for this separation.

---

[11]Genesis 1:27   [12]Genesis 3:6, NKJ   [13]Romans 5:12   [14]Luke 16:19-26

God's Remedy—The Cross

Jesus Christ is the only answer to this problem of separation. When He died on the cross and rose from the grave, He paid the penalty for our sin and bridged the gap between God and man. His death and resurrection make a new life possible for all who believe in Him. First Timothy 2:5 says, "God is on one side and all the people on the other side and Christ Jesus, himself man, is between them to bring them together." When Jesus Christ died on the cross, He made it possible for men to be reconciled to God. He was the bridge across the chasm of sin, back to God. The Apostle Peter said, "For Christ died for sins once for all, the righteous for the unrighteous, to bring us to God."[15] Regardless of popular opinion that there are many ways to get to God, Jesus said, "I am the way and the truth and the life. *No one* comes to the Father except *through me.*"[16] Faith in Jesus Christ, not human effort, brings us to God. There is nothing that we can do to earn our salvation—it is by grace all the way. "For it is by grace you have been saved, through faith—and this not from yourselves, it is the gift of God—not by works, so that no one can boast."[17] Yes, God has provided the only way, but man must make the choice.

Man's Response—Receive Christ

In using an illustration like this, we face the danger of making salvation seem mechanical. We must ever keep in mind that we are not presenting a formula, an outline, or a systematic plan of salvation, but rather the person of the Lord Jesus Christ. We want people to meet our friend and Savior, who dwells in our hearts by faith. When the Holy Spirit is at work, He will make Jesus Christ real to people.

We must, however, get back to the basics: all of us must come to the place where we are willing to admit, "I am a sinner." We need a Savior, "For all have sinned and fall

[15]1 Peter 3:18   [16]John 14:6   [17]Ephesians 2:8-9

short of the glory of God."[18] Pride keeps many people from trusting Jesus Christ. The older we are, the harder it is to be convinced that we are on the wrong track—going the wrong way. But the Bible says, "Repent therefore and be converted, that your sins may be blotted out."[19] To repent means to turn in my thinking and in the direction of my life, to turn to Jesus Christ who is the door to eternal life, the door to God and heaven. Jesus said, "I am the door. If anyone enters by Me, he will be saved. . . ."[20]

The door to forgiveness and salvation is through the cross of Christ. By faith then, we must trust Him—receive Him as our Lord and Savior. When we do, we become a member of God's eternal family. We are born of God. The Bible says, "But as many as received Him, to them He gave the right to become children of God, even to those who believe in His name: who were born, not of blood, nor of the will of the flesh, nor of the will of man, *but of God*."[21]

SHARING THE GOSPEL

All that is necessary to share this graphic illustration is a pen, a piece of paper, and someone who is interested in knowing where they are going to spend eternity. After we have won a hearing for the Gospel, we can share the "Good News" with a friend. Study the following "Bridge to Life Graphic" and draw your own as you share the Gospel.

Facts

First, we should share the facts. On the top of the page, I write "God's Plan—Peace and Life," then I share what I know about God's love. I share my own testimony of what Jesus Christ means to me, opening to John 3:16 and explaining that Jesus Christ came into the world to save sinners, went to the cross to die for us individually, and rose again from the grave the third day. I emphasize the fact that

[18]Romans 3:23, NKJ   [19]Acts 3:19, NKJ   [20]John 10:9, NKJ   [21]John 1:12-13, NKJ

when God breathed into man, He made him an eternal being and that man will live eternally somewhere. He wants us to live eternally with Him, but it is not automatic because man has a problem.

Bridge To Life Graphic

FACTS	INVITATION	PRAYER	ASSURANCE
Romans 1:16	Acts 3:19	Romans 10:13	1 John 5:11-13
	John 1:12-13		Romans 10:9-10

God's Plan	—	Peace & Life
Man's Problem	—	Separation
God's Remedy	—	The Cross
Man's Response	—	Receive Christ

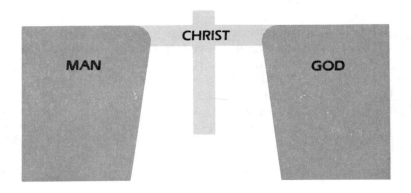

With that statement I write, "Man's Problem—Separation." Then, on the bottom of the page to the right, I proceed to draw the graphic of God on one side of the chasm and man on the other. As I draw, I share the Scriptures that explain how the separation took place. I work my way on through the illustration, showing how the cross bridges the chasm and how man can cross the bridge through faith in Jesus Christ.

Of utmost importance in witnessing is keeping Jesus Christ in the center. We can know a lot *about* a person without knowing him. Multitudes know a lot about Jesus Christ, but they have never met Him in a personal way. They have never received Him into their heart by faith. They have never put their personal trust in Him.

Invitation

I pray quietly as I proceed through this illustration, asking God to open the eyes of the individual with whom I am sharing. Evangelism is the work of the Holy Spirit, and He is able to give spiritual understanding. If I feel led of the Spirit, and the person is responding positively, I proceed to the second point and give an invitation by saying, "If this illustration is true, and I believe it with all my heart, then all of mankind is on one side of the chasm or the other. There are those who by personal faith in Jesus Christ have crossed the bridge and are now in God's family. There are multitudes who may be religious, striving to do good works and are morally upright, but have never committed their lives to Jesus Christ as Lord and Savior. They are still in their sins, separated from God."

Then I ask, "Which side are you on? Here or here?" I have had people put a little check right in the middle of the cross saying, "I think I'm in the middle." I've had others who have put a check just to the left of the cross. I was having lunch with a businessman one day and drew this graphic illustration on a table napkin. When I came to this point, I asked him which side of the cross he was on. He drew a little check mark to the left and said, "I know that I am not a Christian. Right now I'm reading Dr. Graham's book WORLD AFLAME and another one by Catherine Marshall." Then he quickly added, "I'm not ready to make that commitment." There was nothing I could do to lead him to the commitment.

I had been praying for another businessman for some time, and he walked into the office one day. I drew this graphic on a piece of paper, and asked him which side he was on. With a quivering chin, he pointed to the left of the cross. That day, he put his trust in Jesus Christ.

We can plant the seed but we cannot make it grow. Salvation is the work of God through Jesus Christ. We should *never* pressure anyone to make a commitment to Christ, but we can ask, "Is there any reason why you should not receive Jesus Christ today?" If the person is unsure or definitely realizes he is on the wrong side, let him know that he can be sure.

Steps To Commitment

1. Admit your need. (I am a sinner)
2. Be willing to turn from your sin. (Repent)
3. Believe that Jesus Christ died on the cross and rose from the grave.
4. Through prayer, invite Jesus Christ to come in and control your life. (Receive Him as Lord and Savior)

Prayer Of Commitment

Through the ages, many have made commitments without the help of a personal worker. Many, through reading a Gideon Bible, have made their peace with God. Through gospel tracts, radio, TV, and pulpit messages, multitudes have heard the Gospel and have put their trust in Jesus Christ. Romans 10:13 says, "Everyone who calls on the name of the Lord will be saved." Jesus Christ is the door to heaven, eternity, and salvation from sin. Often, I will turn to Revelation 3:20 where Christ is pictured at the door of our hearts. He knocks and we hear His voice as the Gospel is proclaimed by one of His servants. We respond by opening the door and inviting Him to come in.

When my friend desires to make a commitment, I lead him in a simple prayer like this: "Dear Lord Jesus, I know that I am a sinner and need Your forgiveness. I believe that You died for my sins. I now turn from my sins and receive You into my heart by faith. I want to trust You as Savior and follow You as Lord, and live in the fellowship of Your church." Then I ask my friend, "Did you sincerely ask Christ to come into your heart (life)? Then where is He right now?" Once an individual has made the commitment, I can help the person understand what has happened.

ASSURANCE

The Word of God is the anchor for our faith. The devil will do anything in his power to cause doubts. We want the new Christian to be able to say, "God said it in His Word, I believe it in my heart, and that settles it in my mind." We want the new Christian to take God at His word. The following Scriptures offer assuring words for the new believer.

- Revelation 3:20—Christ came in.
- John 1:12-13—I have been born into God's family.
- Romans 10:9-10—I am saved from my sins.
- 1 John 5:11-13—I now have eternal life.

Such an approach may seem very mechanical, and could very well be if the Holy Spirit is not leading. Yet this illustration has been used effectively around the world to introduce people to Jesus Christ. The Billy Graham Evangelistic Association booklet STEPS TO PEACE WITH GOD (similar to the "Bridge to Life" illustration) can be used very effectively in sharing your faith.

STUDY QUESTIONS - LESSON ELEVEN

Witnessing

1. List several facts related to witnessing from pages 157 and 158.

2. Under the title "God's Sovereignty in Witnessing" you will find several vital factors involved in a successful witness. List at least three. (pages 158, 159)

3. How would you improve the "Operation Andrew" plan for witnessing? (pages 160, 161) Suggest two or three ways of making it more personal and practical.

4. Carefully review the "Bridge to Life" illustration on pages 161-164. As you read, circle key words and underline key thoughts. List under each point what you think is the most important truth to remember.

   • God's Plan - Peace and Life (list one important truth)

   • Man's Problem - Separation (list one important truth)

   • God's Remedy - The Cross (list one important truth)

- Man's Response - Receive Christ (list one important truth)

5. Analyze "Sharing the Gospel" on pages 164-168. Please state briefly:

   - What I like about the plan

   - What bothers me about the plan

   - How I would improve the plan

6. Why do most Christians find it difficult to witness?

7. How can this be overcome?

Memorize: Copy Acts 1:8 on a 3 x 5 card. Memorize and review it daily during this study course.

*W*as discipleship a Dawson
Trotman original? Were The
Navigators, an organization he
founded, the ones who blazed
the first trail through the
ecclesiastical wilderness? No, not
hardly. . . . If it had been
conceived in a human heart, we
would have reason to question
its validity. We could opt for a
better way. We might even call it
a fad. But since Christ Himself
cut the first record, the concept
deserves our full attention and
calls for our involvement.

(CHUCK SWINDOLL)

12

Discipleship

Someone asked me once, "Is every Christian a disciple? Is there a difference? If you are a Christian, would you qualify as a disciple? The church is filled with Christians, but is it filled with disciples?" The words "disciple" or "discipleship" are used often these days. We say that a certain pastor is a discipler of men. His church practices discipleship. They have a good discipleship program.

By definition, a "disciple" is a "learner." The word is used to characterize those who demonstrate they belong to Christ by abiding in His Word, living by His Word. The root word denotes one who becomes involved in thought, accompanied by endeavor. Or, more simply, thinking deeply about what God says with the intention of obeying it. Discipleship demands that we identify with Christ and His cross and faithfully follow Him. It demands a daily recognition of His lordship and a willingness to put Christ ahead of every pursuit of life.

BECOMING A LEARNER

A disciple is a follower of Jesus, a learner. To train and equip disciples, we must create an environment conducive to learning and perfect more productive methods of training. We have seen a shift in emphasis in education the past few years. Previously, the key question for educators was "how to teach." Teaching skills were sharpened and perfected as effectively as possible. However, today in many localities, the emphasis has switched to "how to learn." Smaller classrooms with fewer students per teacher and better learning methods are the order of the day. One of the old laws of teaching is right on the mark: "Telling isn't teaching; listening isn't learning; *you learn to do by doing.*" We can sit and listen to the Bible being taught for years without applying the truth. We can listen to hundreds of tapes and read scores of books without applying the lessons. We learn to do by doing. I don't become a generous giver by listening to a message on tithing. I don't practice a disciplined devotional life by listening to a message on Quiet Time. I must make a habit of giving generously to the Lord and practice spending time daily in devotion to Jesus Christ. I learn to do by doing.

One of the major airlines has in their pilot training a program called S.B.O. (Specific Behavioral Objective). In each lesson, the airline instructor has his objective clearly in mind: he wants his class to respond, what he wants them to do. Then they go to the flight simulator and practice prior to actually flying the airplane. We should teach with this same objective in mind—not just as listeners but as doers.

LEARNING FROM THE MASTER TEACHER

A good teacher will realize there is more to teaching than simply sharing a well-prepared lesson. A good teacher will have a vision of investing his life in and through the lives of his students. By teaching life-changing truths and principles, the teacher actually multiplies his life through the lives of those who apply the lesson. This principle is taught in several passages of Scripture, but chiefly through our Lord, the Master Teacher, who was a doer.

The writer of Acts, assumed to be the Apostle Luke, was an eyewitness to much of what Jesus did and taught. He called Jesus a "doer and teacher."[1] In the gospel which

[1]Acts 1:1

Luke wrote, he tells us that Jesus spent a whole night in prayer.[2] On another occasion, Jesus was found in prayer by His disciples. They asked Jesus to teach them to pray.[3]

Jesus taught by example, a method He impressed upon His disciples. Before being taken up to heaven, He gave His last mandate to His disciples: "All authority in heaven and on earth has been given to me. Therefore, go and *make disciples* of all nations, baptizing them in the name of the Father and of the Son and of the Holy Spirit, and *teaching them to obey everything I have commanded you*. And surely I will be with you always to the very end of the age."[4] This mandate, which Jesus passed on to His disciples 2,000 years ago, has been passed on, one generation after another, to us today by His faithful servants. When we stand before a class, we should have investment in our minds and help carry on the biblical process.

JESUS THE MODEL

Jesus lived about 33½ years on the earth. During that time, He spent most of His time training twelve men, or some of the twelve. Mark 3:14 says, "And He appointed twelve, that they might be *with Him,* and that He might send them out to preach." His disciples heard Him give the Sermon on the Mount; they watched Him feed the multitudes, walk on water, still the storm, heal and perform other miracles. They watched Him suffer from day to day. They watched Him pray and learned from His own personal discipline and example. That is what you would call the "WITH HIM PRINCIPLE." You can learn much from being with and observing your teacher in action. You can soon tell if he or she practices what the individual preaches. Someone has said, "I'd rather see a sermon than hear one any day. I'd rather one would walk with me than merely show the way."

To give His disciples further training and to see how much they had learned, Jesus sent them out to put into

[2]Luke 6:12   [3]Luke 11:1   [4]Matthew 28:18-20

practice what they were taught. According to Mark 6:30, "The apostles gathered together to Jesus and told Him all things, both what they had done and what they had taught."[5] As they gathered together from time to time, they must have had some exciting reports to give. No doubt they learned from each other's experiences and could encourage one another.

PAUL THE MODEL

Jesus gave us the "WITH HIM PRINCIPLE." He taught His disciples to multiply their lives through the lives of others they had the privilege to disciple. The Apostle Paul made the "INVESTMENT PRINCIPLE" popular. Paul spent a long time in the desert after his conversion, communing with God. The Master Teacher shared with Paul the best method of reaching the known world at that time: the ministry of multiplication through investment. Paul invested heavily in Timothy's life, for example. In one of his letters to Timothy he said, "And the [instructions] which you have heard from me, along with many witnesses, transmit and entrust (as a deposit) to reliable and faithful men who will be competent and qualified to teach others also."[6] This one verse mentions four different generations of Christians. Paul said to Timothy, "What I teach you, pass on to faithful men, who will teach others also."

Three words stand out in 2 Timothy 2:2 that relate to the Investment and Multiplication Principles: "transmit," "entrust," and "deposit." A disciple, a learner, is being taught life-changing biblical principles and shouldn't bottle them up like the Dead Sea. We need an outlet to transmit or entrust these truths to others. We make a deposit in the lives of others as we would place money in the bank to draw interest.

Lorne Sanny, President of the Navigators, invested in my life during my time in the military service. I had the privilege of investing in the life of Gene Warr, a businessman

---

[5] Mark 6:30, NKJ   [6] 2 Timothy 2:2, TAB

from Oklahoma City. Gene, in turn, invested his life in John Repass who discipled Dr. Chip McWilliams. The process has continued through Chip's ministry. It works. All it takes is a vision, faithfulness, availability, and a practical plan. We don't have to be super Christians to help another; to lead a person, we need only be one step ahead.

THE APOSTLE PAUL'S METHOD

The key to Paul's ministry was his love for people and his availability. He instinctively knew that new Christians need parental care. They need feeding, protection, and training. This care needs to be done *by someone—not something.* He said to the Thessalonians, "But we were gentle among you, just as a nursing mother cherishes her own children. So, affectionately longing for you, we were well pleased to impart to you not only the gospel of God, but *also our own lives,* because you have become dear to us."[7]

It costs something to have children—an invasion of privacy. Before children come, husband and wife can be devoted to each other as they wish. They can do what they please, go where they please, and when they please. Children put an end to all that freedom. That is why many couples would rather have pets. Similarly, the cost of discipling others prevents many Christians from having a ministry. We don't want to pay the price. We would rather be free to do our own thing.

Not so with Paul. He would give his own life to the converts at Thessalonica. To the Galatian converts, who had been sidetracked for a period by false teaching, he said, "My little children, . . . I labor in birth again until Christ is formed in you."[8]

Paul lived for others: first to win them to Christ, and then to nurture them in the faith. He made three major trips as recorded in Acts. The first trip was a missionary journey where God used him mightily in several different

[7] 1 Thessalonians 2:7,8, NKJ   [8] Galatians 4:19, NKJ

countries.[9] His second and third trips were primarily to ground the converts in the faith.[10] Paul spent weeks and months in some cities teaching the Word of God. On one occasion Paul was teaching the Bible in Troas, and he forgot what time it was. About midnight, a young man by the name of Eutychus fell asleep and fell to his death from a loft where he had been seated. The Bible tells us that Paul ministered to the young man, raised him from the dead, and went back to preaching again. Apparently, he taught the Word of God until the break of day.[11]

Paul constantly demonstrated his love and concern by the attention that he gave to individuals and to the church. When he wasn't teaching the Bible, he was writing letters. Most of the New Testament comes from the heart of Paul to individuals and churches. Writing takes time, but we can say a lot in a letter that will comfort and encourage a fellow Christian. Paul's epistles demonstrate how much time he spent on his knees, praying for individuals and for churches. We, too, can pray, and we can write, but it will take time. It will cost us some of our freedom.

TRAVELING BIBLE INSTITUTE

To make it possible for Paul to multiply his ministry, he trained others. Like Jesus, he took many followers with him for on-the-job training. The Bible says, "And Sopater of Berea accompanied him to Asia—also Aristarchus and Secundus of the Thessalonians, and Gaius of Derbe, and Timothy, and Tychicus and Trophimus of Asia."[12] Seven men, from different localities traveled with Paul. They listened to Paul preach and teach; they saw him stoned, whipped, and imprisoned. His life was transparent, an example to those who lived with him from day to day. He could say to Timothy, "You, however, know all about my teaching, my way of life, my purpose, faith, patience, love, endurance, persecutions, sufferings—what kinds of things happened to me in Antioch, Iconium and Lystra, the perse-

[9]Acts 13:2-3   [10]Acts 15:36; 18:23   [11]Acts 20:7-11   [12]Acts 20:4, NKJ

cutions I endured."[13] Training others as he did, we can easily understand how he could send Timothy to minister to the Thessalonians.[14] To comfort and encourage the church at Colosse, he sent Tychicus;[15] to start a church on the Isle of Crete, he sent Titus.[16] Through investing in the lives of these men and many others, Paul was able to multiply his ministry.

Billy Graham has followed this principle of "on-the-job training" for many years. For years his team has consisted of many Associate Evangelists and key laymen from across the states and foreign countries. We have had the privilege of traveling with Dr. Graham to countries all over the world. Listening to him preach, teach, and watching God work in and through his life, has greatly influenced all of us. What we have learned has enhanced our own ministries. He has the world on his heart and is giving all of his energy to touch it through his own ministry and by investing in the lives of other Christian leaders. For many years, a School of Evangelism has been an integral part of every Crusade. Hundreds of pastors and lay leaders have been inspired and equipped through these Schools to be more effective servants for Jesus Christ. To encourage and equip Christian leaders from all around the world, Dr. Graham was the visionary behind two world Congresses (1966, 1974).

Probably his greatest investment in lives, over 4,000 itinerant evangelists gathered in Amsterdam in 1983 to be taught by Dr. Graham and other outstanding Christian leaders from around the world. They took home a new vision, better methods, and practical materials to do a more effective job of discipling their own people. Another such conference took place in 1986 with over 8,000 different evangelists from every part of the world. Billy Graham cannot reach the world by himself, but he has a vision of how it can be done through multiplying laborers.[17]

---

[13]2 Timothy 3:10   [14]1 Thessalonians 3:1-6   [15]Colossians 4:7-8   [16]Titus 1:5
[17]Matthew 9:36-38

Pastors and Christian leaders can learn from Dr. Graham and develop their own team for an investment ministry. By gathering a few staff people for prayer and Bible study, they can use this book—or another—to teach the basics in the Christian life. They can share life and vision as they meet from week to week. They can teach their people the disciplines of the Christian life—making Bible study, Scripture memory, the Quiet Time, witnessing, and discipling others, habits in their lives. Involve them in the outreach and discipling ministry of your church. Take them with you when calling on people in their homes, visiting in the hospital, speaking at other churches and service clubs. Share as you go, and invest your life. Pray for at least one faithful Timothy who will be an extension of your ministry.

INVESTMENT PAYS DIVIDENDS

One of the blessings of a discipling ministry is the by-product. Every Christian has an innate potential that God can develop and use for His glory. Sometimes we can invest in the lives of others who become far more articulate, proficient, and productive in the ministry than we are. For example, I have always had a hard time expressing myself. I have very little talent or expertise in any field. But God has given me the privilege of tapping some of that lay potential that often lies dormant in others. By investing in a few lives, I have seen men come alive who have far more talent and become much more effective in their ministry than I ever could.

In 1956, Billy Graham held a Crusade in Oklahoma City. Through the follow-up of the Crusade, I became involved with a group of men, one of whom had committed his life to Christ during the Crusade. Following the Crusade, I met with these men a few times to share my life and expose them to the Navigator ministry. We agreed to pray for each other daily. To make our prayers more specific, we chose four Scripture verses that we wanted to characterize our lives and ministry:

- Psalm 12:1—Godliness
- Ephesians 5:18—Spirit-filled
- Acts 1:8—Witnessing
- 2 Timothy 2:2—Reproducers

Our goal was to be godly, Spirit-filled, witnessing reproducers. For 30 years we have prayed for each other and
have supported each other's ministries. We meet on occasions to share what God is doing in our lives and to renew
our prayer commitment. The results of this commitment to
discipleship are astounding, as exemplified in the lives of
two of the men.

Gene Warr is an Oklahoma City layman involved in land
development, real estate, and other related interests. Gene,
a contractor, was our Arrangements Chairman at the 1956
Crusade. Today, he is a very successful businessman and
spends much of his time and money in the discipleship
ministry. He is a faithful churchman; for years he has invested in lives through his Sunday School class and led Bible studies in his home. He has developed one of the largest tape ministries in the country and has used it to train
others. Scores of lay people have gone with him to other
cities to conduct evangelistic weekends at host churches.
Presently Gene and his wife, Irma, are investing their lives
in a number of Oriental students attending a nearby university. Gene envisions these students going home as missionaries to their own countries.

Jack Humphreys is another Oklahoma City business executive who was involved in the 1956 Crusade. For the
past 14 years, Jack has been available three to four months
a year to help me train counselors for our Crusades. He has
trained thousands of lay people to share their faith and to
help counsel and follow up Crusade inquirers. Jack, too, is
a Sunday School teacher and faithfully supports his church.

Others in the group are deeply devoted to the discipleship ministry. One has become a pastor of a growing
church. Another has taken an important position with the

Navigator ministry. The others are using their businesses as
platforms for their ministry.

HOW TO INVEST IN OTHER LIVES

Any Christian who has a Bible and can read, can help
someone else. Simply reading through the gospel of John
with a new Christian or young Christian could be a start.
Start where we are with what we have. Are you enjoying
the presence of the Lord in your life? Can you set a good
example by being a doer as well as a teacher? Are you willing to give time to pray for others, prepare a lesson, and
spend time with an individual or small group? Availability,
not ability, may be the key. You provide the environment
conducive to growth, God will work in and through you.
Remember, you only need to be one step ahead to lead.

MULTIPLICATION

Jesus multiplied His life through those He trained. The
apostle Paul caught the vision and multiplied his life, investing in Timothy, Titus, and others. Billy Graham is multiplying his ministry by investing his life in young evangelists
and lay leaders. We can too! Investment starts by focusing
on one or two people, as the acrostic M.I.S.S. demonstrates:

Multiply. We can multiply our lives by being willing to
lose them. By dying a little to self each day we can devote
a little more time to others. Jesus says, "I assure you, most
solemnly I tell you, unless a grain of wheat falls into the
earth and dies, it remains [just one grain; never becomes
more but lives] by itself alone. But if it dies, it produces
many others and yields a rich harvest."[18]

We can live our entire Christian lives without signifi-
cantly touching another life. But if we turn a little attention
toward others and are willing to invest a little of our time
with others, God will honor our efforts with His blessing.

[18]John 12:24, TAB

Invest. You have been reading about several who have had a vision of investing their lives in others. What are you doing to touch others' lives? Have you started your Operation Andrew list? Are you praying for one or more individuals with whom you might share? Are there any younger Christians in your fellowship with whom you could meet for fellowship and Bible study? Remember the "WITH HIM PRINCIPLE" (Mark 3:14) and the "INVESTMENT PRINCIPLE" (2 Timothy 2:2). Get your eyes off the multitude and focus on *one.*

Start with one. Few women have twins, triplets, or more. God knew that one child at a time was enough. And one disciple is enough for effective investment. My wife is one of the greatest examples of one who shares her life with others: a meal for neighbors who are hurting, a trip to the doctors with a suffering child, the lawn mower lent to another new neighbor, or groceries and clothing for a needy family. People love her for her open caring heart.

We can go to the pastor and volunteer our services. There could be a new Christian in a church who needs a "shepherd," someone who will pray with the person, take him to church, and involve him in a Bible study group. If we are there when someone needs to share a burden, we will soon find opportunity for ministry.

Stay with one. After awhile our prayers begin to pay off. Someone trusts Jesus Christ through our efforts, or God brings another young Christian into our lives with whom we can invest our time. As a good spiritual parent, we can help in the feeding, protecting, and training. We can't take the place of the pastor or church, but we can give individual time when it is impossible for the pastor who shepherds such a large flock. As that good shepherd, we help establish the new Christian in the faith and the church.

The most effective method of discipling another individual is meeting one-on-one. We can share heart-to-heart, answer questions, pray over problems, check progress, and instill a discipline and accountability that is rarely learned apart from personal confrontation. The training shouldn't be rigid, forced, or mechanical, but a responsible time of praying and sharing.

We need to involve the new Christian in good Bible study and devotional habits. This book, or one like it, contains the basics in the Christian life. When we invest our lives in others, we help to fulfill "THE GREAT COMMISSION" and prepare workers for the harvest. "When he saw the crowds, he had compassion on them, because they were harassed and helpless, like sheep without a shepherd. Then he said to his disciples, 'The harvest is plentiful, but the workers are few. Ask the Lord of the harvest, therefore, to send out workers into his harvest field.'"[19] As we grow, mature, and reproduce in Christ, we can be the answer to that prayer.

[19]Matthew 9:36-38

STUDY QUESTIONS - LESSON TWELVE

Discipleship

1. In your mind, what is the most important truth about Discipleship found on pages 173 and 174?

   The most important truth is -

2. List one or more outstanding truths relative to Discipleship under each of the following sections. (pages 179-181)

   • Learning from the Master Teacher (discipleship truths)

   • Jesus the Model (discipleship truths)

   • Paul the Model (discipleship truths)

3. Why was the Apostle Paul so productive in his
ministry? (pages 177-179) List three or four reasons.

4. What one thing can you learn from Mr. Graham's
ministry that can greatly enhance your own
ministry? (pages 179, 180)

5. How does investment pay dividends? (pages 180,
181)

6. In summary, write a paragraph from pages 182-184.
The secret of multiplying my life is:

Memorize: Copy 2 Timothy 2:2 on a 3 x 5 card.
Memorize and review it daily. (page 176)

HENRI BOULAD

All is Grace

God and the Mystery of Time

Crossroad • New York

1991
The Crossroad Publishing Company
370 Lexington Avenue, New York, NY 10017

Translated by John Bowden from the German
Alles ist Gnade: Der Mensch und das Mysterium der Zeit,
edited and translated from the French by Hidda Westenberger,
published by Herold Druck- und Verlagsgesellschaft, Vienna,
and the French, *L'homme et le mystère du temps,*
published by Téqui, Paris.

© Herold Druck- und Verlagsgesellschaft 1988

Printed in the United States of America

Library of Congress Cataloging-in-Publication Data

Boulad, Henri, 1931-
 [Homme et le mystère du temps. English]
 All is grace : God and the mystery of time / Henri Boulad ;
[translated by John Bowden].
     p.   cm.
 Translation of the German edition of: L'homme et le mystère du
temps.
 ISBN 0-8245-1081-X
 1. Time—Religious aspects—Christianity.   2. Man (Christian
theology)   3. Spiritual life—Catholic authors.   I. Title.
BT78.B6713   1991
233-dc20   90-24356
                                                       CIP

Contents

1 There are Many Different Times

'They say that I am thirty years old. But if I had lived three minutes in one minute, would I not be ninety years old now?' (*Charles Baudelaire*)

If I asked you whether you knew what time was, you would reply, 'Yes, certainly!' 'All right,' I might say, 'then what *is* time?' At that point you would probably begin to hesitate and would have to think very hard before making a reply. We think we know what time is, and hold on to this belief until we are asked to put it clearly into words. And that's where the trouble starts.

Time is a bit like existence or space. It is one of those realities that is so natural, so everyday, so ordinary, in which we are so steeped that we do not know exactly what they are. If I asked you 'What is space?' you would find it difficult to tell me. If I asked you 'What is existence?' you would not know what to say. I live, I exist, I am, but what does that mean? What is the space within which I move? What is the time within which I develop?

If you could ask a fish 'What is water?', it would tell you, 'I don't know, I've never seen it, I don't know what you're talking about.' Why? Because it's there; it's what the fish lives in.

To know what time is we need to be outside time. To know what water is, we have to be outside water. We need a certain detachment, a certain distance, if we are to know and understand anything. Where there is total coincidence and total immersion, knowledge is impossible. There must be a distance.

I only began to discover and slowly to get to know Egypt the day I left it. That's when I began to say, 'So that's what Egypt is...' It had become too much part of me for me to be able to know it while I continued to live there. I could never have pictured it unless I had spent many years far from it. While one is within

[1

something, one does not know what it means. We only come to know about childhood when we stop being children.

When I talk about love and sexuality, people say to me, 'What do you know about that? How can you talk about something which you've excluded from your life by becoming a priest?' My reply is: 'That's true, but precisely because I am detached from this reality, I may perhaps be able to talk about it better, since I can see it more clearly from a distance and notice some aspects of it better than if I were immersed in it.'

Now if all that I have just said is true, the question arises: 'How can we talk about time if we are completely immersed in it?' But are we so sure that we are completely immersed in time? Animals, plants and even more minerals are certainly immersed totally in time, but part of our being is outside time, above it – otherwise, we could not know what time is, nor could we talk about it.

Human beings are both immersed in time and yet emerge above it. This detachment from time and from ourselves, this capacity to move in and out of time, we call consciousness.

If we are conscious beings, it is because we can see ourselves and think about ourselves. We have an inner space which is the result of a 'step towards reflection', an evolutionary stage that we went through three or four million years ago. Within us we have space to think and reflect. The word 'reflection' is itself significant. It suggests a mirror deep within us in which we look at ourselves, in which we 'reflect' ourselves. If I were stuck to the mirror there would be no reflection; there is a reflection only because there is some distance. The distance is the necessary condition for the images that we make of ourselves, for the awareness of ourselves that we acquire.

Here are some words of Henri Simon, a contemporary French philosopher:

Human beings are animals who can remember and foresee. Because they remember, it is natural for them to reflect and regret. Because they foresee, it is natural for them to fear and hope.

Moreover, it is because human beings have a memory that they can engage in forward planning. It is because they can recall the past to their consciousness that they can project themselves into the future and have a notion of time.

If they lived consciously only in the present, then they would be no more than an absurd series of discontinuous eternities in which they would have neither a sense of personal unity nor the conditions for coherent, active and creative thought.

Let me make some brief comments.

Human memory is the sign of this distance which is to be found within us. When I talk about things in the past, I establish a distance from the present in which I live. So I am not stuck to the present. Moreover, words are the expression of this distance: to express ourselves is to detach ourselves from what we are and to project ourselves forward.

Human beings, I said, are beings who remember. One of our deepest and sweetest joys is to recall old memories. 'Do you remember when...? Those were the days...' And because we remember, we are also beings who reflect and who regret – hence the sense of nostalgia. Animals do not regret, do not have any sense of nostalgia, because they do not have this distance within them.

Finally, human beings foresee: they have a sense of the future, and animals do not. Even the ant in La Fontaine's fable which stores up provisions for the winter does not do so out of foresight, but quite automatically, and by instinct. Because human beings are capable of foresight, it is normal for them to fear and hope.

Human beings are the only animals capable of conscious anxiety and deep care. Why? Because they are torn between their past, which is no longer, and their future, which has yet to come and which they hope for. This tension within them creates an uncertainty and an anxiety which are utterly unknown in the animal world. More than at any other stage in the past, human beings now have an acute sense of their history. The past has never been as present as it is now; history has never been so studied as it is in our day. On the other hand, people have never talked so much as they do today about the future, have never been so concerned to discover what it will bring. And that is the reason why men and women are anxious beings, full of deep disquiet.

Time is not just a series of particular moments, but it is a duration which I assume, because I take a detached position over against my own life.

Human beings are the only animals who know that they are born and who know that they will die, who know that they have begun and who know that they will come to an end, that this is only a 'matter of time'. Beyond question that is the ultimate source of their disquiet and their anxiety.

All animals are born and all animals die. But human beings know only that they have been born. Of course they do not remember being born. I do not suppose that you have any recollection of your birth, though psychoanalysts tell us that the trauma of birth is engraved on our subconsciousness. However, this is not a memory. So I know that I began, that I was born, and I also know that I will come to an end, that I will die. There is no doubt that this death is the greatest question-mark over our lives, the deepest source of our anguish.

The emergence of human beings above their history and their life is the sign of a transcendence over all other realities in the world. This transcendence seems to me to be convincing proof that because we are above time, we are also beyond time, and that means that we do not die completely. Something in us escapes time: part of us, the essential part of us, our self, that which makes me 'me', escapes the flux of time.

As a human being, I am like a traveller standing on a station platform and watching a train go past. The train arrives and departs, but I remain on the station. I look at my life and my history in just the same way. From the fact that I can contemplate my life, I can affirm that in some way I am beyond my life, and therefore beyond my death.

The fact that I am aware of my death is the sign of my transcendence over this event which affects only part of me, the more external part. The essential part of me, what I really am, is unaffected and remains above all this; and that is the case even now. Fr Maurice Zundel comments:

> There is within us an inner permanence by which, in a timeless present, we gather together the fleeting moments whose fate would otherwise be to be lost irrevocably in the stream of time. The stream of time would wash everything away, were there not something above it which prevented all phenomena from slowly sinking into it and dissolving. We would not know that we have to pass away one day if we passed on completely, just as we do not notice the movement of the earth which carries us round with its own motion.

Indeed we cannot sense the rotation of the earth. But why? Because we are caught up in it ourselves. To sense that the earth is rotating, we have to be above it. Similarly, since we feel that our life is running out and that time is passing, we are above that flux which carries us on towards death. We are beyond our deaths and transcend our destinies.

So there is a kind of opposition between time which runs out and escapes us – which brings with it ageing, decrepitude and death – and our inner time, which is spiritual time. This is the time of our consciousness, which develops slowly and, from all that fails and passes away, builds itself up towards a culmination and a fullness of its own. So that means that there are two times: a time which passes away, and the time that will always remain with me, the time which I myself am.

So if in some respects death is catastrophe and annihilation, in other respects it is a consummation and fulfilment of human beings, their realization. As Fr Zundel comments:

Physical death thus coincides with the explosion of an inner life which has achieved its full maturity and is totally freed from time, so that it now surpasses its own limits.

He goes on to make a comparison between a lecture or a speech, which passes away, and its meaning, which remains. If I talk to you for quarter of an hour, you have heard a certain number of words; however, within these words you may have caught something meaningful which will always stay with you. What I said may already belong to the past, but its meaning can remain present and escape temporality. So human beings can be like the meaning of these words which are comparable to their own lives and their own history: their lives, their history, pass away, but they themselves remain.

If we go to a concert we pay attention, listen, enjoy, from the first note to the last. At the end we say, 'What a pity it's over'. But in fact nothing is over, since the whole marvellous concert is contained within us, deep down, in a sphere outside time. Zundel ends by saying:

There would be neither speech nor music if the dead syllables and the dead notes did not survive in a consciousness which does not pass away at all. Time makes sense only outside time.

By dominating time, though a whole part of our being is nevertheless immersed within it, we human beings demonstrate our fundamental transcendence over the course of time and over

[5

our whole environment. We are not imprisoned in time, just as we are not imprisoned in space. The best part of us, the essential part of us, emerges above the flux which carries us away, or which seems to carry us away.

Memory bears witness that we shall not die completely with the fleeting moment. This survival, precarious and limited though it may seem at first sight, would be inconceivable if it did not become part of our 'abiding memories'.

Let us now reflect more deeply on these two notions of time: superficial, external, objective time and internal, personal, subjective time.

Objective time is of linear duration and can be measured by the clock or the calendar. It is five o'clock, six o'clock, seven o'clock, eight o'clock. Each successive hour is of just the same kind as the previous hour and all previous hours; it, too, consists of sixty minutes, and each of these minutes consists of sixty seconds. The same goes for the calendar. Monday, Tuesday, Thursday, any day, each has the same duration, exactly twenty-four hours. Months follow months and years follow years. We spontaneously think of this kind of time when anyone talks of time: it is always the 'external' time of the clock and the calendar, a sequence of measurable moments, from a temporal perspective each precisely the same.

However, modern scientists assure us that this time, which seems to us to be perfectly objective, clear and measurable, is in fact a very relative concept – and is so on a purely scientific level.

To measure time, human beings took the rotation of our planet. The earth revolves upon itself and at the same time revolves around the sun. Starting from this fact, we constructed the day, the hour, the minute and the second. However, we now know that the earth is slowing down, that the speed of its rotation is diminishing by ten seconds every thirteen years. So days now are slightly longer than they used to be: good news for all those who are growing old!

If this tendency is maintained, then in fact days will be perceptibly longer for coming generations, and in the long term that will also have an effect on our climate.

So we know that this standard of time is not stable, and is constantly changing. People used to adjust their watches to the rotation of the earth, but now that no longer works; the earth has proved to be too capricious and we cannot count on it: its movement is too irregular. So our scientists have had to discover another standard. First they used atomic clocks, which work to an accuracy of a thousandth of a second. Quartz clocks are even more amazingly precise: their possible deviation is no more than a thousand billionth of a second a year.

The time of such clocks is based on the vibrations of an atom, in practice hydrogen, rubidium, or above all caesium. Starting from this, the thirteenth General Conference of Weights and Measures held in Paris in 1967 defined the second as 'the duration of 9,192,631,770 periods of emission between the two hyperfine levels of the basic state of the atom of caesium 133'. In other words, atomic time is

$$\frac{1}{9,192,631,770} = \text{TAI (Temps Atomique International)}.$$

Think of that next time you adjust your watch!

So according to scientists there are two quite different times:

I = TAI – Temps Atomique International
International Atomic Time, which denotes the regular continuity of time with the utmost possible accuracy.

II = TU – Temps Universel
Universal time, which relates to the speed with which the earth rotates.

There is no theoretical connection between TAI and TU. The difference between them varies in an unpredictable way and can only be recognized on the basis of previous astronomical observations. It has been decided that the difference between TU and TAI amounts to zero on 1 January 1968. But from that point onwards, TU and TAI have lives of their own. Since then the speed of the earth's rotation has decreased, so the TU principle is moving further away from the TAI principle. By now the TU clock is over fifteen seconds slow, and the difference between the two clocks will go on increasing.

Perhaps you may not be very interested in all this. But it is important for you to know that the time in which the whole of our lives elapses is relative to a great many factors.

Now having discovered that our objective time is relative to the rotation of the earth and even to the vibration of atoms, it has to be added that this time is also relative to space and to speed.

This was the great discovery made by Einstein, after extremely complicated calculations and years of reflection at his desk. In this way he was able to establish a rigorous relationship between time and speed which he expressed in his famous theory of relativity.

However, scientists, who tend to be convinced only by observation, wanted to try an experiment to test this theoretical relationship between time and speed. So on Tuesday, 5 October 1971, two American scientists boarded two Boeing 747s for one of the most interesting flights ever undertaken for the purposes of scientific research. Their aim was to test Einstein's theory of relativity in practice.

Each of them had with him an astronomical clock, weighing thirty kilos and costing $60,000, precise to a billionth of a second. It was Einstein's theory that if you fly two clocks round the earth, in one plane anti-clockwise and in another plane clockwise, while to begin with they will both tell the same time, after a few revolutions a difference will develop between them, and both will differ from a third clock, the control clock, on earth. The clock which goes round the earth clockwise will go slow, and the one which goes round the earth anti-clockwise will go fast. That would seem natural because of the direction in which the earth rotates: one clock is going against the movement of the earth and the other is following it.

But how did the experiment turn out? The clocks which were taken on the planes showed a difference of 300 billionths of a second from the control clock in the laboratory, and the speed at which they had been flown was far, far below the speed of light.

So this new experiment confirmed the idea that time goes more quickly on earth than in space. In that case astronauts who returned from what in earthly terms was a very long interplanetary flight would then logically have to be substantially younger than the families which they had left behind. A father could return younger than his own child or grandchild.

An even more conceivable experiment could be carried out with cats. Suppose one left three kittens to develop naturally and put the fourth into a rocket and fired that off into the universe at a speed approaching that of light. After a year of earthly time the little kitten would return more or less unchanged, while the other kittens who had grown up on earth would have become cats.

This theory has not been tested with cats, but it has been tested with inanimate objects and found to be true. Nowadays the majority of scientists believe it, and the duration of the life of our future astronauts will be quite different from what it is under present conditions. Suppose that I embarked in a spacecraft to explore space for the course of the further twenty or thirty years that I might expect to live. The amount of space that I might cover in this period of time would be ridiculously small compared with the dimensions of the universe: the polar star is forty light years away and the limits of our galaxy are around ten thousand light years away... But scientists encourage me and tell me that I shall live much longer in space. In space, the thirty years that I suppose to be my last would amount to sixty, a hundred or a thousand earth-years. In other words, the duration of my life would be relative to the speed at which my spaceship moved through the universe.

I expect that you have heard of the famous experiment of Langevin's train. Langevin's imaginary traveller gets on an astronomical train, the 'Einstein train'. It is five million kilometres long, goes in a straight line, and has a speed of 240,000 kilometres a second. There are two stations on this straight line, a distance of 864 million kilometres apart. Theoretically, the Einstein train takes an hour to cover this distance. The passenger will be amazed to see that when he arrives, his watch is slow compared with the station clock. But the fact of the matter is that it is not his watch which is slow, but the station clock which is fast. What would have been one hour for someone standing on the station is only one hour minus x for the passenger. This is an enormous challenge to ordinary common sense, but it can be demonstrated by precise mathematical calculations. The knowledge that even the physical concept of time is relative is in fact staggering.

I now want to demonstrate this relativity of time in the sphere of our personal life. The Bible tells us of people who live to be 900 years old. Fine, though I do not know whether I would want to live so long. We would do better to ask about the meaning of our life than about its duration. What is the meaning of a long life of 100 or 900 years or of just a short one of twenty years? The biological rhythm of a human body and the movement of a clock are by no means one and the same, which is why the sense of time of a child of eight is very different from that of a man or woman of eighty. For the child, whose small organism is growing rapidly, an hour is a very long time, since within this period an enormous amount is experienced and assimilated, and in the process of this the child goes through a wide range of the most varied reactions and emotions. I remember my earliest schooldays and the eternity of some of the lessons: the boredom was often torture; I kept looking at my watch and it just would not move. Why? I think that it was because my biological rhythm was going ten times faster than the watch and what went on in school. But the old man or woman, whose biological rhythm seems to go ten times slower than the ticking of a watch, has the impression that the hours are rushing by, so that an hour amounts to virtually nothing.

We encounter the same phenomenon in hibernation. You may well have seen the film *2001 A Space Odyssey*. In it we are shown enormous blocks of ice, at the heart of which we can recognize human bodies, deep-frozen men and women. They are carried through space in a spaceship, to be unfrozen again on earth after a certain number of years travelling. It will then prove that these people have hardly grown any older, since the hibernation has slowed down their biological rhythm, because the body needs only a minimal amount of energy to keep it alive in such circumstances.

Here's an example from everyday experience. If I have breakfast at eight in the morning, I am hungry again by lunchtime. Why? Because I have burned up and consumed the energy provided by my breakfast during my morning's activity. But in the morning I am not usually very hungry, although it is twelve hours since I had supper. That is because the biological rhythm of the body has been slowed down considerably by my sleep. Hibernation works on basically the same principle as sleep. The body temperature is reduced to such a degree that the pulse-rate falls from eighty beats a minute to one every five minutes or even one every twenty-four hours. In these conditions the body consumes hardly any energy and can subsist for a very long time without sleep. We have long been aware of this from the practice of many animals – we call it winter sleep, hibernation. Marmots, for example, gather in groups underground, fill up the space with dry grass, and curl up in their skins to preserve some warmth. Then they go to sleep for up to nine months without food or liquid. In principle the same thing is possible for human beings.

In America there are already commercial companies which offer their clients an extended life through hibernation. For a few million dollars they can be deep-frozen for a period of from a few decades to perhaps several hundred years. Suppose I am fifty and I say that I would like to know what is happening on earth in the year 2090. I go to one of these companies in America and say, 'hibernate me for a century'. After paying the bill, I am put in a glass case, stored in a deep freeze and have a good long sleep. In 2090 I am taken out, unfrozen, tapped on the shoulder and told, 'There you are, 2090!' I should only be fifty-one, since during the century I would have aged only one year. I would be able to see what is happening in the twenty-first century and continue my normal life. Apparently at this moment there are deep-frozen human bodies resting peacefully in the store-cupboards of these businesses.

In fact my twenty-four-hour biological rhythm is inscribed on my organism, and the same is true of plants and animals. How is it that when you decide to wake up at 6 a.m. and set your alarm clock for that time, you often wake up two minutes beforehand? It is because you have an internal organic clock which measures time almost as rigorously as a mechanical clock. Researchers have carried out experiments with life in total darkness, expecting this to produce a different rhythm from our twenty-four-hour one. They lived in caves in total darkness, without clocks. For several weeks they would not have been able to tell whether it was day or night in the world, and yet they lived the quite normal human twenty-four-hour rhythm of sleeping, waking and taking food. This rhythm determines our organism, and it is inadvisable to disturb it.

Air hostesses, who are continually subject to time changes between Tokyo, New York and Paris, have day and night constantly turned upside down. But since their body clocks function by a normal twenty-four-hour rhythm, these continual changes risk disturbing their bodies in a dangerous way.

One of the reasons for the imbalances nowadays is that there is no longer day or night. During the day people are shut up in dark offices and the night is bathed in light and neon. People go to bed at four in the morning and get up at eleven: night is day and day is night. There is respect neither for biological rhythm nor for the succession of day and night. That could be serious. I am not saying that we should all go to bed at sunset like birds or hens, but I think that there is a certain rhythm that we should respect, and that normally we should get up when the sun rises. That is programmed into our organism.

A further example of the relativity of time of which some of you may be aware ought to be mentioned here. We have the impression that the two thousand years which have elapsed since the birth of Christ is a considerable time. In fact, if we put this period in the total history of the universe, we can see that these two thousand years amount to virtually nothing.

To get some idea, we might reduce the thirteen billion years for which the universe seems to have existed to a calendar year of 365 days. On that scale, life will have appeared at the beginning of October. Up to that point the universe was lifeless: nothing but minerals, pure matter. At the beginning of October, somewhere, at the bottom of a marsh, bacteria formed: that was the appearance of life. On 22 December, vertebrates and the nervous system emerged. On 29 December, at around four in the afternoon, mammals appeared, i.e. animals which carry their young within their bodies rather than laying eggs. And on 31 December, at around 9.20 in the evening, human beings appeared! So human beings appeared on earth only just over two hours ago, in comparison with all the former periods of the history of the universe.

And on 31 December, at 11.59 and 55 seconds, Jesus was born. So the two thousand years between Jesus and ourselves amount to no more than just five seconds in a history of the universe totalling 365 days. Therefore when we are told that Christ ushers in the end of time, we can understand that in terms of what I have just said.

Everything that I have summarized here relativizes our conception of time to an enormous degree. And does not the Bible tell us that for God 'a thousand years are as a day' (II Peter 3.8)? It is a phrase which was already used in the Psalms (90.4).

Something else changes the usual picture of time that we have: the use of drugs, which puts people in an exceptional state, in a world without time. A young woman on drugs has told of her experience in a very interesting autobiography entitled *Blue Grass*. In it she says:

> I remember having read somewhere that a thousand years of human life were only a second for the Lord, and I told myself that I had at last found the solution. I was there living my life on the usual time-scale, and at the same time living the life of thousands of human beings in the space of an hour.

I have made the same point in my lectures on death. The last moment in a human life is a total moment, a moment in which all that one has gone through and experienced comes before one and is concentrated at one point. At this point the totality of our personal experience will be summed up, and in the light of this comprehensive view we shall make what Ladislas Boros has called 'the final choice', the last important human decision on which eternal life will depend.

So the value of time is related to the intensity with which we live it. What does it mean to live thirty years, sixty years, ninety years? To talk like that says nothing either about the value of this life or about its true duration.

Time passes at a speed relative to the intensity of the life that is lived and the quality of life that is experienced. Perhaps there are people of ninety who in fact have really lived for only three years of their lives. Why? Because their lives were so empty, so hollow, so inconsistent that they amounted to only a few days or years. These people have not lived; they have just lasted. What is the point of a life which just goes on and on like this over ninety years?

People talk a lot nowadays about living a long life, and scientists and doctors are trying to prolong human life as much a possible. But what is the point of adding years to years if they are all as empty as the ones which precede them, if they have no content? In Arabic there is a greeting, 'Allah yetawwel omrak', 'May God prolong your life!' But I would not wish you a long life if that meant merely an extended life: I would wish you a life filled as much as possible with inner fulfilment. A few years lived out intensively can be more than a hundred useless, wasted years. It is not duration that makes life significant, but its quality.

I'm not interested in knowing how old you are, because I know old people who are as bright as twenty-year-olds and twenty-year-olds who act as though they were eighty. It is your heart which determines how old you are.

I would like to add some thoughts which I wrote down in Lebanon in 1962:

'It is not time that we lack, but heart.' Never say that you have no time. On the whole it is those who are busiest who can make time for yet more, and those who have more leisure-time who refuse to do something when one asks. What we lack is not time, but heart.

'True time is not the time of the clock or the calendar but the time of consciousness.' You may have four months vacation which are worth forty years because they provide such rich and intense experiences that you can live a whole life in a summer. For other people, these four months are worth less than four hours, because this time has been empty, sheer absence. True time is not the time of the clock or the calendar, but the time of consciousness.

'There are moments which are worth hours and hours which are not worth a moment.' In fact, the capacity to live the present moment intensely makes this moment an experience which infinitely surpasses its own limits.

'The concentration of time relates to an intensity of emotion, of life, of sensation and interest.' How is it that in certain courses the teacher has hardly begun to speak than three-quarters of an hour is already up, while in others the clock seems so reluctant to move forward? What's the reason? It is that time is a very relative concept and that it primarily relates to our interest in what is going on.

'Time that one feels passing is time lost.' 'You do not escape time by evasion, but by attention.' Some people try to 'kill time', as they say, and to do so they try to find ways of 'diverting themselves' in order to escape boredom. Quite apart from the fact that this is a criminal waste which dissipates precious capital and potential riches, it has to be added that the enterprise is vain and ineffective because the problem can be solved only by constructive work and purposeful and impassioned activity. It is when I concentrate all my attention on a task which captivates me that time passes and in a way is suppressed. We do not escape time by evasion but by attention.

'Love abolishes time.' The same goes for love. For lovers, time stands still and ceases to exist. One might think of the couple who spend a night in each other's arms, only to feel as the first rays of dawn appear that they have only been there a moment. The long night passes in the twinkling of an eye. By contrast, if while you are with your girlfriend or boyfriend you spend your time looking at your watch, you can be sure that the relationship is nearly over. The same goes for dreaming and playing: children at play lose all sense of time, and that is also true for us if we are concentrating on playing cards or chess. When we really get into a book or are caught up in work which interests us, we can even forget food and sleep. 'There is only one true time, that of love.'

The words which I used earlier, 'intensity of emotion, of life, of sensation and interest', all basically express one reality, that of love. The last function of time is without doubt to blossom and flourish in love, to suppress oneself in it. It is to this change that we are invited, and that is perhaps the ultimate meaning of our life.

I now want to end this chapter with a brief reflection on this change that is taking place in the notion of time today and on its psychological and spiritual repercussions for us.

In our day we are experiencing something like a concentration of time and a contraction of duration: a year today is worth a thousand at other times. I read recently that over the past decade more scientific discoveries have been made than during the whole period of human life on this earth. We are witnessing something like an acceleration of evolution: the motor of progress is under pressure, if not overloaded.

The course of time is accelerating by a geometric progression:

three billion years ago, life;
four million years ago, human beings;
two thousand years ago, Jesus Christ.

The speed of progress is accelerating similarly:

three million years ago the Stone Age;
ten thousand years ago the first civilization;
two hundred years ago the industrial age;
fifty years ago the beginning of the atomic age.

In the near future, the speed of ongoing changes to life may reach a critical point at which the direction changes. Perhaps that will give us a new perspective on things. And along with the acceleration of time goes another phenomenon, namely the contraction of space, and that is again something new. So on earth a process is taking place in which time and space are both becoming increasingly unreal.

When President Sadat of Egypt was shot, the news was immediately known all round the world and in a flash the heads of state had gathered in Cairo for the funeral. In France there is a new train, the TGV, which can go from Paris to Lyons in two hours. Concorde can cross the Atlantic in three and a half hours, and a satellite can circle the earth in an hour and a half. So the concentration of time is closely bound up with the contraction of space, and it seems that time and space belong together in solidarity. It is probably quite unavoidable that, seen as a whole, these phenomena have repercussions on each individual consciousness, causing a state of tension which is likely to increase.

People nowadays find in their bodies and their consciousnesses that everything is going much faster, and this causes tension. I spoke earlier of uncertainty and anxiety. This uncertainty and this anxiety are largely the result of the universal phenomenon of which I have just spoken, which has repercussions deep within the human heart. And if we are to be capable of taking such tension and living with it, we are asked for a true inner conversion, a radical change of being. Without this *sursum corda*, this raising ourselves up to higher things, we risk losing our souls and with them our humanity.

To return to where we started, I would like to stress once again that today the most urgent thing for us is to learn how to save our beings, to save our souls. Faced with this whirlwind which blows us so powerfully along its course, we must more than ever be ready deliberately to draw back, to look at things with a degree of detachment, so that we are not caught up in and torn apart by the mad rush. We must not heedlessly take part in this helter-skelter of our time, climb aboard the relentless carrousel of events, but find our place at its centre.

Here, from the centre, we can watch the movement of the world at the periphery without ourselves coming to grief. Rather than joining in with the world, we need more than ever to keep our hearts quiet and peaceful, to keep our minds calm and lucid, to keep our gazes clear and gentle, and to keep our souls as still as a mountain lake.

If we are to be capable of enduring this increasing tension in the world without dying from it, it is urgent for us to rediscover the inner peace which will allow us to dominate this movement without becoming its slaves or victims. That is not an escape from time or an evasion of the world, but an essential condition for acting in it in truth and depth and in breathing a spirit into it. More than ever we need calm, lucidity, meditation, contemplation and silence:

'What does it serve a man if he gains the whole world and loses his own soul?' (Luke 9.25).

2 The Depth of the Present

'If the moment is mine and I take heed of it,
then He is mine who made time and eternity'
(*Andreas Gryphius*)

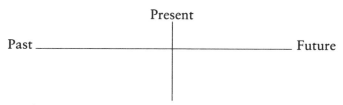

What is the present? Is it not just a simple point of contact between the past and the future, the zero point at which these two time-lines meet? But what is such a point, if not sheer nothingness? A point does not exist. In mathematics a point has no volume, no surface; it is nothing. When two straight lines meet, what is the consistency of their meeting point? It remains a mathematical abstraction, an idea, since it has no real existence. If it had a real existence, it would already be a line, a surface or a volume. But a point is neither a surface, a line or a volume; it is a point.

So if the present is only a point, it does not exist, because the past is advancing and the future is receding, the one occupying the space which the other leaves clear. When I say 'now', this 'now' has passed by the time I have stopped saying it and it already belongs to the past. If I try to catch the coming 'instant', at the moment when I catch it, it is already behind me. So the quest for the present is an endless pursuit of the intangible, the evanescent, which constantly escapes us. The past is no more, the future is not yet, but what is the present? Is it not the future, which is not yet and which is already here, becoming the past, in other words something which is no longer? Everything vanishes before our inner eye, and there is nothing but a void.

Georges Duhamel remarked: 'Between the future and memory,

human beings have to come to grips with what they least possess, the present.'

So we have arrived at an utterly discouraging idea of the present, rather like the experience of someone walking east at sunset and trying to catch his shadow.

But let us look at things a bit more closely. Is the present really only this fleeting moment without existence, without significance? Is it a point which no one can grasp, since its nature is to dissolve, instantly and irrevocably? I said earlier that the present has no existence, no permanence, that it has no reality. Now I want to assert exactly the opposite. Only the present exists and there is nothing else. The present is the only reality and it is imperishable.

The present is imperishable because everything meets and crosses in it. In this sense it is distinct from the 'ephemeral' which is purely evanescent, totally without permanence. The present concentrates time in itself: past and future are resolved in it; the arrow of the future, far from pointing towards an indefinite tomorrow, falls into this 'now' in which everything happens and from which everything originates. The present is that reality which combines the past and the future and gives both of them meaning and value. Because the present concentrates time in itself, to some degree it is beyond the influence of time and belongs to the realm of eternity.

The temptation of many of us, however, is to flee the present and to take refuge cosily in 'the good old days'. The past can be so comforting; provide such a sense of security; we feel so at ease in what we have lived through, like being in a house we have lived in for a long time, that in our return to the past there is always the danger of evasion and a flight from the real world. Now the real world is the present, and nothing but that really exists for me.

People begin to grow old from the moment they close their eyes and take refuge in the past. For young people, the opposite is the case. Their temptation is not to escape the present for the past but to escape into a utopian, marvellous, miraculous future, somewhere on the horizon. This future is called 'tomorrow': tomorrow I will do..., tomorrow I will be..., tomorrow I could... Instead of engaging in today's struggle they risk living out their dreams of tomorrow and the day after tomorrow in their imagination.

Albert Camus commented: 'The greatest fidelity to the past is to give everything to the present.'

In other words, the past is the force which has shaped me and made me, and is now standing at the gateway of the present, where it presses and pushes with all its vigour to move me on further, to shape and to create, to create myself. With all that I have been and all that I have experienced, I am invited to do new things in this present which is given me. So the past exists, but as a power capable of constructing the present.

What I am talking about is therefore an invitation to live out the present in fullness. The word 'fullness' is a marvellous one. It expresses a density of existence in which one can steep oneself and feel filled, satiated, refreshed. We have to know how to dive into the present like a diver diving into the sea, completely and totally. We need to learn how to immerse ourselves with all our being in the here and now.

We have to tell ourselves that every moment of our lives is unique; the moment 'now' is unique. And this moment bears an absolutely unique message. The important thing for us is to seize this message. And this message is neither that of yesterday nor that of the day before yesterday, neither that of last week nor that of last year. Moreover, it is not that of tomorrow or the day after tomorrow or next year. It is that of now. The present moment brings me on a plate a hot, burning, absolutely new and original message which can enrich me infinitely. That is the sense in which I was speaking of fullness. 'Now' bears within it a fullness to which I need to open myself.

I must receive this magic of the passing moment as grace, pluck it like a fruit, take it in both hands and bite it with my teeth to taste and savour it. I do that by an act of concentrated attention: attention to the fleeting moment. To the degree to which I am capable of this act, the most trivial event can leave a deep mark on me and become a true existential experience.

In fact I truly remember only those acts which I experienced intently with my whole being – on such a day, at such a time, in such a place, with such a person I experienced something unique and unforgettable, which was a point of reference for the rest of my life.

Why was that? Because between me and what I experienced there was action and reaction. Because I experienced and savoured this apparently trivial event in the depth of the present. We need to ask ourselves whether we are really present in our lives, whether we are really taking part in the events that we are experiencing.

Do we pass by the real? Do we not often just run parallel to a certain number of the realities which surround us, as strangers and distracted spectators of the world in which we live, a world which does not really get to us?

Here I would like to commend something which in religious terminology is called 'self-examination'. I know that some of you will raise your eyebrows at that unattractive word, which evokes a morbid obsession with sin and a feeling of guilt towards it. However, self-examination is not what you think. Before being a meticulous review of all the mistakes you have made during the day, all your follies, it is first of all a recollection of the moments of grace which you have experienced. For me it is recollection in depth of what has been a unique and singular experience, one which has marked me and transformed me. Only such experiences allow me really to grow and develop. It is to the degree that my being has some contact with reality, action and reaction, that it develops.

Self-examination is the time when I pay attention to those important experiences which have made me grow, to those moments of the present from which I draw all the substance and all the sap, and which because of that form 'moments of grace'. A moment of grace is an ecstatic moment in which I decentre myself completely and plunge into a reality which fascinates, absorbs and fills me. It is a moment in which I open myself to the Spirit and let it invade me.

Self-examination consists in identifying these moments of grace, in finding in my day those 'touches of the Spirit', and at the same time in noting the moments when I became hardened and shut in on myself, when I was absent-minded or distracted, when I passed reality and other people by without wanting to get more deeply into them. Here the Spirit could not reach me because I was not there; I was not accessible to its breath and its grace. For grace is given to us in the present, in the action by which we are present, and make ourselves present to others and to the world. By opening us up to all that is around us, this act of presence also opens us up to grace.

Seen from this perspective, self-examination then takes on an extraordinary richness. It forms the harvest of the day, the moment when we gather those precious moments of fullness which we experienced during the day, to taste and savour them in a mood of thanksgiving.

The mistake of those who calculate time mathematically is to forget that every moment is unique, so that moments cannot be added together one by one. When I say 'one hour, two hours, three hours, four hours', it is as if the first, second, third and fourth hours were all alike. But they are not. These hours are quite different from one another. To the degree that at a precise moment I have had a quite unique experience, this hour infinitely surpasses the concept of sixty minutes and takes on quite a different density and dimension, beause I have experienced something which I did not experience in the other three hours, and this something cannot be compared with all the rest.

The mathematical measuring of time is quite a relative matter. I am not going to return to it, because I spoke of it at length in the first chapter. However, now we can see how the two themes are connected.

What is true on the physical level is also true on the psychological and spiritual levels. Time is relative to the quality and the intensity with which I live out the present moment. The French poetess Countess de Noailles wrote, 'We shall never be able to call our souls our own more than we can this evening.' That's a splendid remark! She thought that the evening she was spending with a friend was unrepeatable. They both experienced it so deeply that they already found it quite incomparable. And I am sure that each of us has had this personal experience in our lives, on a particular day and in a particular place.

If we really enter into this perspective, then we make the marvellous discovery that each moment everything is new. And nothing is old. The old does not exist. The old exists only for those who make themselves old, who want to be old. Everything is new each moment for those who have young hearts. This reminds me of a fine verse by Mallarmé: 'Today is virgin-fresh and beautiful.'

Today is the reality which is born at this moment as it were from nothing, fresh as the dew at the first moment of creation.

Children live in this wonderful world of incessant amazement. Children experience only the present. But as we grow up, we lose this good fortune and look nervously forwards and backwards – and do only that. By contrast, children live only in the present moment. When they play, they are caught up in their games, lost in them. When you tell them a story, there they are, mouth open, wide-eyed, lapping up the story, thinking of nothing else, all else forgotten. When they go to sleep, they are tranquil and restful: 'Sweet dreams,' we say. But when *we* go to bed, we wonder 'What have I done? What have I not done? What am I going to do tomorrow? What should I have done today?' And we get insomnia.

We need to react against what we call habit, and that includes dull everyday repetition. I can make my stereotyped actions new each time if I can turn them into something unique and original.

You may say to me, 'But I cook every day.' 'Yes.' 'I go to the office every day.' 'Yes.' 'So?' 'Today can be very different from yesterday.' 'But it's the same cooking, the same office.' 'Not necessarily.'

'Why?'

'Because you are no longer the same. You are different from yesterday, and by the same token your cooking, your office are also different. The people you will meet today will also have changed; they are not the same as they were yesterday and the day before.'

If I am capable of living out this daily newness, everything will take on an inner light and a new appearance every day. It's a question of soul, a question of inner attitude; it's a question of being young at heart. Keep your heart young, and your life will be new each day. Some people find their life terrifyingly monotonous: yesterday, today, tomorrow; office, travel, sleep. It's all a matter of the attitude with which we approach things. We can restore and refresh ourselves by thinking positively, by curiosity, by enthusiasm. Every day can be something special.

Our discouragement and feeling that everyday life is intolerable comes about above all because we are always dealing with the same people: the husband with his wife, the wife with her husband, children with their parents, parents with their children, teachers with their pupils, employers with their employees, and so on. And so we no longer really see one another. Why is that? It's because we think that we have discovered husband or wife, pupils or employees. A husband may think he knows his wife inside out, that he has squeezed her like a lemon so that there is nothing left but skin and pips. There's no more to get out of her. But we never get to the end of other people. We never get to the end of our husbands, wives, children, friends, colleagues at work. Human beings have inexhaustible depths, and if someone seems to me always to be the same, it is because I have not yet discovered his or her real depths. What we need to do is look again, change the way in which we look at one another.

One day I had this experience with someone who had been living next to me for years. I said to myself, 'Look, you really don't know him.' 'What? I know him very well.' 'No you don't. Look at him today as though you were meeting him for the first time.' So that day I did, and something quite essential dawned on me, something very important that I had not yet discovered about this person I thought I knew.

What I have said about meeting other people I could equally well say about getting to know myself. I think I know myself. But in fact I scarcely do at all. The essentials escape me. So there are some people who have had too much of themselves, who feel tired of themselves, who are discouraged, like the prophet Elijah who collapsed under a tree and said, 'It is enough, Lord. Now take away my life' (I Kings 19.4). That was the point at which God, with a morsel of bread and some water, gave him new strength which enabled him to go for forty days and forty nights to the mountain of God.

There are people who think that they have exhausted what they are. They have to be told, 'Look deep within yourself, and at the depth of your being you will discover new strength, unsuspected riches.'

Look at other people, look at yourselves, look at your country. When we look at our country we may well be deeply pessimistic, hopelessly disappointed. And very many people may be unable to believe in a revival, believe that things can get any better. A negative past can often make us react to the present in an excessively negative way, write causes and people off and not give them a chance. So we need to tear down walls, to look for a new being and allow it to emerge.

Great educators or great spiritual figures are those who release people from their past, put them in the present, and from that position show them a new perspective on the future. These are the people who believe that life can begin again and who create confidence in others. 'Today your life is beginning again; today everything is new and you can make a new start. Do you believe that?' 'Yes, I do.' 'Your past no longer exists. I have forgotten it. You forget it. Your life begins now. Now. Do you believe that?' 'Yes, I believe it.' That is rebirth and resurrection and radical transformation.

That is what is called a conversion, i.e., according to the etymology of the word, a 180-degree turn in which instead of looking backwards a person suddenly looks forwards, and as a result becomes a completely new being. Psychology all too often encloses people in their past, their childhood, their education, their instincts, their heredity, their sub-conscious, and this past weighs so heavily on the present that people become its slaves and its prisoners. This is where faith comes in, stronger and more true than any psychoanalysis: the word of faith which says to people, 'You are not a prisoner of your past or of your subconscious or of your heredity or of your education or of anything that you have experienced so far. And today, now, your life is beginning.'

That is resurrection faith. Not a future resurrection at the end of history, in a more or less uncertain future, but resurrection 'today, here and now'. That is the good news, the joyful news, the great news of the gospel:

The lame walk, the deaf hear, the blind see, the dead are raised (Matthew 11.2-15; Luke 7.22).

Arise, take up your bed and walk (Mark 2.9).

Lazarus, come forth (John 11.43).

That is the liberating word of Christ which we have to take account of and repeat after him to all those lying around us, dead tired, the victims of their past. Grace is offered to us, here and now, to begin our lives all over again.

When St Augustine discovered God in his life he exclaimed, 'What beauty, existing from eternity yet always new!'

Our God is the God who is new each day and who renews men and women each day, giving them new strength and new youth. 'I will go to the altar of God, the God of my joy and gladness,' runs Psalm 42, which began the old Latin Mass.

Another idea which I want to go into more deeply is that of contemplation, because there is a close relationship between the present and contemplation. Contemplation is the capacity to steep ourselves in the present, to look at the world and others in an entirely open way, so freely and disinterestedly that it can easily penetrate to the heart of reality.

The difference between contemplation and action is that in action, as soon as I see anything, I say, 'What's that for? What can I do with it? How can I use it? How much does it cost? Where does it come from?' This is a utilitarian and pragmatic attitude, based on intelligence.

By contrast, contemplation does not seek to know the use of something, what I can do with it, the profit I will gain from it, but is content to look on it with tenderness and love, and that creates the possibility of penetrating slowly right into its depths. Contemplation is steeped in the present; it is a welcoming of being into itself without any afterthoughts, the love of the other simply for the other's sake.

Our relations with one another are often purely utilitarian: 'Good morning, sir. What are you doing? Where are you working? Can I have your visiting card?...' And I make a note in my book: 'This man works in such and such a company; one day he may be able to help me out.' You may smile, but that's what happens. Our relationships with one another are often centred on interest and profit. We ask ourselves how we can exploit or make use of a particular person. And that can be true even when we gather together in church meetings.

Quite gratuitous, disinterested encounters, meetings with another person just for that person's sake, are very rare. 'I'm interested in you just for your own sake, because I enjoy your company.'

This attitude develops in us an interest in other people: concern for other people, attention to other people. And that's what contemplation is.

Contemplation is not necessarily a matter of thinking of God. Contemplation is a matter of immersing ourselves in the heart of reality. And to anyone who is capable of taking the plunge, reality suddenly unveils itself, presents itself in its truth, reveals its truth. But this revelation is possible only if our gaze is pure enough to penetrate this secret sanctuary without violating it or seeking to possess it.

Contemplation is an attitude of mind which does not need either a monastery or a desert to be practised in. We can develop this contemplative gaze which penetrates to the heart of reality in order to reach its soul in the midst of our ordinary everyday life. Contemplation is the capacity to live out the present fully.

John Dewey, the great American educational theorist, stressed the sovereign importance of experience in education. 'Only living experience shapes and determines a child's development.' In Egypt, almost all education is based on memory and the effort of memorizing. Instead of letting pupils have experiences, teachers make them learn by heart the results of the experiments of others. Now Dewey tells us that anything that children have not worked out for themselves is nothing, pure zero. It does not leave any mark on them and slides off them like water off a duck's back. At the end of the child's education we have an empty, dried-up being, who has learnt a good deal, but whose heart has remained empty because he or she has experienced nothing, felt nothing, experimented with nothing. That is why so many schools leave so little mark on children: their real life is elsewhere.

John Dewey says to us: 'Each of us must think back and ask ourselves what has become of all the knowledge that we accumulated during our years at college.' What did you learn during your years at school? Dewey went on to ask: 'Why are we obliged to relearn everything afterwards? Because this teaching was not based on an immediate and actual experience of reality, but on notions aimed at preparing for experiences to come.'

At school we may be prepared for future experiences, but we may not have present experiences. But the only thing that counts is an intense present experience. Dewey again comments:

> It is at the moment when one has an experience that one derives from it all that is possible to retain. If, by contrast, we sacrifice the present for the future, as happens in traditional schools, we ruin everything and this supposed preparation for the future is a sheer waste of time.

> We always live in the present moment and not in any other, and it is only by deriving the maximum from this passing moment that we really prepare ouselves for the future. Living the experience of the present moment to the full is the only thing that matters for our future formation.

Let me add something from my own experience. If you want to give a lecture, do not think about what you are going to say when you give the lecture, but try, rather, to feel intensely what you want to say, to live out the subject in depth to the point of being literally possessed by it. You may then be sure that the lecture will go well. Why? Because the lecture will become a living spring, deriving from a real experience. That is why the Lord said to us, 'Take no thought for the morrow; the morrow will take thought for itself' (Matt.6.34).

Live the present to the full! Live out the moment! Immerse

yourself in experience! That is the best guarantee for your preparation for tomorrow.

Making the substance of the present a personal experience by steeping oneself deeply in it is the best guarantee for whatever is to come. You may perhaps have read the famous novel by Nikos Kazantzakis, *Zorba the Greek*. It made a great impression on me and I quote it often, because I find the figure of Zorba quite extraordinary; for me he is a unique figure in world literature. This is what he says:

> I've stopped thinking all the time of what happened yesterday. And stopped asking myself what's going to happen tomorrow. What happens today, this minute, is what I care about. I say, 'What are you doing at this moment, Zorba?' 'I'm sleeping.' 'Well, sleep well.' 'What are you doing at this moment, Zorba?' 'I'm working.' 'Well, work well.' 'What are you doing at this moment, Zorba?' 'I'm kissing a woman.' 'OK, kiss her well, Zorba! And forget all the rest while you're doing it; there's nothing else on earth, only you and her. Get on with it!'

And later:

> When she, Bouboulina, was alive, you know, no one had ever given her so much pleasure as I did – old rag-and-bone Zorba. Do you want to know why? Because anyone else in the world, while they were kissing her, kept thinking about their fleets, or the king of Crete, or their stripes and decorations, or their wives.But I used to forget everything else, and she knew that, the old trollop. And let me tell you this, my learned friend – there's no greater pleasure for a woman than that.

Ask yourself the same questions as old Zorba did and live in the moment. Follow his example, his complete interest and genius in every form of work and occupation.

Now I want to develop some important ideas of the German philosopher Martin Heidegger, for he too stresses the unique value of the present as the context of action. For Heidegger, the present is presence, presence in the world. 'Man is a being in the world, but he is not in it like a coat in a cupboard.'

We are beings who act; we are in an interrupted process of action and reaction with our world. Science, too, tells us that every reality in the world, even matter, is in action and reaction with the rest of the universe, if only on the basis of universal attraction, the law of gravity. A piece of chalk that I hold in my hand, which evidently does not have the least thing in common with a table, in reality has a good deal to do with one. Everything is related and akin to everything else, and is in interaction with it: you as a person and the Eiffel tower or the pyramid of Cheops are related to this piece of chalk in my hand. In a most mysterious way the part is bound up with the whole, what we call the universe. There is even a real relationship of action and reaction between this chalk and the remotest star, for 'to be' means 'to be active': all being is active.

That is true to the greatest extent of human beings, who are never purely passive. Human beings, Heidegger says, are not just a part of this world but above all are in it. And being in the world means being constrained to act, to take an attitude, to be responsible for one's existence and the possibilities for which one opts. The future is a matter of coming to oneself. The future is the projection of our possibilities of realizing ourselves from what we are, i.e. from our past. At the beginning of my project I take on my past and project it on my future as a flow of energy. My project is what I already bear within myself, what I really am, and what one day will be realized. Then I shall have 'come to myself', I shall have 'become myself'. So, strictly speaking, the present is my birth; it is the moment at which I bring myself to birth, the moment in which the project takes shape and comes to maturity. Therefore in the end neither the past nor the future count, but only this germ of the self in me, which is the project of my life and which will develop slowly through successive acts of presence.

So past, present and future, these three temporal spheres, are simply the development of the depth of my being and the realization of the decisive plan of my life. Heidegger says that time is simply the 'development of a project in space', the realization of a plan. Time as a task! These thoughts fit very well with a splendid passage from the biblical book of Ecclesiastes, of which I am very fond:

There is a time for every matter under heaven:
a time to be born, and a time to die;
a time to plant, and a time to pluck up what is planted;
a time to kill, and a time to heal;
a time to break down, and a time to build up;

a time to weep, and a time to laugh;
a time to mourn, and a time to dance;
a time to cast away stones, and a time to gather stones together;
a time to embrace, and a time to refrain from embracing;
a time to seek, and a time to lose;
a time to keep, and a time to cast away;
a time to rend, and a time to sew;
a time to keep silence, and a time to speak;
a time to love, and a time to hate;
a time for war, and a time for peace.
What gain has the worker from his toil?

I have seen the business that God has given to the sons of men to be busy with. He has made everything appropriate to its time; also he has put eternity into man's mind, yet so that he cannot find out what God has done from the beginning to the end (Ecclesiastes 3.1-11).

Because there is a time for everything, immerse yourself in the present, and do completely what you are doing, with all your heart.

Another idea of Heidegger's is the relationship which he establishes between the present and presence. There is no present in itself, but only present for a presence. It is my presence and your presence here which give the present its substance. This view of Heidegger's about time is resolutely personalist. There is no time without presence, and it is the person who incarnates the present, by being capable of being present to himself or herself and to reality. There is no present in itself, but there is a presence or presences in presence.

I would now like to say something about three modes of presence:

1. Being present to ourselves;
2. Being present to the world;
3. Being present to our fellow human beings.

To be present to ourselves, which is something on which we have already reflected at length, is to refuse to escape into the past or into the present, and instead to enter into the present moment, to reflect on oneself, to gather oneself together. But modern men and women find it extremely difficult to live out this act of presence in this way. The characteristic feature of our age is the discontent, the anxiety that we meet in ourselves; we escape from ourselves.

Everybody complains about the noise, but what do we do when we are given a moment of peace and quiet, when we can be alone? We rush to the radio, the video, the television - or to the telephone, so that we can fill our solitude with sound and pictures. We suffer under the stress of events, but when we are by ourselves we bring this stress upon ourselves yet again by means of the television, in a more concentrated and louder form. We flee from our own presence, which is tangible in the stillness; we feel anxious about being alone with our selves and looking at our own image face to face.

How difficult it is to devote ourselves to prayer and meditation! I know some young people in a meditation group who have been trying to spend half an hour each day in silent prayer. If you ask them how easy it is, they will tell you that it is very difficult. Nevertheless, out of experience they recommend others not to turn silence into emptiness, which has to be filled at any price. Put your book aside and turn off the music. Sink into yourself. Only if you do this will the most important things be revealed to you and will you see the source in which you will find your origins. Those who are capable of being present to themselves in this way in prayer will find that in everything they do and say later, they will achieve a power which is almost limitless. Their language can become light and fire, and all their activity will prove effective. Why? Because they have immersed themselves in their being there; they have concentrated their thought, breathing, speech, action and being; and this concentrated power of being releases energy, so that their words and actions become amazing powerful.

A saint is a person who has found the unity of his or her being and who radiates and becomes effective from this focal point. His or her gaze penetrates others and moves them deeply; his or her words can quite simply move mountains, change society, help to renew our world. But the majority of us live in quite the opposite way; we prefer dispersion, distraction, which means that we apply only five or ten per cent of our true being to what we are doing and saying. That is why our action is often so superficial and ineffective.

There are techniques borrowed from Yoga or Zen, based on bodily feelings, to remedy this state. If you feel that your mind is wandering all over the place and is running off in all directions, turning to memories or plans; if you feel that a whirlwind is carrying you far away from the present in its spiral, become aware of your body again.

My body, my arms, my legs. Look, I have two arms. I have just seen them. I wasn't aware of them until just now and I can feel them resting on the table. I can feel my body resting on a chair, my legs on the carpet. I brush my hand over my face and I suddenly discover that I have a forehead, cheeks, a nose, ears. Little by little I feel a sensation of calmness and my mind slowly reintegrates my body and brings me back to myself. It's simple and very effective. Try the exercise for yourself, and you will see. Whole books have been written about it. I find particularly interesting the Vittoz method, which is based on 'bodily sensation'; it's a really good therapy for anxiety.

The phrase 'being beside ourselves' conveys the same sort of thing. We feel alienated from ourselves. And if we are going to come to ourselves again, we have to get ourselves under control. That means first of all controlling our bodies. Modern men and women can lose themselves, no longer be in full possession of their bodies, their senses; often they don't know one which way to lie to go to sleep. 'So many demands are made on me that I no longer know who I am.' No, for there is a time for everything, as we heard from the Bible, a time also for stillness and absorption – our fuel tank.

So the first priority is for us to be present to ourselves; this is our experience of our own presence. Secondly, we must be present to others, present in the world. It is not enough for us deliberately to make contact only with our own bodies, as we are taught by the methods I have mentioned; it is equally important to be in contact with our environment, which means constructing it and constantly developing it. We should become increasingly attentive to the details of the things and the beings around us, even to those things which seem insignificant, since nothing is without significance. We have to see everything and take it in. That will make our present ever richer and more precious, and we shall make contact with the reality of being.

We have plenty of time for this approach in our everyday life. If you are waiting for a bus or a train or a plane which is late and you are becoming edgy, look carefully at the people around you. Look at the cut of their clothes, the colour of their hair and the hairstyles, whether a man has a moustache, and so on. You may say that that doesn't interest you. In which case I must tell you that it should interest you, and that it is very important at this particular moment to know whether a certain person has a moustache or not.

If you do this, you will suddenly feel a great calm sweep over you and you may find something else in view, like a beautiful tree spreading its branches and saying to you 'admire me'. Or there might be a young woman a little further off with a certain air about her as she walks which says 'admire me'. You will find deep inside you a profound peace as you discover the reality that you are trying to escape. And then when what you have been waiting for actually arrives, it will be a pleasant surprise.

I recently had just this kind of experience. I had to celebrate mass at the Jesuit house at six and it was already twenty past. I couldn't find a taxi or a bus and I had to walk quite a distance from the central station to take a tram. Normally I would have been seething as I sat there in the tram, telling myself that there were fifteen people waiting for the mass. But at that point I said to myself, 'What's the point of sitting in your tram seething?', so I began to look at the people and the things around me. At one point I noticed that the tram station had not changed for forty-five or fifty years, since I was a child. I watched the stationmaster blowing his big whistle, but the tram didn't move. I smiled. Finally it set off, but it went very slowly and I said to myself, 'Just think of it – a tram that goes slowly!', and I smiled. Then I looked at the students getting on and strap-hanging. It all made me very calm.

I arrived at the mass thirty-five minutes late. But even if I had been in a bad temper, I would still have arrived at the mass thirty-five minutes late. Nervousness, excitement, anxiety often make us lose precious energy which we are just squandering. By living in the present, we concentrate all our potentialities, all our strength, all our energies, and exploit them to the full. There is a deep wisdom here.

This attention to concrete, ordinary reality can help us to make some extraordinary discoveries. We may notice with amazement that things are more beautiful and more interesting than we had thought. The artist sees that, and by concentrating on the most ordinary things can discover in them a hidden beauty which escapes us.

You will know about Van Gogh and his famous picture of the basket chair. Van Gogh turned this chair, which none of us would dare to offer to a guest, into a masterpiece. How did he do it? He knew how to look at it with love, knew how to look at it in a certain way, and this chair suddenly became beautiful. For most of us, 'beautiful' means sophisticated, ornate, gilded, decorated. People make frightful sitting rooms with gilding and imitation Aubusson tapestries and artificial bronzes, and we say, 'How beautiful!'

There are those who can only admire museum-pieces. They rush to Florence to see Michelangelo's David or to the Louvre to stare in admiration at the Mona Lisa, because someone has told them that these are beautiful and that they must be seen. But why go so far to admire beauty? Why go to museums to contemplate works of art? Your everyday world is bursting with works of art; they are all around you. Go to the seashore, sit on the sand and look at a small shell – it is far more beautiful than anything in the Vatican museum. Go into your garden, on to a balcony, into a park, and look at little plants beginning to grow, perhaps moving gently in the morning breeze. Is that not far more beautiful than anything in the Louvre?

This morning I spent a long time sitting on the concrete steps which lead down into the garden watching a cat surrounded by its six kittens. It was a real party. The kittens were literally laying siege to their mother: they were pouncing on her, nestling up to her, looking for milk from her, never leaving her alone for a moment, turning somersaults all round her. It was a marvellous sight, and I told myself that it was better than any of the films of Fellini or Rossellini. Why go to the cinema? Why switch on the television? I had much more.

The artist is the one who knows how to look; the mystic is the one who knows how to contemplate.

There are people who cannot appreciate their local countryside. They have to go to some remote place and discover the beauty of that. They have to consult their travel guides to know what has to be admired and when you have to say 'That's beautiful'. And they have to send postcards with exotic postmarks on them. But in virtually any place there is beauty for those who have eyes to see. The great photographers are not those who take pictures of magnificent countryside or majestic monuments. Anyone can do that. The real artist is the one who can make a masterpiece of a water jug, a rainy day, an old chair or an old dead tree. Why?

Because artists can open their eyes and their hearts to the most ordinary reality and find it extraordinary.

I have spoken about presence to the body, which is a matter of being present to ourselves. And I have also spoken of presence to the world, which is a matter of being present to reality. Now I have to talk about 'presence to the other', which I already mentioned earlier. This presence to the other is first of all 'presence of mind'.

Presence of mind is not just the capacity to mobilize our intellectual faculties to confront a critical situation, a fortuitous and unforeseen event. Quite apart from this practical aspect, presence of mind is presence to the other, the capacity to devote my whole attention to the person I encounter, to put myself wholly at his or her disposal.

If I am to do that, I have to convince myself that the person before me deserves my whole interest, my whole attention, my whole being. Some people are capable of this intense presence which makes one feel understood and known, makes oneself feel that what one is going to say has already been anticipated; such people are capable of vibrating to whatever one has to say: they can experience your drama or joy, drink in your words. You can feel that by their looks, their expressions, their actions and their words.

By contrast there are people who receive you in their office between their telephone, their diaries, their books and their files, and who say, 'Go on, I'm listening.' They will be listening to you while looking over the last report typed by their secretary, or the telephone book, or their eyes will stray to the morning paper. Oh yes, they're listening! When I find people like that I just get up and leave.

A great deal of misunderstanding and incomprehension, a great deal of tension, arises because we are not present to one another. We are there with our bodies but not with our hearts or our minds. We are there like wallpaper on a wall, or, to use Heidegger's phrase, like a coat in a cupboard.

'Being there' is not a physical act, but a spiritual act which involves our whole bodies. Being present to other people means giving them our time, our attention, our minds and our hearts. Presence of mind is also presence of the heart and of all our being. It can be seen in looks; it can be seen in smiles; it can be felt in handshakes or embraces. If that happens, there is true communication, action and reaction, and our presence to the other becomes an active and transforming presence.

I can spend two hours with a person without anything changing between us, because there has been no real encounter; we have spent two hours in parallel, as strangers to each other. By contrast, I need spend only five minutes with someone else to experience him or her with such attention, such intensity, such a 'presence of mind and heart', that these five minutes have truly been an 'event'. Something has happened because there has been real encounter. An encounter is not a juxtaposition of bodies but an osmosis of souls, a presence of minds, a fusion of hearts. All that happens only in the depth of the present as a place where things happen.

So only the present counts, for only it is true, only it exists. The present is the place of history; it is where history is made or unmade. It is here, today, now, that the destiny of the world is played out. What I say, what I do, here and now, changes the orientation of things, changes the course of history. Can you believe that? If you can, your present will take on an extraordinary density, fullness, force. Every instant, every moment, every present in my life means a change in universal history. It is not just elections that change our history. Nor is just discoveries like Einstein's theory of relativity that change history. Each one of my choices, each one of my moments, represents this turning point in universal history, since because of them history takes another course and by my action my present takes on fullness, seriousness, importance.

Once that has been understood, life changes meaning and becomes a passionate adventure. I once said to someone, 'Life is beautiful, isn't it?' He replied, 'No, it's not beautiful; it's fascinating.' The word beautiful is indeed inadequate to express the density of our existence. This existence is beyond beauty; rather, it is of another order, the tragic and sublime, and it is for me to make it so by living it to the full with all its intensity, by making each of my moments a present that I seize with both hands, an act of presence which immerses itself in the heart of reality.

Those who can understand that will help to transform the face of the earth.

3   Eternity at the Heart of Time

Jesus said to them, 'My Father is working still, and I am working' (*John 5.17*)

Eternity is a word which is largely out of favour at present. At best it is avoided or overlooked, and it can be totally denied. It is assumed that the category of the eternal is diametrically opposed to the temporal; it is thought that it is a kind of refuge, beyond the historical and physical world, into which people feel themselves born. Eternity can only mean 'somewhere else', in which many men and women take refuge, an opium of the people, a flight towards a distant and inaccessible unreality.

This criticism is certainly justified if applied to a particular conception of eternity, which tends to assimilate it to an atemporal, abstract order, to something which takes place up there beyond the clouds. There is no way, no communication, between the temporal and the eternal: in this view temporal and eternal represent two parallel lines which never meet. In order to attain the eternal, human beings have to abandon the temporal and escape this earth to find 'heaven'.

Another reason why eternity has fallen out of favour is that it has been conceived of as eternal duration, losing itself behind us in the darkness of time, from well before the creation of the world, and then reaching forward and disappearing before us into the mists of an indeterminate future, 'for ever and ever', as we say in our liturgies. That would make eternity a monotonous and boring eternalism which will never stop going on.

Moreover, such a conception suggests a phenomenon of repetition and morose tautology in which God indefinitely repeats himself *ad nauseam*, in incessant self-repetition, from one identical thing to the next. This is rather like the teaching of the fifth-century BC philosopher Parmenides: indefinite and immutable permanence of pure identity with itself.

The notion of eternity sometimes evokes a picture of God eternally contemplating himself with complacency and satisfaction, incessantly admiring himself as in a mirror: 'How beautiful I am! How great I am, how strong and powerful I am! I am God, always the same, always myself, for ever and ever.' And the saints in heaven, in beatific admiration, would have no function other than to praise, glorify and flatter this magnificent perfect God, beatifically enjoying the compliments that his heavenly court heaps on him.

I want us to try once and for all to get rid of this aberrant idea that we carry around in one form or another in our sub-conscious, and replace it with the true notion of eternity, which is the fullness of the present.

Here we pick up the theme of the previous chapter, which I would ask you to keep in mind as we go on.

When God reveals his identity in the book of Revelation, he says:

'I am the Alpha and Omega, the First and the Last, the Beginning and the End. I am he who is and was and is to come... the Living One' (Rev.1.8; 1.17; 22.13).

The eternity expressed by all these words can be summed up in the last of them: the Living One. God is 'the Living One'. That is how he already describes himself in the Old Testament. For Christians, the idea of the living God necessarily meets up with the idea of God as Trinity. God can only be living if he is Trinity. Why?

The gospel reveals to us that God is not pure identity with himself, but otherness and dialogue in the oneness of his divine essence. It is in the dialogue of the Father and the Son, in this outflowing of the Father into the Son, by the Spirit, that God is alive. God would not be a living God if he did not have within him this possibility of continually letting his living nature flow into that other self who is his Son, who lives within the divine heart, where the One is indivisible.

God is the living spring, the source of life. We have to say that before all creation, before any external expression of God's divine life, God is the source, the source in himself, of his very being. But without approaching the mystery of the Trinity, it is impossible to see how God could be the source in this way. The source of what? The source for what? It is equally difficult to see how God could be Love. Love of whom? Love for whom?

God is the source because God is Love, because God is Trinity. This eternal birth of God to himself in the mystery of the Trinity has as its cause the divine altruism which is at the same time an 'infinite capacity to love'. If God were not love, infinite love, God would not be eternal, God would not be sparkling life, would not be a source, a spring.

God is a living spring – and 'spring' is so rich, so profound a word that the church fathers often used it to talk of God. A spring is always new, always bubbling up, always flowing; it never exhausts itself, never grows old. So to say that God is a spring is to say that he is always young. The secret of God's youth is that God constantly empties himself – and constantly renews himself. God's being is not an indefinite repetition of himself, an eternal monotony, but a constant renewal. God never repeats himself. The being of God is always new. The face of God is always new. It is the interchange within the Trinity that is the secret of the perpetual being of God, making God an ever-flowing spring in the inexhaustible wonder of infinite ecstasy and self-giving.

The French writer Charles Péguy wrote a very beautiful poem which shows God contemplating his work at the beginning of creation, the brand-new world which has just emerged from his hands. God looks at it with wonder as the reflection of his own newness and his own youth:

And God himself, both young and eternal,
looked upon the flower of youth.
Like a father, he looked with paternal eye
on the world, gathered together like a humble village...

And God himself, both young and eternal,
looked upon time and age.
Like a father, he looked with paternal eye
on the world laid out like a beautiful village...

And God himself, both young and eternal,
looked upon time and space.
Calmly, gazing down with paternal affection,
he saw the image of God...

God is young and eternal. He is young because he is eternal, and he is eternal because he is young. There is a tendency to depict God as an old man with a beard, coming from the distant ages with all the weight of past centuries on his shoulders. But the reality is exactly the opposite. God, rather, should be represented as a child, as a baby, as a dawn, as a morning. It is not God who is old; we are old. God is eternal youth, the capacity for constant rejuvenation.

It was by discovering this eternal infancy of God that another French poet, Paul Claudel, was converted to Christianity one Christmas night. In this child in the manger, this newborn of Bethlehem, he discovered with wonder and amazement the most perfect expression of the very being of God, and his whole life was transformed as a result.

Christmas is the precise moment at which this eternal youth of God, this eternal childlikeness of God, irrupts into our world and establishes itself there for ever. In Jesus Christ, eternity has penetrated to the heart of time, the heart of history and the human heart.

In Jesus Christ a new and eternal covenant has been made between God and humankind. Note how Jesus brings together these two words, new and eternal.

We sometimes get the impression that in the incarnation God came to pay us a visit and then withdrew again into his heaven. The incarnation seems like a parenthesis which is opened at Christmas and closed again at the Ascension. God comes to live with us for thirty-three years and then says 'Good-bye' and returns home.

But that's not true. God has not come just to pay us a visit. Christ did not leave at Ascension; he simply disappeared from our eyes. For just before he 'went up to heaven', he told us, 'I am with you to the end of the world' (Matt.28.20). That is to indicate to us that his incarnation is a definitive act, an act by which he has inserted himself once for all at the heart of time and of history.

We say, 'The Lord came' (in the past) and we say 'The Lord will come again' (in the future), but what we should really be saying is 'The Lord is coming, coming, coming' (in the present).

'I am he who is, and was, and is to come...' (Rev.1.8). The Lord is the one who does not cease to come, because he is here. The Lord is here, we sing in the French mass, in a marvellous hymn which follows the consecration:

[39

Christ has come.
Christ was born.
Christ has suffered.
Christ died.
Christ is risen.
Christ is alive.
Christ will come again.
Christ is here.

Yes, indeed he is here with us. Between his first and second coming, between the 'has appeared' and 'will come again', both of them visible and tangible, between this past and this future, there is the daily and continual coming of Christ in each one of us; there is the actuality of his active and hidden presence in history to bring this history to its consummation.

Another fine hymn which we know and love in the mass runs,

You are here at the heart of our lives
You make us live.

Here we have the presence of eternity at the heart of time, through Jesus Christ who gives meaning to time and history and who completely fulfils and renews them because God cannot enter into human history without turning everything upside down, without renewing and transforming everything. With this mystery which has been accomplished once and for all in Jesus Christ, at a stroke history has reached the level of eternity, anticipating its final destiny in what has been called the fullness of time. That's a very fine expression!

The fullness of time, which is the coming of Christ, does not simply mean that something precise happened at H-hour and D-Day. The expression 'fullness of time' means more than that. It means that in Jesus Christ there is a summing up, a recapitulation of fullness:

For in him all the fullness of God was pleased to dwell...

For in him the whole fullness of deity dwells bodily (Colossians 1.19; 2.9).

In the historical event of Jesus, time in some way contracts, concentrates itself, adds itself up. Jesus Christ embraces all history within himself and sums it up. In other words, this history which unrolled itself before him and which will prolong itself after him is wholly present in him, and that is why he has been able to redeem it.

To say that Jesus is the Alpha and Omega presupposes that the thirty-three years which he lived are in fact, in a mystery which is beyond our comprehension, the total history of humankind, time concentrated in its totality. If this were not the case, Christ would not be the Alpha and the Omega; he would be simply a man who was born in the year 4 BC in the reign of the Emperor Augustus and who died in the year 29 under the Emperor Tiberius and when Pontius Pilate was governor of Judaea: a historical, temporal and finite being – like you or me.

The reality of Christ infinitely surpasses the narrow limits of historical life. Men like John and Paul were able to recognize in this being of flesh and blood called Jesus of Nazareth the head of humanity, the one who embraces history in his person and then transcends it. Now the mystery of Jesus, the Alpha and Omega, the First and the Last, the living one, illuminates our mystery and makes sense of our lives. How does it do that? To answer this question we must first reflect on the significance of time.

Time is the place of the creature, the place of becoming; it expresses the distance between 'us' and 'us'; it is a space in which we fulfil ourselves. We are in time because we are created. And because we are created, we begin and we end. But we begin in the form of a seed and we end in the form of a tree which has realized all the potentialities contained in the seed. Between our beginning and our end, between our birth and our death, there is a development and a growth by which we become what we are; we realize that we were only potential. Time allows this transition from the potential to the actual. That is why time is creative.

The time in which my existence unfolds is not just a duration in which I can simply live, subsist; it is a time which realizes and constructs something. The time of the living being, the time of the human being, is a time which creates, which arouses, which brings about development. One might ask why God, rather than making us seeds, did not make us trees all at once, in other words why he did not make us beings who from the start had completely realized themselves. That would have saved us all kinds of troubles and difficulties. Why did he impose on us this puzzling and laborious process of making our own selves? Why go this long way round, with all these complications? Why not create us at point Z instead of at point A?

The reason is that if God had created us at point Z, we would no longer be human beings, but completely finished things, stable, immobile, immutable. By contrast, human beings are those who, as Sartre put it, make themselves, create themselves, decide themselves, choose themselves.

Human beings choose themselves, and time is the sphere in which they have the possibility of making this choice. In this sense we call time creative, since it is to time that human beings owe the possibility of becoming and shaping themselves.

In God, the distance between 'us' and 'us' does not exist, since God *is*; God does not *become*. That is why we say that God is eternal. If God were subject to a process of becoming, he would be temporal, he would be a creature as we are, he would be caught up in a duration as we are. Hegel wanted to introduce the notion of becoming into God, making history the sphere in which God realizes himself. For Hegel, the absolute Spirit realizes itself only in the succession that we call history. That is unacceptable. God is God from all eternity. He is the Alpha and Omega from all eternity. God does not undergo any development.

However, by creating a world, this God who is himself from all eternity involved himself in it so as to allow it to come into being, and that is what explains the transition from the less to the more which we call development and evolution.

How is it that in the creaturely world we can observe such a movement from the lesser to the greater? How can it be that the lesser gives rise to a greater? How can a small, hard and bitter seed grow into a tree full of sweet fruits? How can a tiny embryo result in a tall, intelligent human being?

According to the strict laws of logic, mathematics and physics, it would seem impossible for the greater to emerge from the lesser. That is inconceivable. But in evolution we are confronted with this riddle: starting from atoms and pure matter, we have life, plants, animals and finally human beings. This development, this progress, this ascending movement is strictly inexplicable, since the lesser cannot produce the greater. However, it is in fact evident every day that the tree shoots up, human beings grow and mature, the world evolves. How can that be?

The answer is that it is possible because eternity is at the heart of time.

Let us reflect on creation and becoming.

Classical philosophy has accustomed us to consider the world as a static entity, the existence of which is self-sustaining down through history. This conception gave rise to two terms in scholastic theology: 'creation' and the 'sustaining of being'. The world was once created by God and since then God has kept it in being as it is. God cares for its preservation, its existence.

The disadvantage of such a view of the world is that it overlooks the fact that creative being at the same time underlies the becoming, the development of the world. It is not the case that the world is; rather, it is coming to be.

It is to the great credit of contemporary science that it has struggled so hard with this coming to be. The world was not created in its present state, as our ancestors believed, but is the result of a long upward process which not only involves the sheer transformation and metamorphosis of being, but also clearly displays a real progress.

Between the atom and the cell, as between the cell and *homo sapiens*, we can observe not only an alteration and an interesting transformation of being, but above all a change from the lesser to the greater. This change is not a quantitative but a qualitative progress.

But why should a qualitative progress call for a lesser cause than a quantitative process? Why do people expect a greater creative power for the creation of a piece of matter from nothing (*ex nihilo*) than for the creation of life from matter (*ex materia*) or for the appearance of the spirit from the living flesh (*ex vivo*)?

My view is that the immense distance between nothingness and primal matter is relatively small, compared with the infinite distance between matter and spirit. I believe that the fact of a qualitative growth applies equally to both the idea of creation and the 'production of matter' from nothing. The great Islamic theologian Ali al-Ashari, who died in Baghdad in 935, was right in suggesting that anyone who wants to prove the existence of a creator God need only contemplate the qualitative growth of life.

The one thing which makes us hesitate to say that the way from the lower to the higher, from the lesser to the greater, is as inexplicable as that from nothingness to being, is purely and simply the frequency with which we encounter it. In our environment, and in our own persons, we are so accustomed to this 'process of nature' that we regard it as normal. But if we attempted to renew our capacity for wonder, then we could become philosophers and sages. And then we would soon concede that in the whole of 'natural evolution' there is a qualitative increase from the lesser to the greater, and an explanation has to be found for this. Anyone who puts a bet on 'nature' will win nothing; that does not explain the problem but simply shifts it elsewhere.

Do we not find the only satisfactory answer if we say that all events have one and the same cause? The primal matter produced at the origin of cosmic existence contained the substratum for the whole of evolution, but at the same time also that inner quality of many-sided growth which was to lead it to its goal. From beginning to end of this development the cause is one and the same, both in its quantitative extension and in its inner development and maturing.

So the goal of created being is not just its preservation and increase in a quantitative sense – such a view of things would be too simple for this grandiose enterprise of creation; it would not be enough. God not only sustains a being which he has created but allows it to become. And this becoming is both creation and preservation; the two things are identical.

Creation takes place every day before our eyes; we experience it every day, and it is far from having come to an end. Creation, evolution, incarnation, history and eschatology are essentially one and the same event. All follow one and the same movement, and above all, have one and the same cause. This one cause is God, who at the origin of the world produced a crude, formless and inwardly empty matter from nothing and made it fertile with his spirit, so that it could slowly be encouraged to rise upwards and after a twofold metamorphosis achieve its crowning glory – in the kingdom of God.

Time and history have a higher principle than themselves which makes possible this rising development from the lesser to the greater. It is really inconceivable that I should develop and grow as much as I do both physically and in other respects if there is no more in me than myself. If there were no more in me than myself I would always be the same, in a state of perpetual stagnation. But since there is growth and development, then there is within me a principle of growth and development, an element within me which is more than me and which acts as a catalyst, a motive power that drives me forward and upward.

God's eternity at the heart of time is the condition which allows time to be creative, and allows the world to grow and evolve. In fact, time exists only in relation to other things than itself. It is because the eternal is within time that time takes on a value. So, far from devaluing time, eternity gives it value – provided that eternity is understood as a mystery within time.

But if time is separated from the eternal which gives it life from within, the movement is reversed, and time, far from being creative, becomes destructive. Time is not automatically creative. Time is creative only when it is indwelt by eternity and animated by it. If it is separated and detached, it becomes a time of regression and death or a time of sin.

We do not have to believe that eternity is at the heart of time like a destiny which forces time to progress and rise higher. That may perhaps be true until the appearance of human beings, but with human beings a new element appears, that of a choice for or against this inner thrust, for or against this growth and self-conquest, a movement towards being more.

The time of choice is the time of acceptance or rejection, and if there is rejection, there is regression, a fall backwards towards death, which is what we call sin. In the time of sin there is no longer creation, but de-creation, to use a term of Simone Weil's. There is dispersion, decomposition.

By contrast, the time of grace is the time when human beings open themselves to eternity, which lures them from within and allows them to be borne up by it. Those who do this arrive at another dimension of being, beyond themselves, and participate in the very eternity of God. As Péguy put it:

And eternity itself is in the temporal,
And the tree of the race is deeply rooted,
goes deep into the soil and reaches right to its foundation,
and time itself is a timeless time.

This fusing of time and eternity came about historically in the incarnation, thanks to which the living spring of God has become our spring! By opening ourselves to it, we share in God's life and in this spring. In two texts from St John, the story of the woman of Samaria (4.10) and the story of the Feast of Tabernacles (7.37-39), Jesus expresses this profound truth: 'He who believes in me, out of his heart shall flow rivers of living water... The water that I shall give him will become in him a spring of water welling up to eternal life.'

The faith which is this acceptance of God as the spring at the heart of my life means that in turn I become what God is – a spring. This is the unheard-of mystery of faith and hope at which we arrive thanks to the reality of the incarnation.

God is at the heart of history.
God is at the heart of time.
God is in the human heart.

God is there as an explosive force which gives our life a new dimension and our existence an infinite value. From now on each of our moments is full of his presence, since eternity is at the heart of time. The irruption of eternity into time confers upon time a fullness of being, a weight of reality and being, a density of meaning which it is incapable of having by itself. From now on nothing in our lives is insignificant or ordinary; the most trivial act can be transfigured by this truth of faith.

We have tended to divide our actions into achievements and ordinary activities. To be in charge of a school or a business is an achievement; to sweep a room or to cook are ordinary activities. Starting from this conception we have established a hierarchy without taking account of the fact that what gives value to an action is not the action itself but the spirit in which it is done. Nothing is trivial, nothing is ordinary for someone whose life draws on the eternal.

I can still hear upset nuns complaining at having been assigned to cooking or to kindergarten when they could have been superiors or taught in secondary schools. They felt diminished, misunderstood, humiliated. What nonsense! Did the Virgin Mary do anything other than cook, go to the market and sweep the house? She did not have any glorious achievements, did not perform any miracles! And yet she represents the supreme figure of human history.

The gospel constantly reveals to us that what is lowest is in fact highest, that the last shall be first and the first last. If we understood that and really accepted it, how many of our complexes would disappear! The essential thing is not what I do but the significance that I attach to what I do. Once that happens, nothing is ordinary any more, and the most trivial reality is transfigured and takes on a divine and eternal dimension.

Another idea emerges from this involvement of the eternal in the temporal: each of our moments is unique. Time is irreversible; it passes and never passes by again. It escapes us, and it is no use running after it to try to catch it, like someone running after a shadow at sunset. There's no point in running after your shadow: you'll never catch it up. It's also the same for those who run after time. There is no point in being foolish or panicking. The irreversibility of time is not a catastrophe; on the contrary, it is something which gives importance to each of my choices. What gives the action that I do here and now its eternal value is what gives my existence its value and its weight.

In the previous chapter I quoted the beautiful verse by Countess de Noailles, 'We shall never be able to call our souls our own more than we can this evening.' I did not want simply to express a vague and more or less sentimental nostalgia, but to convey that each of our moments is unique. Now is a serious moment, since it is the place where I am going to perform an action which involves all my being, and consequently takes on the value of eternity. So for us the irreversibility of time is the occasion for taking the passing moment seriously.

In his fine book *Existence and Eternity*, Fernand Guimet remarked:

> The irreversibility of time, in the Christian perspective of existence, has a different meaning from this succession of hours, all of which hurt us and the last of which kills us. It allows us to measure the seriousness of an existence which is given us only once, an existence in which every day and every hour counts, and in which every day and every hour does not cease to be the day and the hour when we respond to our eternal vocation.

This is a very powerful idea, because it provokes us. When I think that I am in my fifties, I ask myself: 'Lord, what have I done with the past fifty years of my life? And what will I do with the years to come, in which each month, each day, each hour, each minute, bring a unique message?' Each passing moment I have to do something full, something overflowing. If time is irreversible, it is no use complaining and telling myself, 'It's terrible, time's passing'. I have to seize it with both hands and involve all my being in it so as not to waste the slightest bit of it.

What makes me mad here in Egypt is the total absence of a sense of the value of time amongst the majority of people. What value can it have for men aged thirty, forty or fifty, spending hours every morning playing tric-trac or smoking water pipes in cafés?

Does time have any value for them? Between June and October several million young Egyptians ask themselves what they are going to do with their holidays. They spend four months on a mat on the beach and at discos in the evening, to kill time. Four months wasted – completely lost – in the full flush of youth. Can you imagine it?

Time is a treasure to be exploited, capital to bring profit, a talent to develop. What do we do with it? What have we done with it? For us the irreversibility of time is a challenge to accept, a challenge to provoke us. In the last century the French poet Lamartine dreamed of stopping time as Joshua is said one day to have stopped the sun. But you don't stop time by stopping the sun; you stop time by plunging into it and surpassing it. For the sun to stop doesn't change anything – it is men and women who have to stop and learn how to penetrate the heart of time in order to find eternity in it.

This brings us to the way in which we experience time: it can be both cyclical and linear. Cyclical time is a movement of indefinite repetitions in which nothing new happens. This idea is expressed very well at the beginning of the biblical book of Ecclesiastes:

Vanity of vanities! All is vanity.
What does a man gain by the toil
at which he toils under the sun?
A generation goes, and a generation comes,
but the earth remains for ever.
The sun rises, and the sun goes down,
and hastens to the place where it rises.
The wind blows to the south, and goes round to the north,
round and round goes the wind,
and on its circuits the wind returns.
All streams run to the sea, but the sea is not full;
to the place where the streams flow, there they flow again.
All things are full of weariness, a man cannot utter it;
the eye is not satisfied with seeing, nor the ear filled with
    hearing.
What has been is what will be,
and what has been done is what will be done,
and there is nothing new under the sun.
Is there a thing of which it is said,

'See, this is new'?
It has been already,
in the ages before us.

The Hebrew Koheleth, author of this biblical text, is quite pessimistic: 'Nothing new under the sun.'

'Nothing new under the sun...' That reminds me of a surprising conversation which I had one day up at the top of the Great Pyramid with a guide with whom I had climbed up. He assured me that the ancient Egyptians had already discovered all the inventions of our age five thousand years ago: rifles, rockets, planes, the atom bomb and the rest of it. And he added, 'We have not discovered anything which did not exist before. We have simply lost trace of it.'

Nor is he the only one. Many pseudo-scientific books and journals claim the same thing and enjoy wide circulations. We are told that everything had already been discovered in the past, but that this brilliant civilization was swallowed up by a terrible cataclysm. Humanity then began to develop all over again, and nowadays we are simply rediscovering what our ancestors had already discovered in times past. But what is equally old is this cyclical concept of time. Here is a text from antiquity: the author is Nemesius, who lived around AD 400.

Socrates, Plato and each individual will live again with the same friends and companions. They will have the same experiences and the same activities. Every city, every village, every field will be restored to its former state. This restoration of the universe will not be done once for all, but will have to be done again and again, ceaselessly, for all eternity. The gods, who are not subject to destruction, having observed the course of events in a period, will know what must happen in all subsequent periods. For there will be nothing new – and nothing will happen which has not always existed down to the smallest detail.

Here we can find the same tone that we heard in the Hebrew Koheleth, the preacher of Ecclesiastes, and in modern times Nietzsche says precisely the same thing.

'O Zarathustra,' said the animals then, 'all things themselves dance for such as think as we: they come and offer their hand and laugh and flee – and return.

Everything goes, everything returns; the wheel of existence

rolls for ever. Everything dies, everything blossoms anew; the year of existence runs on for ever.

Everything breaks, everything is joined anew; the same house of existence builds itself for ever. Everything departs, everything meets again; the ring of existence is true to itself for ever' (*Thus Spake Zarathustra*, 'The Convalescent').

So your life has already been lived hundreds, thousands, millions of times, and you are simply beginning your existence all over again. In a book called *The Myth of the Eternal Return* the famous ethnologist Mircea Eliade has given a magisterial account of this cyclical concept of time as history eternally beginning all over again.

In any case, does not astrology suppose that our destiny is predetermined? The stars, which have been witnesses to what happened on earth in former times and in our former lives, can reveal our future to us. So there are people who avidly scrutinize their morning paper to know what kind of a day they will be having. As if my day was already pre-programmed, was no more than a predetermined destiny to which I have to submit!

But that is not the case. My morning paper does not tell me what kind of a day I'm going to have. My day will be what I make it. 'What's going to happen to me today?' That's something that I shall be deciding, and this morning will be mine: it will not belong to Mars, Neptune or Jupiter. I am utterly opposed to the astral fatalism which is emerging again in our day; it is simply an expression of our avoidance of responsibility and our fear of freedom, the fear of personal commitment.

This cyclical concept of time as an eternal return of phenomena has deep roots in the countryside and in rural society. For all their lives peasants experience this repetitive cycle of nature. The sun rises and the sun sets; the Nile rises in August and falls in October; night follows day and day follows night; the same rhythm of the seasons is repeated every year: spring, summer, autumn, winter. Birth yields to death and death yields to birth. All this gives country people the feeling of eternally new beginnings in which nothing really new ever happens.

By contrast, city people, those who live in industrial societies, have escaped the fatality of a cyclical time and discovered the linear dimension of time. With the coming of the modern age, time takes on a direction, is aimed towards an end, develops towards a goal, tends towards a realization. Time becomes a history.

For example, try to imagine the revolution that the Aswan Dam has brought about for the Egyptian peasants, who for millennia had become accustomed to the inundation from the Nile every summer and had regulated their lives by it. Suddenly, by the decision of a man called Nasser, the Nile has stopped rising every year, and as a consequence the whole countryside is electrified, completely upsetting the very cycle of day and night. All this represents an enormous revolution in the mind of the Egyptian peasants within a few years, utterly overturning their view of the world.

Human beings suddenly discover that they themselves make history, that they themselves decide on their lives, that they themselves can make day or night by switching on the electric light, that the Nile can rise or fall at their command, that it will rain or not rain, depending on the techniques that are applied. It is no longer the case that human beings are subject to time, but rather that time is subject to human beings. Human beings escape the fatalism of the cycle and become masters of history.

In such a conception, God no longer finds his place in history as the one who governs nature, since from now on human beings have taken his place. So it is no coincidence that atheism has appeared along with the birth of the modern age and the industrial era. Here human beings escape the fatalism of a 'natural' time and create their own time, a 'human' time, that of work, of machines, factories, choice, freedom. And at the same time they discover that time has a value: time is money. Unfortunately those who frequent the cafés of Egypt have not yet made this discovery; they are still living in the other time, the old time, when nothing happened. Time is not money for them!

I have made a distinction between cyclical time and linear time. In fact, neither expresses the objective reality of time. Time is neither cyclical nor linear, but spiral; that is to say, we simultaneously begin again and go forward. We do not just begin again by returning to the starting point, but as we go round in circles, we gradually rise to a higher stage of development. The sun which rises today is indeed the same sun that rose yesterday and will rise tomorrow, but everything happens within time: the earth is different, human beings have changed, history has developed. And yet there is repetition – however, it is a repetition which brings about progress, which produces a plan, which tends towards an eschatology.

This idea of eschatology seems to have originated in Judaism and Christianity, because it is said in the Bible that history has a beginning and an end; it is enclosed within an Alpha and an Omega. Ontology becomes an eschatology. The Christian conception of time is an evolutionary conception in which time is creative, history has a goal and temporality acquires a meaning. In this perspective, the incarnation is a unique event which cannot be repeated; the cross is a unique event which cannot be repeated; the life of Christ is an event which cannot be repeated; and human life is also a unique event which cannot be repeated.

In this context, I would like to quote a passage from the Letter to the Hebrews which may shed light on what I have just said:

> Nor was it to offer himself repeatedly, as the high priest enters the Holy Place yearly with blood not his own; for then he would have had to suffer repeatedly since the foundation of the world. But as it is, he has appeared once for all at the end of the age to put away sin by the sacrifice of himself. And just as it is appointed for men to die once, and after that comes judgment, so Christ, having been offered once to bear the sins of many, will appear a second time, not to deal with sin but to save those who are eagerly waiting for him (9.25-28).

This idea of unrepeatable time demonstrates the unique character of the phenomenon of the incarnation and the unique character of our own existence. So the idea of eschatology frees us from the fleeting nature of time and the nightmare of entropy. According to the law of entropy, the world is constantly involved in an irreversible and irreparable loss of energy. Electric lights consume energy which is lost for ever. Every day the sun burns up energy which is lost for ever and cannot be renewed. The world is therefore orientated on a progressive loss of energy which means that we are all threatened, sooner or later, with the prospect of the eternal cold. Science tells us that the world is growing old, is using itself up, is impoverishing itself irreparably, and that one day this process will result in the total death of the universe. Such a view, which is true, real and scientific, cannot but engender in us pessimism, despair and darkness.

However, at this point faith comes in, announces itself, and demands a hearing. Faith tell us that such a dying of the world and human beings is a transition to another sphere or state, and that something is already going on behind a 'curtain'; something new is in preparation. The believer 'knows' that, so we talk of our knowledge of faith, that goes a long way, even extending to eschatology.

To explain all this more closely, Teilhard de Chardin describes the working of two kinds of energy: tangential or material energy, like the sun or an electric light bulb, and radial or spiritual energy. Tangential or material energy is subject to constant loss because it is subject to the phenomenon of entropy; by contrast, radial or spiritual energy does not cease growing and increasing in inverse proportion to material energy. So there is a rise in the spiritual and psychical in our world, an exchange between these two forms of energy, in favour of love, in favour of a rise of consciousness and a development of consciousness. So we are told by Teilhard de Chardin, who behind the apparent decline of our world recognized and experienced its true rise – its radial growth. Eternity at work in history is in process of giving birth to a new world, an eternal morning. And that is just what Easter means. Easter is a morning which does not pass away, an eternal morning.

The resurrection of Christ is a triumph over death and the basis of human history, making it flow into the eternal and the definitive. In Christ, the passage of all humankind to the other shore, to life eternal, to triumph over death, is accomplished once for all, since Christ is the Alpha and the Omega, who sums up all human history in himself.

Because Christ is man, Son of Man, perfect man, total man, what happens in him has already happened in each one of us. When St Paul claims that 'You are risen with Christ and your life is hidden in God' (Col.3.13), he is making a very profound statement. Christian hope is based on the conviction that the definitive act of salvation in human history has already been performed, already achieved, already accomplished in Christ. It is based on the conviction that in him we escape death and night, that beyond this transitory world there is another world inside this world which does not pass away, crossing it and transcending it. So the eternity which breaks into time with Jesus Christ and which has culminated in the resurrection gives the present all its density.

Here is another quotation from Fernand Guimet:

Our present is now no longer this ridge walk along a knife edge which we are constantly invited to cross, between the slope of a past which is no longer and that of a future which is yet to be.

Beyond the very order of fugitive time, in a kind of *stasis* which is as it were a potential *ekstasis*, ecstasy, it is rather, or at least, called to be the phenomenology of the presence of God and his grace. In faithfulness to the Spirit, it is the place of our encounter with God, the place of a conversion in which everything is always open to us, by the very grace of the Easter mystery, the place of a passage from this world to the Father.

Eschatology has already become present in history. The definitive triumph of humanity in Christ is already achieved and present. That is why Christ can say that 'The kingdom of God is within you... The kingdom of God is among you... The kingdom of God is here' (Matt.12.28; Luke 17.21).

Christ knew that he bore human history within himself; he knew that his coming was the definitive coming of God on earth; he knew that his resurrection was also the resurrection of the world.

Finally, here is one last idea. The presence of eternity at the heart of time, by the incarnation and the resurrection of Christ, is a principle of continuous development and renewal in human beings and in history. The irruption of God at the heart of the world evokes the unexpected, the inexplicable, the unforeseen, which escape all scientific forecasts, including those of that modern science which calls itself futurology.

In the world there is always more than the world; in history there is always more than history; in human beings there is always more than their human nature.

Who could have foreseen John XXIII or the Second Vatican Council in the second half of our century? That was an utterly unexpected event, and one which changed the course of history. Who could have foreseen Einstein, whose theories overturned modern science? Who could have foreseen the developments in our time which have utterly confounded all our predictions? What will the next discovery be? What will the human race look like in twenty years time?

We are told of all kinds of disasters and upheavals which will take place in the year 2000. What will we know about them? Some people tell us that the world is so evil that the end must be very near. Others say that our human race is so old that its end is imminent. But God works wonders with the elderly! He raises up men and women, prophets, saints, geniuses, new ideas, new inventions, at the most unexpected moments and among the most critical periods.

Christ told us, 'Do not be anxious for the morrow' (Matt.6.34), and when he said this he meant both individuals and humankind. Certainly, we need to be warned about the future, but within reason. Above all we must have trust. The one who has borne up the history of the universe for twenty billion years will bring this history to its conclusion. The past is the guarantee of the future. The Lord already tells us in the gospel, 'Be of good cheer, I have overcome the world' (John 16.33). I have already won the battle. I have already gained the triumph.

If Christians have an optimistic view of history, it is not as a result of simplistic bliss or passive expectation, but in the name of this certainty of faith that the divine has broken into the world in Jesus Christ and that this new element brings with it an immense hope. From now on, history surpasses itself, thanks to this divine ferment.

> The kingdom of heaven is like leaven which a woman took and hid in three measures of flour until it was all leavened (Matt.13.33).

> The kingdom of God is like a grain of mustard seed which is the smallest of all seeds but which becomes a great tree (Matt.13.31f.).

This seed hidden in the earth on the evening of Good Friday is in process of growing until the fullness of the kingdom which is to come. 'When I am raised up from the earth I will draw all people to me' (John 12.32).

Something enormous is going on within our history. The Lord has come. The Lord will come again. The Lord is coming. That is our hope.

I recently held a retreat in Alexandria during Lent on the theme of 'Human Hope and Christian Confidence'. I tried to explain that human hope is a short-term feeling which counts on known realities that often get out of hand. No wonder, then, that we are all dismayed at what goes on around us. By contrast, Christian confidence is focussed on realities which do not yet exist, which are in process of coming to be and are not yet manifest. It is an act of faith in the future, a bet on the one who made the world, who sowed the stars, the suns and the galaxies in space, and who is quite capable of raising up children of Abraham from these stones.

God makes fun of our prognostications, our predictions and our forecasts, since the one who creates heaven and earth does not cease to make us grow every day. 'My Father is working still, and I am working' (John 5.17). Christian faith is an enormous matter, a principle of hope and dynamism capable of overturning everything and moving mountains.

I believe in humankind because I believe in Jesus Christ.

I believe in the future because I believe in Jesus Christ.

What this future will be I do not know. Do not try to make plans for the future city. Do not try to describe the kingdom of God which is to come. The Apocalypse, which seeks to do this, necessarily remains vague and full of symbolism. We must not try to over-interpret these symbols; it is good that they remain vague.

The future is unpredictable, and even Karl Marx, who spoke of the future city, refused to describe it. For who could describe what the world and humankind will be like at the end of their evolution? Who could conceive of this kingdom which awaits us at the end of history?

Eye has not seen, nor ear heard, nor spirit imagined what God has prepared for those who love him (I Cor.2.9).

History is constantly new because the Spirit which is at work in history is constantly new. This Spirit constantly at work in the world is grace, the 'supplement of the soul' constantly breathed by God into the world. To live within the movement of the Spirit is to live in a state of grace, in this spirit of youth and childhood, which is to share in the eternal childlikeness of God. The child is someone who believes everything, hopes everything, dreams of the impossible; the child is someone who lives in a fairy-tale world, a utopian world, in the belief that it is all true – and children are right:

Truly, truly, I say you that unless you become like little children again, you will not enter the kingdom of God (Matt.18.3).

4 The Wisdom of Time

'Combine action with inaction and you won't go crazy'
(*Russian proverb*)

I want to begin with Saint-Exupéry's story of the little prince. The little prince had left his little planet, somewhere in the sky, and went to visit some other planets across the universe. The first of them was inhabited by an ambitious king and the second by a conceited man. The little prince had just been to the third planet, which was inhabited by a gloomy drunkard. The drunkard drank, he said, to forget that he was ashamed of himself. On each visit the little prince said, 'The grown-ups are certainly very, very odd'; on his travels he came to the fourth planet:

The fourth planet belonged to a businessman. This man was so much occupied that he did not even raise his head at the little prince's arrival.

'Good morning,' the little prince said to him. 'Your cigarette has gone out.'

'Three and two make five. Five and seven make twelve. Twelve and three make fifteen. Good morning. Fifteen and seven make twenty-two. Twenty-two and six make twenty-eight. I haven't time to light it again. Twenty six and five make thirty-one. Phew! So that makes five hundred and one million six hundred and eighty thousand seven hundred and thirty one.'

'Five hundred million what?' asked the little prince.

'Eh? Are you still there? Five hundred and one million – I can't stop... I've so much to do! I am concerned with matters of consequence. I don't amuse myself with balderdash. Two and five make seven...'

'Five hundred and one million what?' repeated the little

prince, who never in his life had let go of a question once he had asked it.

The businessman raised his head.

'During the fifty-four years I've inhabited this planet, I have been disturbed only three times. The first time was twenty-two years ago, when some giddy goose fell from goodness knows where. He made the most frightful noise that resounded all over the place, and I made four mistakes in my addition. The second time, eleven years ago, I was disturbed by an attack of rheumatism. I don't get enough exercise. I have no time for loafing. The third time – well, this is it. I was saying, then, five hundred and one millions...'

'Millions of what?'

The businessman realized that there was no hope of being left in peace until he answered this question.

'Millions of those little objects,' he said, 'which one sometimes sees in the sky.'

'Flies?'

'Oh, no. Like glittering objects.'

'Bees?'

'Oh, no. Little golden objects that set lazy men to idle dreaming. As for me, I'm concerned with matters of consequence. There is no time for idle dreaming in my life.'

'Ah! You mean the stars?'

'Yes, that's it. The stars.'

'And what do you do with five hundred million stars?'

'Five hundred and one million, six hundred and twenty-two thousand seven hundred and thirty-one. I am concerned with matters of consequence; I am accurate.'

'And what do you do with these stars?'

'What do I do with them?'

'Yes.'

'Nothing. I own them.'

'You own the stars?'

'Yes.'

'But I have already seen a king who...'

'Kings do not *own*, they *reign* over. It is a very different matter.'

'And what good does it do you to own the stars?'

'It does the good of making me rich.'

'And what good does it do you to be rich?'

'It makes it possible for me to buy more stars, if any are discovered.'

And so on.

That's the story of the businessman. He counts the world, he counts the stars. He's busy, occupied, serious.

But the little prince isn't serious. He has time to spare, time to dream, time to look at the stars. The other man is serious. He counts, and counts again.

This story of the businessman reminds me of another story that you'll know.

One day another businessman was going to work when he saw a bedouin from the desert sitting under a city palm tree resting and dreaming, as so many people do in Egypt. He stopped and said to him,

'What are you doing there?'

The bedouin replied,

'As you can see, I'm dreaming, resting...'

'You know that you could be earning money if you were working.'

'What would I do with it?'

'If you earned money you could open an office.'

'And then?'

'Then you could earn more money and build a factory.'

'And then?'

'Then you could own a fine villa.'

'Good! And then?'

'Then you would still have money to put in the bank.'

'Yes. And then?'

'Then you could sit down and rest.'

'But that's what I'm doing at the moment.'

There are those among us who keep putting off the time when they can sit down and rest and in the end never get to the point of doing it: they never have time to sit down and rest because in fact they never finish their work. Just think about that a moment. When can you say that you've finished your work? Work never ends, whether you're a manager, a teacher, a worker, a director, a monk or a nun. There's always more to do, there's always work around, and you never finish it. If you wait until you've finished your work before you begin to live, you will never live. Take time to live! That's a wise thing to do. Hence the title of this chapter, 'The Wisdom of Time'.

This businessman is certainly intelligent, cultivated, serious, but perhaps he has not learned something that the bedouin at the foot of his tree has understood. He has not understood that time is something that one takes: otherwise it takes us; otherwise it is something that possesses us. Take time to live!

And the Lord who gave the commandments gave a third commandment: 'Keep the Lord's Day holy.' How do we do that? By going to mass? Not necessarily. Not primarily. There is no mass in the Old Testament. Then by doing what? By resting. Stop working. Not just you, but your manservant and your maidservant, your donkey and your ox. Give them time, time to live themselves.

So there is wisdom in this rest on the seventh day. The fact that the Lord gave a commandment about it should make us think. A divine commandment, one of God's ten commandments, is devoted to it, given over to the art of resting. So perhaps we shall see that there is a very close link between resting and praying. Rest itself is already prayer, and it is often because we have not rested that we do not know how to pray.

I spoke just now of finding time to live. And that is something which we people of the twentieth century, busy and overburdened, need to do.

Now I would like to talk about finding time to love. Let's go back to the little prince:

The fox gazed at the little prince, for a long time.

'Please – tame me,' he said.

'I want to, very much,' the little prince replied. 'But I have not much time. I have friends to discover and a great many things to understand.'

'One only understands the things that one tames,' said the fox. 'Men have no more time to understand anything. They buy things all ready made at the shops. But there is no shop anywhere where one can buy friendship, and so men have no friends any more. If you want a friend, tame me!'

'What must I do to tame you?,' the little prince asked.

'You must be very patient,' replied the fox. 'First you will sit down at a little distance from me – like that – in the grass. I

60]

shall look at you out of the corner of my eye, and you will say nothing. Words are the source of misunderstanding. But you will sit a little closer to me every day.'

Time to love. Friendship takes time. Love takes time. And often love dies for want of time and friendship dies for want of time. If we want to build up life together, and we do not give it the time it needs, that life will wither and die.

There used to be family meals at least once a day. A white tablecloth, flowers, napkins, glass. You went in before the meal, chatted, laughed, sat down. And then after the meal there was time to smile, to chat, to stay together. Now we have snack bars, fast food, self-service. Between-times you grab a sandwich, drink a Coke, on the go. You get home in the evening and either you aren't hungry because you've eaten too much or you eat straightaway without waiting for the others. Then you start work or go to bed. The others get in and do the same thing. People all eat when they want to, get up when they want to, have breakfast when they want to, go to bed when they want to.

The family meal is dead. You're lucky if there's time to have a meal together once a week. The proclamation of family life nowadays will not be found in great declarations; it is primarily and above all a way of being together, a way of living together.

Time is an indispensable element in forming a family; forming a family takes time. That is one of the demands of family life and at the same time one of its greatest joys. If you cannot count on giving time to your family, don't get married, because you will cheat your children and your spouse if you marry while knowing very well that you will have no time to give to them. To get married is to be prepared to give time to others: and that applies to giving time to husband or wife as well as to children. In fact, it is clear that if husband and wife themselves set an example in doing this, the children will join in: they will want to be there, they will enjoy being together, the family will attract them. And where there is a happy family life, the children develop well. Where there is no family life, the children have problems. Problem children are those with no real family life, who have seldom enjoyed a family meal, who have seldom experienced family reunions.

Time for loving also means outings together, walks, trips to the country or the shore, holidays abroad. That sort of thing brings the members of a family together. The fact of travelling together, of being elsewhere, in the midst of strangers in a strange world, immediately welds the family together. But that takes time.

If everything has to be expressed in terms of money, productivity, cash value, all this kind of time is lost time. But if we have another criterion of value in our time, if the ultimate value is not time and efficiency but joy and love – things which cannot be weighed or measured, which do not count – at that point we are capable of sacrificing. There would be loss on the one side but gain on the other, and this gain would be infinitely more precious that what we would have lost. There is always something to sacrifice; that's the price to be paid. Family life has its price, a couple's life together has its price, friendship has its price, love has its price – but one might say that it all pays off.

And the time we have to give cannot be condensed. We cannot concentrate compensation for hours or days of absence into a few short minutes' conversation. Any attempt to do that will seem like a grudged gift. No real encounters can take place in hasty meetings: they cannot result in mutual understanding. We live in an age of miniaturization, when everything is condensed: *Reader's Digest*, telex, multivitamins in a pill. I expect that one day we shall have the amazing opportunity, instead of taking three meals a day, wasting half an hour over each, to gulp down three pills which will save us this loss of time. Think of the satisfaction of working sixteen hours a day, of saving these three half-hours, of losing only three seconds to gulp down the pills! And roast turkeys with stuffing, apple pies and the rest will no longer exist – they will have been replaced by pills!

I hope that that age never comes; I hope that there will always be old wooden tables with glasses and napkins and the smell from the kitchen and long family meals. Don't dream of a concentrated family life, to which we give the absolute minimum, simply to reassure ourselves, to appease our conscience, to tell ourselves that we are doing our duty. Love cannot be condensed. We all need to ask ourselves whether we are taking time to love, to be with others, to enjoy ourselves with others. That's important.

I say that firmly to the clergy and to religious, because here I'm well aware of what I'm talking about. In the religious life you've never finished working; there's always something to do. But relax! If you are given time for recreation, spend it being with others, with your companions; forget your newspapers and magazines, put all your work on one side. Unwind with other people, chat, laugh, listen. I know someone who as soon as he comes into the common room picks up a newspaper. You talk to him and he replies, 'Yes, no, ah, well...' I'd like to pick up the newspaper, throw it out of the window, and say, 'Let's get rid of that. You can read it some other time. There's a time for laughing and a time for reading. Now's the time for laughing; you can read later.'

We might ask ourselves whether many problems in the family or between couples do not arise because they don't take time to be together.

I've spoken of family life. Let's talk for a while about the life of married couples. Husbands and wives must find time to be by themselves, perhaps at home, perhaps in their room, perhaps in a restaurant, perhaps going for a walk. Many marital problems arise and develop because the couple never talk. Things mount up, become burdensome, and poison life because they've never been talked about. And when they *are* talked about, they come out like cannon fire. Of course, it's inevitable that there should be such exchanges, but the cannons should then be given time to cool down. Perhaps the conversation will begin with complaints and home truths. Then, 'All right, what else do you have to say? and I'd like to tell you...' All this goes on, not just for quarter of an hour, but for two or three hours. Everything has to come out, the volcano has to erupt and calm down, the lava has to flow, so that the sun can shine again behind the volcano. Finally the couple can say, 'But in the end we can get over it all.'

We need time to listen: time to listen to our children, time to listen to one another. Parents need to take time to listen to their children when they've just come back from camp, from an excursion, from a trip. The children want to talk immediately, because they are full of their stories and their experience. They want to share what's happened, now! Never say to them, 'Not now, I'm busy. I'm tired.' When that happens, the days go by, the weeks go by and the child no longer wants to tell the story. There was just one occasion to hear it, and to deepen the relationship with your child, and you will have missed it.

Many problems with children arise precisely because there is no communication between parents and children. There's no time to listen. Listening is not easy and takes time. If you're in a hurry you won't listen. I'm incapable of talking to someone who keeps looking at his watch. To listen presupposes that one has time, all the time in the world, is perfectly relaxed, really present.

When someone asks me as a priest, 'Are you free?', I say, 'I'm always free.' One becomes free when that's important. I used to say: 'Free? How can I be free? I've a thousand things to do. I'm overburdened with work. You must be joking.' But it's important. I really am always free. In fact I'm always free and always busy. When it's important, I become free. The person in front of me must be given the impression that all my time is at his or her disposal. Some problems take ten minutes and don't need more. But these ten minutes are minutes given, minutes during which there is truly a reciprocal presence, communication. At that moment I've really given my ten minutes. There are other problems which take two or three hours. In fact, when you begin an interview you're never quite sure how long it's going to take.

I remember one of my friends telling me that there are problems for which the time-factor is indispensable if a solution is to appear. Psychologists are aware of that. Someone talks, and often says nothing. He or she talks and talks and talks. After an hour, an hour and a half, two hours, the real problem begins to emerge and there is a crisis: floods of tears. Often the problem is hidden and the person in front of me is unaware of it, or is afraid to mention it, is ashamed to speak of it – so the problem takes time to come out. And if you haven't taken the time, you will have sent the client away; he or she will have left with the problem and nothing will have been resolved. It's hard to take time to listen; it's an ascetic discipline, and at the same time it's an area in which one can hope to work at depth.

In psychology there is what is called logotherapy, from the Greek *logos*, word, and *therapein*, to cure. All psychology is based on that. An analysis can take three, four or five years, with sessions lasting two to three hours. I sympathize with the analyst. I remember a cartoon with the patient stretched out on the couch and the psychoanalyst asleep in his chair. The client was talking away and the analyst was fast asleep. Analysis takes a long time. One of the diseases of our time is the absence of communication, the lack of communication between people, communication in depth. Logotherapy aims at helping people to express all that they were unable to say, all that is bottled up inside them.

I have spoken of time to live, time to love and time to listen. Now I would like to say something about time to grow and mature. People only grow in time, and one cannot economize over time in growth or education. We know that all education requires a certain amount of time. But many ambitious parents do not know that by forcing their children through school too early or by arranging for them to jump a year they are not giving something but taking it away. As a result these children may become more aggressive, since they are too young for their class, suffer as a result, feel more pushed than the others and inferior to them. It could be a valuable help to such children if a skilled and sympathetic teacher 'failed' them and made them repeat a year, for in that way the child could gain self-confidence. The French Jesuit sociologist Desquéyrat commented that the quickest learners are not always the best twenty or thirty years later. Artificially accelerated development never helps anyone.

There are working-class boys who have never had a chance to go to school or university. At fourteen or fifteen they are little men. They began working as apprentices at the age of ten or eleven, earned money very soon and had family responsibilities. At fifteen they talk like men of twenty-five or thirty, but they always lack something. These personalities which have been formed too quickly have never known childhood, or adolescence, or youth, or the slow growth at the end of which a human personality is formed. They have matured too quickly on an improvised basis. They have not had their share of life and love, play and joy. Children who have never played can be very lively, but not having known childhood will have robbed them of something: it's a serious matter not to have been a child.

Children have to take their time; adolescents have to take their time; and in a way education, which retards maturity through school and university, is a good thing. The maturity comes later. Among the people I've just been talking about, a boy is mature at eighteen. In our societies, with school and university, a boy begins to become mature at twenty-five. I'm not insulting anyone here; it's not an insult – quite the contrary. The time you take to grow up isn't time lost; don't try to be grown up earlier than you need be. Adulthood will come all in good time, and when it does it will be a fully developed maturity, fully achieved, which will have taken time to come about. Things are better that way.

When I felt I had a vocation, I made inquiries to see whether I should become a Jesuit. When they told me that the training took fourteen years, I thought to myself: 'My God! I've had enough of school. Another fourteen years? These Jesuits must be crazy!' And then I understood. I understood that the Society of Jesus sacrificed a certain immediate efficiency, a rapid return (for I wanted to give, I was anxious to produce, to work, to act), for something deeper but longer-term. So I accepted the delay, this slow and patient growing to maturity, this long period of austere study for something more profound. There is wisdom there, and nothing to be regretted.

What do Bedouins write on the walls of their tents? 'Patience is the key to joy', or 'Patience is sweet'. Here's the same sentiment in another passage from Kazantzakis's *Zorba the Greek*:

> I remembered one morning when I discovered a cocoon in the bark of a tree, just as the butterfly was making a hole in its case and preparing to come out. I waited a while, but it was too long appearing and I was impatient. I bent over it and breathed on it to warm it. I warmed it as quickly as I could and the miracle began to happen before my eyes, faster than life. The case opened, the butterfly started slowly crawling out and I shall never forget my horror when I saw how its wings were folded back and crumpled; the wretched butterfly tried with its whole-trembling body to unfold them. Bending over it, I tried to help it with my breath. In vain. It needed to be hatched out patiently and the unfolding of the wings should be a gradual process in the sun. Now it was too late. My breath had forced the butterfly to appear, all crumpled, before its time. It struggled and, a few seconds later, died in the palm of my hand.
>
> That little body is, I do believe, the greatest weight I have on my conscience. For I realize today that it is a mortal sin to violate the great laws of nature. We should not hurry, we should not be impatient, but we should confidently obey the eternal rhythm.
>
> I sat on a rock to absorb this New Year's thought. Ah, if only that little butterfly could always flutter before me to show me the way!

We, too, are sometimes too hasty with our children, want them to mature too quickly, become wise too quickly, reasonable too quickly, adult too quickly. A child is not an adult; it is not even a small adult; it is a child. It has a rhythm to respect. And you don't make your child an adult by talking; there are some things which only come with time.

Paul Claudel has a fine phrase, 'You don't open a bud with your fingers.' That's splendid. You have a rosebud and you say, 'I want a flower, an open rose.' You pull on the petals with all your might, and all you get is a sorry mess. It's the same thing with children. Children don't open up through advice, or orders, or talk, or lectures: children open up when the climate is ripe. A child is timid because the climate in which it lives does not help it to open up. You say to the child, 'But don't be timid, shy and silent. Smile, talk, relax!' The more you press the child, the more he or she will remain shut in. You don't make a child open up like that, any more than you do a flower. Like a flower, the child needs an atmosphere of warmth – human warmth and confidence, a fond smile, a kind look; those help the child to blossom. It's not so much a technique as a climate, a matter of taking time.

I learned more about that when I was regional superior of the Jesuits in Egypt. I wanted to change the Society of Jesus in Egypt far too quickly, immediately. I arrived with plans and projects, and I saw that people were not following my rhythm. So I asked myself whether I wasn't making a mistake. You can't make people go as you can make machines and automobiles and locomotives and such things go. Human beings have their rhythm, their character, their temperament. Taking account of all this is a matter of wisdom, and I think that there is a time factor in all government. Being in charge of people means taking the time factor into one's calculations.

'The best fruits are those which fall by themselves when they are ripe,' said Ricciotti. To discover that is to accept the law of growth, the time of growth.

Now I want to talk about creative time, since time creates. An artist who has not been pregnant with a work for many months, has not had it circulating in the blood and beating in the heart, may produce something, but it will not be a real masterpiece. Why? Because it has not matured in time. Perhaps this is the explanation why so much contemporary art is valueless, however much people discuss it and however much they pay for it.

You may know Pascal's remark, 'He wrote a big book because he did not have time to write a little one.'

That's also true. Pressure to publish may produce a book which gets bigger and bigger because it has not had time to mature; the material increases as an attempt at a solution. Nowadays authors make use of the most modern technology to get a book out in record time. But where is the time that it needs to mature?

I once saw the corrections which La Fontaine made to his classic fables – they were extraordinary. A simple little fable which seemed to have sprung straight from La Fontaine's pen was in fact the result of scrupulous correction and patient labour. This simplicity is the result of a very long effort, painful asceticism, and infinite patience.

We can go back over centuries and millennia and note that nothing changes with regard to the great significance of the time factor for growth and maturity. Here I'm thinking of the book by Isha Schwaller de Lubicz, *Her-Bak*, about Pharaonic Egypt, which contains a conversation between Her-Bak, an apprentice potter aged thirteen, and his master.

'What's a masterpiece?' asked Her-Bak. The old potter reflected and then said, 'A masterpiece is something that one creates with one's soul, that one has conceived with one's heart, that one has formed with one's body, from the skin to the entrails, that one has experienced, that one has carried around until its due time like a ripe fruit. It is brought to birth with the fingers.'

Her-Bak pondered.

'Does it take long to make a masterpiece?'

'Generations prepare for it. A man, their heir, produces it.'

'What do you have to do to be such a man?'

'Listen to the voice of the ancients, observe nature, and keep quiet.'

This is a very fine text. The old artist expresses what he sees: the work is deep within him, in the confused state of a feeling, an emotion, an intuition. What form will it take, what appearance will it assume? He does not yet know. The work has to mature slowly, with a long period of gestation. The artist is like the pregnant woman who feels that her time has come. And like the child, the work of art then emerges of its own accord.

The same thing can be said of poetry. The great Austrian poet Rainer Maria Rilke once said that to write a single verse one had to have seen many cities and known many people, have a good understanding of animals and plants, so good that one could feel what it was like for a bird to fly or for a flower to open up in the morning. A verse should be the plunder of a full life: all that one carries around with oneself concentrated in ten lines. If that happens, then the ten lines will be good.

Rilke might have been exaggerating a bit, deliberately, but at least he points out the need for a very thorough observation of the world and quiet meditation. You have to let the outside world come into your body to taste it, to let it enter your heart, to contemplate it there and nowhere else. Only then can this world be born a second time, shining like a star, in the words of poetry. A true poem is a marriage between the world and human beings, between nature and the human heart. Only from this marriage of love can the true poet create.

All creation has its roots in time. It is in time that we have the soul of all things. How does it happen that we rediscover ourselves in one or other work of an author? 'That's just what I would have wanted to say: it's a perfect expression of how I feel.' In fact, by reaching to the very depths, the writer meets the point at which we all converge, at which we all meet, the focal point of all human communication.

Now I want to talk about the time of knowing. Not learning, but knowing. Paul Claudel showed how the French for knowing, '*connaître*', can be read as '*con-naître*', being born with. To know someone is to be born with that person, to share a new beginning with him or her, for all knowledge immerses us in time.

Nature itself gives us abundant examples, for nature is a school. Look at the sun. It is dawn, it is mid-day, it is sunset. Hardly has the sun appeared above the horizon than it rises a little, slowly, slowly, imperceptibly, until it has gone right round the sky. The sun is never in a hurry; the moon and the stars are never in a hurry. Nature is never in a hurry. Everything revolves in this world, everything moves, and no one notices it.

Look at a tree. Between yesterday and today the tree has not changed, and yet it has changed. A plant has not changed, and yet it has changed. Something very profound is going on. Slowly the roots are penetrating the soil, slowly the branches are stretching towards the sky, but you can't see it; you never notice it. True growth is slow and imperceptible. True knowledge also immerses us in time.

Once, after giving a lecture in Alexandria on the Trinity, I was asked how long it had taken me to prepare. I replied, 'Thirty years' – and that was true. For the two or three hours' immediate preparation for the lecture were simply a gathering together of ten thousand elements gleaned from my whole life: thoughts, feelings, emotions, experiences long savoured and loved which I had only to put together as a bouquet, as a sheaf. You don't prepare for a lecture in an hour or a month, but all your life. Unless words emerge from the depth of one's soul, from the depth of one's being, they have no value, no savour. There is a whole difference between a truth learned and a truth lived.

Unfortunately, in most schools truths already learned are handed on, no more, and that is why they are so quickly dead as far as the pupils are concerned: accumulated knowledge, catalogued truths, an indigestible and inassimilable farrago which the pupils rapidly spew out and reject once the examination is over. That's a good thing, because if it remained in their stomachs it would kill the poor things. Any knowledge which has not entered into your flesh, your skin, your heart, remains external and alien to you. Reject it, because it will do you more harm than good. Learning 'by heart' is not a matter of accumulating knowledge in the reservoir of memory or dulling the mind with figures, dates and names; it is primarily learning 'with the heart', savouring, enjoying. Then such knowledge becomes an integral part of one; it becomes oneself.

That's the difference between culture and erudition. Culture is growth of the being by organic assimilation and the living integration of knowledge which is deeply loved and enjoyed. By contrast, erudition is a collection of miscellaneous and undigested baggage. The erudite person is a walking encyclopedia.

We should not be surprised that our young people do not enjoy going to school and are not keen to learn. There is nothing amazing about that, since school has become a vast collective enterprise engaged in dulling the mind, in intellectual sterilization and mental intoxication. The word for study in current Egyptian is *zakara*, i.e. to memorize: a formidable storing up of unformed and badly assimilated knowledge.

When I began my training as a Jesuit I discovered a new world. I left school sick and tired of all that I had learned. And suddenly I found an extraordinary delight in reading, getting to know, studying. A profound truth slowly began to take root deep with me, developing and growing; it helped me to mature and filled me with immense joy. I said to myself, 'How enjoyable learning is!' That's culture: a tree that grows, not a truck one fills; this new knowledge can be a sparkling spring.

Here are two quotations from the contemporary Swiss theologian Hans Urs von Balthasar:

> Patience is the prime virtue of anyone who wants to learn. Only what has disappeared in the ear can be born in the heart.

And I would add:

> Only what has been born in the heart can be repeated by the tongue.

Rudyard Kipling made the same point in his famous poem:

> If you can trust yourself when all men doubt you,
> but make allowance for their doubting too;
> If you can dream – and not make dreams your master
> If you can think – and not make thoughts your aim,
> If you can meet with Triumph and Disaster
> And treat those two impostors just the same...
> you'll be a Man, my son!'

But who can take time to do all these things? Who can take time to dream, to think?

Saint-Exupéry said:

> My people need time, if only to look at a tree. To sit down each day on the threshold in front of the same tree with the same branches. And little by little the tree reveals itself to them.

One day is not enough. It takes days and days until, little by little, the tree reveals its soul to us. It's the same with human beings. It takes time to get to know us, to discover us, because human beings do not reveal themselves all at once; they take time to uncover their souls. And that presupposes a look, a long look; waiting, long waiting; patience, long patience: until the other reveals himself or herself in a truth and a mystery which is very different from what we had originally imagined.

It's the same with God. It takes time to get to know God and discover God. And that presupposes that one takes time to pray. God does not reveal himself to anyone who is in a hurry. To penetrate his mystery, you have to take time, all your time.

Remember Jacob's ladder. Jacob went to sleep and in a dream he saw a long ladder reaching up to heaven with angels going up and down it. He woke up and exclaimed, 'God was there and I did not know it' (Gen.28.16). Jacob had to stop, rest, go to sleep, dream, before he suddenly realized that God was there.

It's the same with us. We have the impression that God is the great absentee figure. 'Lord, where are you? Reveal yourself!' We want God to reveal himself to us, like the light which comes on when we press the switch. We live in a mechanized world in which everything obeys our commands: the century of technology, the century of electronics, the century of switches and buttons. We want rapid, effective, automatic reactions. 'Lord, what do you have to tell me? Tell me quickly, in three words.' It's like someone saying to a beloved, 'Come on, quickly, do you love me or don't you?' People want meditation pills in three minutes, mini-meditations. Since everything is condensed in the modern world, why doesn't the church make little prayer pills that you can swallow in the morning?

Prayer, like love, takes time. But it is freely available, free like all the basic values of our life: music, poetry, the air that we breathe. And these are the things which build us up inside and constantly nourish us; they alone allow us to grow to be truly human. We would do well to recognize that we must give time to these values, to prayer, love, contemplation, dreaming so that we do not grow inwardly hard and rigid, and then pray only mechanically and love only artificially.

Only if we become aware of the living spring that we have can it refresh us and nourish us. Then our work will become much more productive, we shall be much more relaxed, will find it much easier to get on with people, smile more genuinely, and feel a warmer love. Why? Because we have spent half an hour in the morning with God, the source of our humanness.

If you have cloudy liquid which you want to make clear, stirring it with a spoon only makes things worse. What you have to do is leave the liquid for a while. Then the impurities sink to the bottom of the glass, and the water becomes clear and transparent. Some people say to me, 'Show me God! Prove that God exists.' I tell them to be patient. God is an experience to be had; they must calm down. 'Why?,' they ask. 'You'll see. God will reveal himself to you. I can't give you God on a plate; if he does not spring up from within you he is not the true God, but a word, an idea, an idol. God is a reality which springs up from the heart of our being and fills us. It's inexplicable. You just have to experience it. It's an experience you have to have, to have new every day. God is not given once for all; God is not proved once for all. Unless God is new every day, he is no longer God, but something else. God is always new, always being reborn.'

Prayer, too, must always be made all over again. And so must love. Louis Aragon remarked that human beings never acquire anything permanently.

Here are some remarks by the Greek Orthodox monk Metropolitan Anthony Bloom:

> You can only pray when you find yourself in the presence of God in a state of quietness and inner peace which transcends the notion of time. Here I don't mean our objectively measurable time, but our subjective experience of the passing of time around us and the certainty that we ourselves are timeless.

> If you embark on prayer, or love, or play, while at the same time looking at your watch, stop! Don't pray, don't make love, don't play. It's not worth it. When you begin to pray, take an alarm clock, set it to the time you want to devote to prayer and forget everything. It's like sleep: if you say 'I want to sleep just an hour', and look at your watch every five minutes, you won't sleep well. Like prayer, sleep is abandonment in which you lose all sense of time. All vital activities presuppose a forgetfulness of time, a forgetfulness of the clock.

Anthony Bloom goes on:

> We know what happens when we are on holiday. On holiday, there is nothing we need to do, even if we walk quickly, cheerfully and at a rapid pace, even if we run... We do not have the impression of being in a hurry, because what counts is the walk and not the destination.

We need to learn to live as though we were always on holiday. You will tell me that that's impossible. Are you sure? Have you tried? I tell you that it *is* possible: I am always on holiday. That means that whatever I do, I do it as though I were on holiday. There is a way of walking when one is on holiday which does not necessarily consist in going more slowly, because I can walk fast, but without strain, without being in a hurry. There is a difference between being fast and rushing.

Rushing is a source of tension, anxiety, whereas we can be fast while at the same time being calm and relaxed. In everyday life, I do what I have to do without feeling time pressing. You may tell me that time does press. In that case I would reply that that is all the more reason to do what you have to do slowly, gently, calmly. Try putting on a dress or a shirt when you're in a hurry. What happens? The buttons come off, the dress tears, the shirt comes apart at the seams. You haven't gained any time, you've lost it. Try putting on your trousers or sweatshirt. What happens? You get your leg in the wrong hole and the sweatshirt is inside out. That shows that there is a rhythm to be found in existence: a holiday rhythm. That is the wisdom of time.

There is a great wisdom of time. And it is because we have not found it that we are anxious, tense, nervous, disturbed, neurotic, bad-tempered, aggressive. It would be so easy to live in a different way. And then what we do, we would do better. Much better and much quicker. For once you acquire this inner rhythm, this relaxation, this holiday rhythm, you end up treating everything as a game. My work's a game; my cooking's a game; my shopping's a game; my lecture's a game; this meeting is a game. Everything is a game. I'm always on holiday, I enjoy everything, I'm relaxed, and so I do it well.

Here's another suggestion of Anthony Bloom's:

Sit down and tell yourself: 'I'm doing nothing. I'm going to do nothing for five minutes.' Relax, and during this time repeat, 'I am in the presence of God, in the presence of my own self, in the presence of all the furniture around me. I am peaceful, not moving.'

I've tried that exercise and I can recommend it to you. I didn't have much time to pray one morning, and when I arrived at my desk around ten there was a pile of work: proofs to correct that would take days, a lecture to prepare for that very day in another city, lots of letters to write. So I said: first, I'm going to pray, to do nothing for quarter of an hour. I could have spent that quarter of an hour like a lion in a cage: nervous, tense, exasperated. But I told myself: 'You've quarter of an hour's holiday, quarter of an hour for yourself, to dream, to love.' So I lost fifteen minutes, from ten to ten-fifteen. It's difficult to tell you what I gained in that quarter of an hour. It was extraordinary. At 10.15 I began work, and all went well.

Try it! Try it when you're most tense, most wound up; when you've most to do. Say: 'I'm going to have five minutes off, five minutes' holiday.' You may say, 'That's crazy', but I assure you that it's wise. Spend the five minutes at the window. Open it and look at the sky, at the trees, at the birds, at whatever you can see. Take a few breaths of fresh air and look at nature. After five minutes you will find that the world is beautiful, and you'll be ready to start work. And it will go very well.

This necessary and healing time into which you sink so peacefully belongs to God. That's what Anthony Bloom tells us. He comments: 'The only real hindrance to prayer comes when you are buffeted by the tempest, when you let the tempest get inside you instead of letting it rage around you.' And he cites the example of the disciples in the boat with Jesus. Jesus was sleeping on a cushion, and the storm was raging around him. Little by little it entered the heart of the disciples, and they panicked. They woke Jesus, who said, 'Why are you disturbed?' And then he stood up and stilled the storm (Mark 4; Luke 8).

Never panic. The moment of an accident, when things are at their worst, is the time to relax, to take a deep breath, and to calm down. Real leaders are no more intelligent than others, nor more gifted than others, but they are people with a calm head and solid nerves. When the world is panicking, they say, 'No trouble, it will all get sorted out.' And then everyone calms down. The situation may indeed be serious, but that is why there's a need for calm. That's the only way in which problems can be solved.

In our twentieth century we are threatened by what is called stress. Panic situations are not just accidents, exceptional situations. All the time we are in a state of stress because of the rhythm of life, and we have constantly to tell ourselves to keep calm and not to panic.

Imagine a wheel constantly going round and round. If you're on the edge, you will go round with it. But if you get to the hub, the axle at the middle, what happens? Everything revolves around you, but you do not revolve; you stand firm. Prayer is precisely the act in which we rediscover our centre, our axis. The world revolves, people go crazy around you, but you can be like a mountain lake, still and calm.

Unfortunately many people nowadays have no centre, no direction, no head. They live on the circumference and not at the centre. But the whole secret of life is to find a centre and never to leave it. The ultimate aim of prayer is not just to give half an hour to the Lord. What counts is not this half-hour, but the action by which we set ourselves up at this centre in the morning and do not leave it for the rest of the day.

What I have tried to express in this chapter by reflecting on the time of loving, the time of listening, the time of living and the time of praying, is a certain way of existing, a certain life-style which establishes an attitude of mind that is prayer itself. Once it is acquired, this attitude steeps all that we do in a certain climate, and life becomes a game, poetry, liturgy. I like the word liturgy, because in the liturgy everything is done with calmness and dignity. To make my life a liturgy is to raise it to the level of celebration, of festival. When I eat, when I drink, when I am talking to someone, when I am walking, coming and going, everything must be done with a certain rhythm, a certain atmosphere, which will make my whole life radiate peace.

5 The Past Goes On

'The past is not dead. It is not even past'
(*William Faulkner*)

Remembering is a mysterious process! What are we doing when
we remember, and what happens to us? Are those past hours or
days completely obliterated or do they belong to dimensions
which lose themselves unattainably and irrevocably in the dark
depths of time? Or are they still tangible for us in some form; do
they still have live in themselves? When we become preoccupied
with our past, we say that we are losing ourselves in 'old'
memories, 'old' times; the past seems 'old'. Is that the case? Has
my past gone by like a clock, which I can never put back? In his
extraordinarily rich book, entitled *Existence and Eternity*, which
I have already mentioned, the French theologian Fernand Guimet
answers this question in the negative:

> Memory is never a retrospect on the past, pure and simple. It
> is never a matter of restoring the past in its pastness. It does not
> perish with the event that gave it birth. It is a spiritual activity
> within us which, in the awareness of time that it gives us, is not
> in itself of the order of time. It escapes time by this power which
> it has to represent the past, i.e. to make it present, without
> telescoping or confusing the present with the past as it is grasped
> again by the memory, the past which we remember, in another
> dimension than that of pure temporality. One might say that
> memory is not *passé*. It simply allows the application of the
> past to all that it touches, to all that constitutes its object
> because it is within it. It simply recalls itself in a particular way,
> *sub specie aeternitatis*. By making the past present to us, it
> cannot but make it eternal. It is because within all our memories
> there is a beginning of eternal life that memory can be so
> valuable for us, indeed is priceless.

By memory, Guimet is saying, the past is renewed at the heart of the present, is realized in this present. Human beings have a special capacity to be able fully to recall a past event. We bring something up from the past, allow it to blossom again, give it a time in which to live and breathe. Guimet speaks of another dimension: there is more than the sphere of pure temporality, by which he means the general succession of moments of life which no one can cling on to, which escape us. He thinks that our recollection is not just a vigorous concern to recall things from the past; this activity in our minds takes place in the light of eternity. We eternalize the past by making it present.

Only memory is ultimately in a position to help us to understand the meaning and depth of an event, since we have to adopt a particular perspective and a degree of detachment if we are to decipher its meaning.

You will certainly be aware of all the discussions there are about the Gospel of John. It is said that this Gospel is not as historical as the other three. St John is criticized because instead of reporting events as they happened, he tends to interpret them, although he is always very precise in everything that he says. It is said that St John's Gospel is not historical, but an interpretation of the life of Christ, and therefore is not real history.

Now what is said of St John could also be said to a lesser degree of all the other Gospels. The Gospels are not stories about the life of Jesus, but the interpretation of these stories, at a certain distance which has been established between the event 'Jesus' and the moment at which the evangelists were writing. So it can be said that these writings are not historical because they are only memories, interpretations with all the distance which separates them from the time of the experiences that they contain. How does one reply? Is memory a betrayal of the event, or on the contrary is it a restoration of it at its deepest level?

Pick a particular event from your store of memories. For example, I might think of the moment of my religious vocation. I was sixteen years old; it was 8 May 1947, around three in the afternoon. I was reading a book, and for the first time the question occurred to me, 'Henri, why not become a priest?' This happening was a matter of no more than an hour. If I had described it the next day I couldn't have said much more, but I could have said more a month later and even more a year later. If you were to ask me about it now, nearly forty years later, I could write a book about it. This event, which did not take long, was clearly no minor matter in my young life. That hour was not an hour like thousands of others, but was deeply rooted in a very particular past, and soon took on a different dimension in terms of the future. The full significance of the message contained in this hour and all the events of our life, significance in a real and special sense, becomes evident only as one sets it in the context of everything that happened later. At that moment it comes alive and is linked to all the rest.

True history can only be written after a very great interval of time. One only becomes aware of the significance of a historical event when one can relate it to all that follows. Only from the time when one considers things in this perspective does light begin to fall on a past event, does it begin to speak to us, so that we recognize the way in which it fits into the web of existence.

St John is the evangelist who wrote his Gospel last. Matthew, Mark and Luke also wrote their Gospels at some remove from the life of Jesus, but perhaps the interval was not great enough. St John wrote his Gospel later. When the gospel had gone beyond the Palestinian and Jewish world, when it had penetrated the whole of the Mediterranean basin, when theological reflection had begun and developed from the first beginnings, the mystery of Jesus appeared in a new light, with new clarity. The Gospel of John is in a way much more historical than the other three, precisely because it has penetrated to the heart of the interpretation of three generations.

Memories reveal the truth of an event. And what is the Bible, if not a memory, a history? God does not reveal himself in a theology, a dogma or a creed, but in a history. History is revelation. If an Israelite child wanted to know who God was, he was not given a catechism with questions and answers; he was told stories, stories of God's dealings with men and women. You cannot really know people without knowing their history, and you cannot know about God without knowing about God's history.

As I give my lectures, when I look round the room, the faces I see are just blobs of colour. What do I know of the individual stories which underlie these blobs of colour? People do not know much about one another, because they do not know one another's stories. Those whom I have known personally for a long time become increasingly profound; they become 'more' and 'richer' for me, since they are now taking on depth. The superficial picture gradually gives way to time that we have spent together – their past. There can be no real knowledge without the dimension of memory. I only grasp that part of a being, that part of a thing which I can recall later; it is recollection which gives a being or an event the necessary consistency. In the history of Israel, when people asked God for his name, God refused to give it to them. That means that God refuses to be fixed in a word. No word can express God. God is alive, and because God is alive, he only reveals himself in life. Penetrate the history of life, penetrate human history, penetrate the history of the chosen people, and you will find God. God is unfolded in a history. To know God is not to name him; to know God is to recall his mighty acts. In our French mass we sing the Great Hallel, Psalm 136, 'Give thanks to the Lord for he is gracious, and his love endures for ever...', which goes on to relate in a splendid series of verses the 'divine works' from creation to God's intervention in human history. All God's actions are named with gratitude and celebrated in a hymn.

We can see how in all this God discloses his face, reveals his personality, to make it accessible to us. It is by recollection that we are capable of discovering God. The Virgin Mary did precisely the same thing in her song of thanksgiving. The Magnificat (Luke 1.46-55) is a hymn of thanksgiving which takes up Psalm 136 in a denser, more concentrated form. And the Christian creed is similarly a recollection: a recollection of creation, incarnation, redemption, resurrection; a recollection of the whole of the life of Christ, the sending of the Holy Spirit and the history of the church. Here again, faith is expressed in history.

Those who read the Bible constantly ask, 'Who is this mysterious God who withholds his name from human beings and does not explain his actions, who leaves unanswered the human longing to get to know him?' They ask, 'How does God manifest himself in history? What being is acting there, and what attitude do we constantly see anew?' But readers of the Bible also want to see God at work in their own lives; they try to find God at times of meditation on the gospel. But you can do this in another way, by reading and meditating on the history of your own life.

I recently read somewhere that 'human beings are the best translation of the Bible'. This means that we really have two Bibles. The first is the history of a people, human history experienced in the transparency of the assured guidance of God; the second is our personal history, which we recall back to the earliest days of our childhood. People believe that the revelation of God is to be found in the first Bible, and that is right; but we also have our private Bibles in which we find the revelation of God addressed to us, and hear our word of God. This Bible is also important for us and infinitely rich in its own way: in it we recapitulate our own histories in order to find the trace of God in them, just as we do with the other Bible.

For me, the finest of all prayers is that in which I re-read my own life. Nowadays the term 're-read' is very much in vogue. One 're-reads' a past event and investigates its background. I also re-read my own life. What does it have to tell me? Try it yourself! Pick up your life, as you might pick up a book, and read it carefully page by page. Look in it for the significance of this or that event and personal experience, and go back as far as your memory takes you, right back to your childhood.

When I was four years old I was at a kindergarten in Alexandria; I can still see myself as that small boy. They had been showing us how to make little paper boxes, and suddenly for the first time I heard the chilling cries of the Muslim mourning women passing by the house on the way from a funeral. Standing on a chair, I was able to glimpse these uncanny figures, dressed in black veils, which seemed to me to be the heralds of the most fearful disaster. Even now I still have this vivid memory from childhood.

I can also picture the local playground. One day, a bigger boy than I, Simon M, pushed me headlong into a hole. I just missed an iron bar, which could have shattered my skull. I tell myself, 'Lord, you could have let me be killed at the age of four, but you saved me.'

Each of us can recall such events even after fifty years; each of us has this sort of experience. I could also faithfully depict less dramatic events than the two I have mentioned, memories from school, but they would not be of general interest. Yet how vivid such moments are! Every now and then what is supposed to be ordinary takes on an extraordinary dimension as a result of the depth of experience. So I re-experience my past with the devotion of a prayer, and in it have the spiritual experience of the presence of God. I recognize and feel that the Lord is here, the Lord is always present, in the depths of our consciousness and the ground of our being.

Now, in my fifties, I re-experience the past in quite a different, new way, and understand how my life is rooted in all that past, is immersed in it and draws on it, so that it all becomes prayer. When I take up my past history, it is not simply a memory for me, a vague nostalgic memory of my infancy. There is more than that: in memory there is more than memory, and in the past there is more than the past. And the story of my vocation, which I mentioned and which I could recount in detail, was an open window on the beyond; it was a climax to my existence.

When I want to find spiritual nourishment, I can open my Bible and meditate on the mighty acts of God with his people, the crossing of the Red Sea, and so on. But I can also open my own book, my own gospel, the story of my life, to wonder at the mighty acts of God with me, since I have my own history with the Lord.

There are two ways of looking at our past: the secular way which reduces life to a succession of flat and one-dimensional events, and the sacred way which sees in existence the secret and continuous act of God. Only the latter approach shows the basis and background to life and reveals its religious dimension, its dimension of eternity. My history then takes on meaning, acquires a particular savour, and my past becomes near, present, current.

What I can say of the course of my life, I can also say of the course of my day. How did I spend today? What has it shown me? What has it brought me? There are people who never have time to remember, to look back on their lives, to stand back and see all that has happened, what they have experienced – people with no depth-dimension. They live in the moment without ever emerging from it. Their life never reveals its meaning, and will never reveal God to them. We need to take time every evening to look back on our day, to weigh it up, to savour it and to discover those moments of grace in which God touched our heart, for in each one of those days there are moments, encounters, events which have marked and touched us.

There is no such thing as an 'empty' day, because no day in human life is without God's grace. There are all kinds of ways in which this can come to us, and it is the cause of particular insights and recognitions; it can be found in anything that has touched us. At the time these things happen I am not aware of their significance, and it is only afterwards, as a result of a certain distancing from them, that I can discover the particular flavour, the profound importance of such events.

What I was saying about St John could be applied to all of us.

Each day brings us a message. It is not a verbal message and cannot be put into words. It is a message which is perceived from the heart and kept in the heart. Remember the Gospel phrase about Mary: 'And Mary kept all these things and pondered them in her heart' (Luke 2.51).

We need to be capable of taking up our day, our existence, into our hearts. Remembering is bringing a past event into our hearts to give it new life. Language itself tells us this. In Latin, *recordare* means 'recall', and it is derived from the Latin word for heart: *cor, cordis*. We talk about a tape recorder. Language has a whole philosophy; it goes very deep. So recalling is not just an abstract activity of the brain, but a matter of the heart – and I would say that only the heart can recall fully. If only the traditional schools, both teachers and pupils, could understand that! What we call learning 'by heart' is nothing of the sort, because the heart is not involved at all; all that is involved is thought-mechanism. Language is understood wrongly and applied wrongly.

The heart is an organ which is capable of recall. In fact I can only remember what has gone through the depths of my heart. How long ago this happened is immaterial. But anything that leaves the heart uninvolved is soon forgotten, and ultimately becomes valueless, even if it was written only a short time previously. However, once it has reached my heart, it will become my flesh and blood, it will grow with me, become part of my inner self, part of my existence, will become my own self.

Seen in this way, my review of the day becomes a profound meditation, a way of perceiving God in my everyday life. That is what Mary is said to have done by keeping all these things in her heart; in that way she discovered the profundity of the mystery of Jesus. Having meditated on this for several decades she handed it on to St John, who had adopted her as his mother. The mystery of Jesus which passed through the heart of Mary also passed through the heart of St John. That is why the Fourth Gospel is so great and splendid a Gospel. It passed through two privileged hearts, the heart of Jesus' mother and that of 'the disciple whom Jesus loved...'

When saints want to write about God, they first of all look very carefully through their own lives. St Augustine's masterpiece is not his sermons, his homilies, nor even *The City of God*, but his *Confessions*, which are the story of his life, the web woven by God in his existence, the story of his quest for faith. In the

Confessions his life becomes a long invocation, a long conversation, a loving dialogue:

> Lord, do you remember my youth, when I was immersed in sin and I sought those delights which left me unsatisfied? Do you remember when my mother spoke to me and I did not listen? Do you remember when I finally felt your hand, which held me and guided me? Do you remember?

Deliberately to take up my own existence in the light of God is to embark on a dialogue, to discover a presence, the presence of the one who has followed me from the first moment of my conception to the present, the presence of the faithful companion who has taken me by the hand from the first moment of my life.

Later, in the sixteenth century, we have the memoirs of Peter Faber, a co-founder of the Jesuit order. He also set down his meditations on paper when he wanted to talk of God. He sought to demonstrate the guidance of God in his past. Nearer still, in the twentieth century, is the *Story of a Soul* by Thérèse of Lisieux, which is another set of reminiscences.

If you are suffering from spiritual aridity, instead of taking a theological or spiritual book, pick up a biography, the life of a saint. There you will find substantial nourishment, because in a biography it is the living God who speaks, whereas in theology we have a dead God. When you are talking to children you should always tell them stories, because it is through stories that they will understand, and not through concepts or ideas.

Above all, hang on to your personal memories, for they are something sacred. Modern men and women no longer have any roots; they continually move from place to place because of their work, constantly changing their homes, their cities and even their countries. In the United States people can live in as many as twenty different cities during their lives, and the same thing is beginning to happen in the Near East. There are people who have lived in Iraq, in Libya, in Saudi Arabia, in Kuwait, and so on. In this merry-go-round of modern life it is increasingly important to keep roots. In former times it was normal, natural, to have roots. People visited or lived in their ancestral home all their lives. Our old home in an area of Alexandria, where I spent my childhood, still exists, and naturally I stop and look at it every time I go past. The wall is falling down, the iron gate is rusting, but every window speaks to me, every step, and the two pillars to the right and left of the entrance. And the little garden. It all speaks to me of my childhood. We should all regularly make a pilgrimage to our roots, should return to our childhood homes, if not physically, at least by means of photographs, letters and mementoes. People may call this sheer nostalgia or sentimentality, but it is more than that. Certainly I am not excluding sentiment or nostalgia, but it can be given another depth, another dimension.

Those who are of my age may remember a sentimental French song which went, 'Memories, memories, sweet and tender, of happiness which seems almost forgotten'. And then it goes on: 'Memories, memories, the past cannot die as long as it remains a memory in our hearts.'

Certainly the past cannot die, and memories keep this past alive, present. That is why memories are so sacred. Human beings are their past. I am my own past. What I am now is what has been formed slowly over the years. I am a tree with concentric circles, and each passing year has made its mark deep within me. I am a pyramid built up of layer upon layer, the result of my infancy, my education, my family, my religious training, my travels, and so on. All this crystallizes around the small being that I am; all this has shaped me, made me, formed me. My being is my past; I am my past; that is why it does not pass.

The slightest past event has shaped us in a particular way, has marked us for ever; that is why it is part of our eternity. We shall always be what we have been, what we have experienced, what we have felt. And all that will one day rise again and be eternally alive.

One day I reminded my mother of a journey we had made to Lebanon in 1944. I told her that all its happy memories, the villages which we had gone through, the events that we had experienced, would never pass away, but were inscribed in God's eternity. The journey would last for ever. For me, access to eternity consists in passing through the gate of death to rediscover a concentration of our lives on the other side. There we shall experience all the fullness of the eternal past. One day all our events will lie before us like an open book, like a present reality. The past will come alive again. Nothing passes away, nothing disappears, but all is gathered together in God's great storehouse. If God is eternal, and if we become eternal with him, it is in order to rediscover in him all our past life, no event of which can disappear.

That is an extraordinary hope for me, for each of our relation-ships, each of our friendships, each of our loves is more than an unforgettable story, an inestimable treasure. One of the most important messages to hand on to people is the message of hope and trust:

All that you have experienced is of value, is important, is serious – so serious that God preserves it and gathers it together. And one day he will say to you: 'You have not just lived your life in the past, but you will live it always. It will be yours, you will take it up again in the eternal light of the beyond, but with quite a different clarity, quite a different density.'

That's marvellous! You may call it wishful thinking, but I would reply that that is just not true. If a stone, a simple stone, can exist for billions of years without decaying, would you want something that is infinitely richer, infinitely more important than a stone, to disappear one day completely? If God can preserve a simple small stone for billions and billions of years, is he going to delete the whole of my past existence at a stroke? No, this spiritual existence is there for ever: it has been, it is, and it will be.

None of it is ephemeral. Nothing is ephemeral for anyone who lives his or her life at this level. However, here the question arises: 'At what level?' Look at this diagram of a cone. You can live your life at the base, in the middle, or at the point. It is at the point that everything is concentrated, that everything is eternal. The point is my real being, my essential being, which does not pass away.

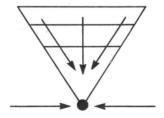

It is at that level that all my life is concentrated; it is there that it will be taken up and kept for ever. That is where eternity is. To be eternal is not to perpetuate oneself in the final state one has reached, i.e. a human ragamuffin at the end of life. I am not interested in perpetuating myself as an old man; that is not eternity.

What is capable of living at this level is a force. I do not have the strength of my body, but the strength of my life. Those who concentrate all their past in the present moment are not simply the human beings that they are now but human beings with all the irresistible thrust of their past. That is a way of living in a state of synthesis, of totality. If I only live as I am now, I am only the thinnest of films on the surface of my being. But if I live with all the weight and all the thrust of what I have been, my life takes on quite a different dimension. Those who remember are those who have given all the weight of what they have been to their existence.

There is such richness, such fullness, in our past, that it would be a pity to live only in the passing moment, the fleeting instant, without devoting to it all of our past lives. In other words, I can experience the instant uniquely on the surface of the cone, but I can also involve the whole pyramid in the present act and make it bear the whole weight of my past existence on the point of the cone, here and now.

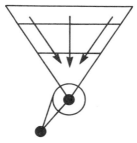

The word that I speak, the act that I venture, can be the concentration and sum of all my past. At that moment living becomes a total act of all being. There is extraordinary power there. But to avoid misunderstandings, there are some things that we should remember.

By eternity I do not mean holding on to our final state, which is what some people are afraid of: the sorry end of our existence. Who of us would be happy if we supposed that we would go on for ever as an old man or woman? No, eternity is something quite different. When Mary appeared to St Bernadette at Lourdes, she had the attractive appearance of a girl of about fifteen. According to historical tradition, Mary died in Ephesus as an old woman of eighty-five. So among other thing Lourdes is a sign to us that human beings continue for ever in the best form that they had on earth, and that the rest of their lives will be absorbed by this form, which illuminates and supplements them from within.

What will we look like in the life to come? That is a question which crops up again and again. What impression will we make there? Don't worry. You will look as you did in the prime of life, and will not reflect any stage of your bodily decline. The resurrection body will reveal the best of you; the highpoint of your existence will be raised to true life; it will blossom, develop fully and be brought to full maturity. Possibly this new appearance will not be immediately recognized by others, but it will be our true face, since we shall be living with God in the truth. Our eternal appearance is the appearance of our youth in the higher sense, our true youth, and that means that it will be the appearance of our deepest being.

Anyone who already lives and breathes this vision becomes a source of power for others. I am not the power of my body but the power of my being and the life that I live. Those who integrate their past into the present moment and concentrate it there are made up not only of the human nature which is visible at a particular moment, but of more: at the same time they embody the whole inner drive of their past. There is an art of living in a state of synthesis, in a state of totality.

By contrast, if I see only what I am now, I am no more than a tiny speck on the surface of my being. But if I live with all the weight and all the impetus of what I have been, I shape my life in quite a different way, and it takes on another dimension. Those with good memories at every moment give their existence another dimension by holding on to their previous experience. What reveals the meaning of the present is a reference to particular events which were experienced intensively at some point in the past.

Here is an example. Last time I was in the church of St Joseph in Cairo I spent the whole of mass watching a mother and her child in front of me. The child was standing on the edge of the pew, and the mother had her arms around the child while it was swinging, walking, and so on. Every now and then she would put it on the ground. The child did what it wanted, and all the time the mother carefully kept an eye on it. She was praying, but she never let the child out of her sight. It could have fallen a hundred times during the mass, but never did. At the last moment, the mother, by a tiny movement, would catch the child or hold it back by its coat. You might say that I was watching the child instead of praying. But it was my best prayer! The whole mass was a marvellous contemplation of the love of God.

This small incident is in the past, but it is now present for ever and has become a point of reference for me. This trivial event, which I experienced deeply in my heart, is the catalyst for quite a new experience in this sphere. Just looking at a mother carrying a child or holding its hand brings back memories of that other experience in church to produce quite a different feeling and quite a different depth. Memory feeds the present and fills it with incomparable riches. There is a richness of life in our past, a richness of expression, which it would be a pity to leave on one side. This richness can be with us all the time and become nourishment, delight, enjoyment. That is what memory is.

Memories nourish our present with their savour and their fire, and they fill us with inestimable value. So we should not regard our wealth of experiences as museum-pieces and leave them lying unused, but should deliberately make active use of them. That is what I understand by the spiritual activity of recollection.

Old people are those who have this wisdom of memory. An old person is someone who remembers, and that is splendid. You might say that this is a waste of time, but I would reply that it is the most important thing for old people: remembering for themselves and remembering for others. There is a wisdom, an intensity of life in memories. Memory is never an empty experience, but something full, something which plunges its roots into the heart of existence.

I said earlier that human beings are their past. But what past? The individual past or the eternal past? Science shows me that my past is not only my own past but the past of all the earth and of all humanity; it puts down its roots very, very wide and very, very deep. My past is the world of minerals and the world of vegetables, the world of animals and the human world; my past is most deeply rooted in the earth and in the centuries.

I bear within myself all this history of the universe and of humanity. When people say in scientific, technical terms that ontogenesis recapitulates phylogenesis, they mean that the history of the individual recapitulates that of the species. The little embryo in its mother's womb undergoes in nine months the stages undergone by the whole of life over its evolution. If you analyse your body, you will find in an infinitesimal form the ninety-two elements which exist in nature. Human beings are microcosms; each body is a concentration of the universe.

When I make contact with the earth, I make contact with myself and remember my past. That we experience such an attraction to earth is not simply a result of gravity; it is because there is a profound relationship between human beings and the earth. I am a son of the earth and the earth is my mother. I come from it, because it bore me and it is my own past. The tree is my past, the plant is my past, the flower is my past, the forest is my past. I have been that way before; we have all been that way.

We feel the same thing in the proximity of animals. The affection and the attachment that we feel for animals is not just sentimentalism; there is a profound affinity between them and us. We are made of the same stuff, we are brothers and sisters, we are one. The creaturely world forms one family because we have one past. What is modern genetics concerned with? What is heredity? It is this being moulded by experiences which extend far back in time. That is what Lamarck's theory about the transmission of acquired characteristics is all about. All the experiences of flowers, birds, cats, apes and so on in the past have been stocked up, accumulated in certain cells, and have been constantly transmitted over millions of years to make us what we are today. We are the result of this long past, this long earthly history. Evolution is ineradicably inscribed upon us and we bear it with us. Heredity is the memory of our species, the recollection of the whole cosmic ascent towards us.

Education is akin to this; it is the reappropriation by each child in a few years of all the past experience of humankind. Everything that has been experienced and thought between Adam and Einstein, all the work of discovery and knowledge by the peoples of antiquity, the philosophy of Plato and Aristotle, the thoughts of St Thomas and Hegel, all the philosophers, sages and poets, are presented to the child on a plate from which he or she can help themselves. It is a gift of past humankind, a memento of all generations, an everlasting present, for the young person to take.

But how is a child to remember all this with enjoyment, by heart and with heart? There is an art in relating history well. Unfortunately this art is all too often reduced to broad, superficial knowledge and the hasty transmission of dates and synoptic tables of facts. But that is not history or remembering. History has to become a story, a true story: 'Once upon a time...' At that moment the child listens and the story enters into its heart. Relating history is an art. There are many history teachers, but very few of them have mastered it so that they know how to make the past live again, make the heart of their pupils beat faster.

Thus through evolution, through heredity, through education, little by little, we inherit a whole primal wealth which slowly becomes ours. To remember ourselves is to take possession of this priceless treasure.

What is an educated person? Not someone who has knowledge but someone who has roots. For many people culture is often no more than an accumulation of knowledge, an encyclopaedic mind; a culture person is thought to be someone capable of saying everything there is to be said about a subject, or something about everything, depending on what it is... Such a person is a walking dictionary; but we don't need walking dictionaries because we now have electronic brains which work much better. Rather, an educated, cultivated person is someone who lives with all the past generations, who lives with all the humanity of former days, and who lives with all the wisdom of the ancients, who puts roots down into the world of yesterday and today. The aim of education is to transfer into myself the universal human being, to become this person of all other times and all other places, thanks to the memory of the heart.

The memory of the heart allows us to experience love between one another. We find ourselves back in a common past. What is a culture? What is a civilization? What is a nation? A nation is not a countryside; a countryside is a geographical entity: mountains, valleys, rivers, frontiers. But a nation is rather different: it is a common past, a common history, common experiences.

What is Alexandria? Alexandria is all these faces, a quite specific mentality, different from that of Cairo, different from that of Upper Egypt, different from that of Lebanon, different from that of France. It is a mixture of all these things at once and it is also something else. There is a distinctive culture in Alexandria, a distinctive civilization and mentality, a very special spirit. It is the shared past of shared experience which helps us to communicate, to feel at ease with one another; there is a family spirit. At national level, at the level of a city or a village, there is this sharing of past experiences which are our riches, which are our power of communication.

To end with I would like to demonstrate that all this is not a collection of ideas, theories, dreams; it has an existential dimension. Some years ago, when I was lecturing on death, I raised this question:

> What is the past of humankind?
> Where are the dead to be found?
> Where are those who have preceded us? What is their abode?
> In heaven? In hell? In purgatory? In limbo? With God?
> With the devil? Where are they?

I replied to these questions by saying that there is in fact only one humanity, the humanity of today, here and now.

When I was small, after my grandmother had died, my mother told me that she was now in heaven. I wanted to take a long, long ladder and climb up to my grandmother. Since then, I've come to realize that I don't need a long ladder, for our dead, those who have gone before us, are there – there in me, in you, in us, here and now. There is no other world than our own; there is no other universe than our own; there is no heaven anywhere above, and no hell anywhere below. What exists is today's humanity, which bears within it the humankind of former times as a mother carries her child in its womb. We are the summing up of all former humankind: we are its living and present memory. Our present existence bears this fruit, hundreds of thousands of years old, which the earth has slowly brought forth.

More than twenty years ago I wrote this, about death as a restoration and a return to earth:

> Death is the moment at which each of us flows back into the great stream of life from which we emerged. This reintegration is not a dissolution into the anonymous but an ascent into the personal; it is not a return to primal energy but a transcending of ourselves in love; it is not a return to the timeless but an entry into eternity; it is not a matter of being consumed, but an ascent; it is not sinking into the unconscious but an ecstasy of the superconsciousness; it is not destruction but realization.

Then the dead begin to be active. They attach themselves to the living and give them additional life. The dead do not withdraw into a sphere of the universe outside the earth, to lead a life there among their like, but through every act of their dying they find themselves restored to the flow of life which gave birth to them.

The dead now experience an intensification of their present. Their death does not take them away from us, but makes them intimately near to us, and this nearness is many times more definitive than it could ever have been before.

In their spiritual power they become a ferment for those of us who are alive. Through the presence of the dead, human society raises itself step by step and will one day find its fulfilment. The dead are the motive power of development and all progress. Through them evolution slowly makes its way through time towards its goal.

The other world is within this world; the beyond is here. Former humankind adds itself to humankind today through the great reintegration of death, by the restoration of the dead. Present humankind is none other than a summation of all the human beings who have ever lived. We bear in ourselves the living but concealed presence of all the human beings of the past.

Each of us is supported by the whole line of his or her ancestors. This is not symbolic, figurative language, but a real ontological fact. All the dead are really alive, and they continue to live in us.

My dead live in my heart, in my body and blood; they live my life with me. I recapitulate them, I am their last word, they speak through me, they work in me, they remain active in me as the ongoing past which is the present – in all of us, in each of us.

So there exists in us and in today's humankind a sort of pressure from within, the pressure of all past generations waiting to see what we will make of them, what we will do with this world from which they too came forth, which they know. They confidently whisper, 'Take over the baton, take up the succession, take on the task.' We are responsible for a world which was entrusted to us by others. Are we acting accordingly?

There is only one humanity and there is only one human person who has existed over the millennia of history. I am, we are, this person. To the degree that we are inwardly watchful, sensitive and responsive to the inner call of all those who preceded us, this recollection of all that is past will bear fruit – not just for me or you, but for the whole human species. If we notice any progress in humankind, then we also note the reason: its good memory.

What I said about inheriting, which is quite simply the accumulation of experiences from the past in the mechanisms of memory made up of genes and chromosomes, I am now also saying about humanity in its spiritual and ontological dimensions. In our spirits, in our bodies, in our hearts, in our consciousness and our sub-consciousness, we experience this irresistible thrust of all the past generations who are expecting from us the fruition that they have a right to expect. This fruition will be the new humanity which must come to birth in us one day 'when the times have been fulfilled', when human beings have reached their full maturity and stature.

Once we have arrived at this final point, this omega point, the whole of past history will be actualized for ever in eternity. Heaven is only this eternal moment of remembering again all that we have been, all that we have experienced in the presence of God.

6 The Redemption of Time

'I am worth more than my life'
(A young man before execution)

After I had given a lecture on the theme discussed in the previous chapter, one of those present was quite disturbed and came up to me: 'Father, you say that the past does not pass. As far as I'm concerned, that's a terrible prospect. My life is a series of mistakes, an ongoing tragedy, and in heaven I wouldn't want to find that I had to begin that all over again...'

I told myself that she was right. For those who have had a happy childhood it is good that the past does not pass, but I can understand how those whose life has been one long *via dolorosa* can say to themselves, 'My God, no... Please make the past past, let this nightmare disappear, so that I can at last turn the page and forget...'

That is precisely the problem I want to deal with in this chapter, which I have called 'The Redemption of Time'. I could also call it 'Obliterating the Past'. So does that mean transitoriness?

In no circumstances should the concept of an everlasting past be understood in terms of a retrospective destiny which takes our breath away and weighs heavily upon us. However, to some people the past evidently seems to be an eternal destiny which ties and binds them to what was, to what they can no longer change, to their failures in life, or to what has gone very wrong. Suffering gnaws at them, and they ask themselves, 'Are we helpless? Can we never break loose from this chain, break out of this darkness, to reach a freer, clearer sphere in which we can pick up again the whole of the life that we have lived and come to grips with it afresh, so that we can put many things right, make up for what we have not done and rescue what we have lost?' Is there no magic formula for what Marcel Proust called 'the search for lost time', for the work to which he gave this title seems to recapitulate his whole life in time? But what is the meaning of the redemption of time? What is making good? What is the redemption of the past?

In a famous text, Nietzsche contemplates with furious rage and despair this past against which he feels impotent, this past which is beyond his grasp and which escapes him. Nietzsche, the one who based all his philosophical work on the will-to-power of the superman who can overcome his destiny, comes up against the wall of the past, which raises itself before him like an insuperable obstacle. He says:

> To redeem the past, and to transform every 'It was' into 'I wanted it thus' — that alone do I call redemption.

These lines from his *Thus Spoke Zarathustra* inspired me to the title of this chapter. So we shall now try to see the meaning of the redemption of the past and whether this redemption is truly possible.

'It was': that is what the will's teeth-gnashing and most lonely affliction is called. Powerless against that which has been done, the will is an angry spectator of all things past.

The will cannot will backwards; that it cannot break time and time's desire — that is the will's most lonely affliction.

It is sullenly wrathful that time does not run back: 'That which was' — that is what the stone which it cannot roll away is called.

And so, out of wrath and ill-temper, the will rolls stones about and takes revenge upon him who does not, like it, feel wrath and ill-temper.

Thus the will, the liberator, becomes a malefactor: and upon all that can suffer it takes revenge for its inability to go backwards.

This, yes, this alone is *revenge* itself: the will's antipathy towards time and time's 'It was'.

Can there be redemption when there is eternal justice? Alas, the stone 'It was' cannot be rolled away: all punishments, too, must be eternal! Thus madness preached. No deed can be annihilated; how could a deed be undone through punishment? That existence too must be an eternally-recurring deed and guilt, this, this is what is eternal in the punishment 'existence'!

These thoughts of Nietzsche's are fearful. No act can ever be undone, and everything lasts for ever. That is also suggested by the title of a novel by Paul Bourget, *Our Deeds Follow Us*. That phrase contains a terrible obsession, a feeling of fright and anguish in the face of this ineluctability of an action which, once performed, follows us and pursues us indefinitely. Even punishment, says Nietzsche, cannot do away with the fact that the action has been performed. It is there as a curse.

All 'It was' is a fragment, a riddle, a dreadful chance – until the creative will says to it: 'But I willed it thus!'Until the creative will says to it: 'But I will it thus! Thus shall I will it.'

Here in a strange way Nietzsche attempts to do away with this fatality of the past by proclaiming in the attitude of a philosopher: 'Yes, that is basically what I wanted. I failed, but basically I wanted that to happen. I am not in a position to obliterate the past, and so I explain it to myself in a different way and tell myself that this is really how I wanted it, how I want it now and how I shall want it in the future.'

But in acting in this way I am fooling myself. This Stoic attitude is no solution, for the will always comes up against the wall of time, the wall of the past, without being able to cross it.

This leads us to reflect on the significance of the feeling of guilt. Here I would refer particuarly to a remarkable book by a contemporary French philosopher Jean Lacroix, *The Feeling of Guilt*. Lacroix distinguishes between two different, not to say opposed, attitudes: remorse and repentance.

I have done something bad, a wicked act that I regret. But this regret can take two forms: either remorse or repentance. For most of us, these two words are equivalent and almost synonymous. To say that 'I feel remorse' or 'I repent' seems to us to be two ways of saying the same thing. But in fact here we have two feelings which are not only different, but diametrically opposed to each other.

Remorse is a useless and ineffective regret which consists in wishing that the fault had not happened and suffering from one's inability to suppress it. Men and women torment themselves inwardly, saying, 'Oh, if only I had not done that! Oh, if only that could never have been! Oh, what a shame that it happened!...' And in so doing they shut themselves up in a vicious circle of useless regrets.

There is a proverb which goes, 'Too late is too late.' Those who are eaten away by remorse are undermined within by a feeling which gnaws at them and consumes them, by a kind of morbid and unhealthy anguish which devours them. Then follows self-condemnation in hopeless questions about guilt, for within the feeling of guilt there is the rejection of whatever has been done and its condemnation by our conscience.

Do you ever notice the spontaneous gestures which people make when they suddenly become aware of a mistake, gestures which you yourself also make? The hand goes to the forehead, the fist hits the table or the wall, someone claps her hands, someone tears his hair or beats his breast. Remarkable reactions! What do they mean? They mean that we want to punish ourselves: we chastize ourselves, we take vengeance on ourselves. Do you know that beating the breast goes back to the time of the desert fathers? In order to satisfy their need for repentance, they would pick up a stone and hit themselves on the chest with it, very hard. This gesture survives down to the present day in our mass. Our fingers gently touch our chests when we say – unfortunately more or less mechanically – the confession:

I confess that I have failed to do good and done evil. I have sinned in thought, word and deed through my fault, my own fault, my grievous fault.

However, mild though it has become, our gesture of self-punishment still expresses the same thing – a need for atonement. People think that they can atone for their guilt by pain and punishment, and it is here that Nietzsche strikes. Stubbornly and desperately he describes those who grind themselves down in sick anxieties and meaningless self-accusations; he knows how useless the whole exercise is: too late is too late. This behaviour comes near to masochism: masochism has many dimensions, but one of them is the spiritually painful feeling of guilt which one continues to nurture. Guilt feelings can take on morbid forms, even extending to a delight in moral pain, which people carefully preserve by constantly savouring their misery all over again. Here the sufferers persuade themselves that their suffering is good and redemptive in itself. But it is only good and redemptive to the degree that it has a meaning, brings with it faith, confidence and love.

A person suffering from remorse may seem to be an embittered being, but this bitterness is disguised; in a veiled way it seeks to give the impression that God finds pleasure in this suffering of the conscience. We all know from our childhood days that spirituality of sorrow which sought to convince us, 'The more you suffer, the greater is God's joy.' It is precisely at this point that Sigmund Freud's famous concept of the 'sadistic father' comes in – a God who takes pleasure in human suffering. This phenomenon can go so far as to become an obsession, a form of neurosis consisting in the compulsive repetition of an action, as though those in its grip were driven by inner shadows which did not allow them any rest.

Another type of neurotic and obsessional act is the scruple, which is also associated with remorse. Pushed to extremes, the scrupulous attitude can bring about the most disturbing form of neurosis, which is called manic depression or melancholy: in ordinary language, a nervous breakdown. Here lies one of the dangers of self-examination, which for many people consists in going over the past time and again in a sterile way, so that it becomes a source of discouragement and bad conscience: a more or less obsessional mental rumination which paralyses and raises obstacles. Remorseful people feel steeped in their failure, imprisoned in a enclosed world from which they cannot escape, plunged into a morass, all the time arguing with themselves and shutting themselves in. They normally end up in despair and even suicide.

Remember Judas! He felt his guilt penetrating his whole being, fettered and imprisoned by this past hour of betrayal; he could no longer see a future; his past became a future which had nothing else in view but his own guilt. As the psalm puts it, 'For I acknowledge my misdeeds, and my sin is ever before me' (Ps.51.5).

So people's lives can come to an inner standstill, since they experience not only their past but also their future as past, as they are caught in the past. For what is life, if not constant new departures and inward rejuvenation, a new flourishing in the power of eternal resurrection? However, those who are torn apart by remorse are incapable of all that. Their wings seem broken; it is as though they have stopped real life and put themselves outside it. In banishing themselves they recognize themselves as victims of their guilt, fettered to the past, over which Nietzsche laments, having made the unchangeable past a rigid time which eternalizes itself for them.

Let us look more closely at that Christian spirituality of past days which has celebrated grief. Nietzsche could help us to understand Sartre's analyses of God as the spy whose eye is fixed permanently on men and women to torment them. For Sartre a look is that which fixes someone or something. To look at someone or something is to fix it in an immovable image, to transform it into a 'statue of salt', to make a new Lot. Those who suffer remorse look at themselves and at the same time they feel that they are being looked at, since there is a close relationship beween these two attitudes. In looking at oneself, one feels one is also being looked at by others and by God, and this look is at the same time condemnation, a definitive judgment without any appeal.

Victor Hugo wrote a famous poem about conscience, from which I quote a few lines:

When with his children, clothed in animal skins,
dishevelled, livid, in the midst of tempests,
Cain fled before Jehovah...

Having killed his brother, devoured with remorse, Cain flees the implacable gaze of God, across plains, mountains and valleys, steppes and forests. Every time he looks back, he sees this gaze fixed on him. He hides in the depths of his tent, but the gaze is always there. He asks to be buried alive in order to escape the terrible vision. The earth slowly covers the body, the neck, the eyes, the head, down to the last hair. When it was all finished,

The eye was in the tomb and looked on Cain.

Today we shudder at such a story of God, at such a view of God: God as a spy, a police inspector, an inquisitor, whose gaze follows us step by step, whom nothing escapes. In some churches this eye looks down from the ceiling with a vividness one cannot miss, a wide open eye which sees absolutely everything. Is it surprising that such an image of God inevitably also prompts a tendency towards atheism? Here is how Sartre relates an experience from the time of his adolescence:

God sees me, I feel his gaze within my head and my hands, horribly visible, a living target. Indignation saved me: I was furious at so gross an indiscretion, I blasphemed, I murmured as against my grandfather: Holy name of God, name of God. He will never look at me again.

Sartre's atheism is precisely the rejection of this inquisitive look which violates human intimacy and in the process deprives it of all liberty. God sees me, so I am not longer free. Moreover, this impalpable look, anonymous and omnipresent, is like the unification of all human looks, the regard of all spaces infiltrating into the human heart.

For Sartre, God is a 'voyeur' in the sense that contemporary psychology gives to this word. God is the one who tries to see through the keyhole what is going on in my room, what is going on in my heart. God is inquisitiveness itself. At the same time as God fixes human beings in their past, he also fixes them in their bodies, which are also their past. What is our body? Our body is not ourselves; it is only a certain image of ourselves. It is our past rather than our future; our animal nature rather than our humanity. It is that by which we participate in the animal world, the material world; that which does not have the possibility of changing from one day to the next, despite all the make-up. A woman keeps the face she has. An old man will never succeed in making himself a child's face.

This look, then, by fixing us in our past, becomes a kind of death sentence for us.

Nietzsche is the one who is mostly behind this. He is the one who has principally prompted analyses of the regard of God. In his book *The Gay Science*, he tells of a young girl in the bath. Her mother says to her, 'God sees everything'. The girl's reaction is, 'How indecent! What right has he to see me in my bathroom?'

At another point Nietzsche cites the example of Judas, on whom Jesus looked twice – at the last supper and at his betrayal. At the supper he gave Judas a piece of bread and looked at him – knowing all – with the words, 'What you do, do quickly' (John 13.27b). Then, when he approached Jesus to betray him in the garden of Gethsemane, Jesus looked on him again and said, 'Judas, do you betray the son of man with a kiss?' (Luke 22.48). For Nietzsche, the motive for this betrayal was Jesus' look. This intolerable gaze had to be extinguished, and that meant the death of Jesus.

Now let us look at Nietzsche's Zarathustra.

On his journey, Zarathustra encounters the desolate, terrifying valley called 'Serpent's Death' and there encounters the ugliest man, Judas. Judas discloses to him the true cause of his crime:

Zarathustra! Zarathustra! Read my riddle! Speak, speak! What is the revenge on the witness?

But he – had to die: he looked with eyes that saw everything -

he saw the depths and abysses of man, all man's hidden disgrace and ugliness.

His pity knew no shame: he crept into my dirtiest corners. This most curious, over-importunate, over-compassionate god had to die.

He always saw me: I desired to take revenge on such a witness - or cease to live myself.

The god who saw everything, even man: this god had to die. Man could not endure that such a witness should live.

So Judas commits two murders which cannot be separated from each other: the murder of Jesus, aimed at destroying this look which he cannot stand; and his own murder, his suicide. The two go together, and in this double murder of Judas lies the proof of what I affirmed earlier: remorse brings condemnation of self by self, of self by others and of self by God. Judas did not simply suppress Jesus' gaze on him, for this gaze would have pursued him beyond death. No, to get rid of it he had to do away with himself. 'The eye was in the tomb and looked on Cain.' God has to exist. His eye burns in the midst of the human person and sees all. For man to live, God must die.

These interpretations shake us, since they reveal a real tragedy of misunderstanding. So let us now pass to rather brighter perspectives and speak of repentance.

What is repentance? It, too, is the recognition of personal guilt, but at the same time it goes beyond it and overcomes it.

Repentance seeks to by-pass the past by looking forward, by looking to the future.

Remorse directs us towards the past. Repentance projects us towards the future.

So there is a world of difference between the two. The idea of redemption and restoration by means of a particular action is an integral part of the concept of repentance. Here we are not held eternally captive in the past, but are given the possibility of going beyond it. That is the marvellous good news we are given. In the end, nothing is ultimately lost and there is never occasion for total despair. Everything can be taken up again and fundamentally reshaped; everything can be blotted out or purified. Everything can rise again in purity.

That sounds incredible, unbelievable. Nevertheless, the good news to men and women is indeed that there is no death.

There is no death. Not in any form. It is wrong to think of death as final defeat and the utmost unhappiness for men and women. This view is false: it lacks reality, it has no existence, because the new element in this world news which has reached us is the redemption of human beings and the redemption of time. It is the news of our future which discloses itself to us and leads us to brighter realms of life. It is the news of the liberation of men and women from all time, so that they do not remain indissolubly entangled in the mistakes which they made in the past. It is the news of the redemption of men and women from a guilty past.

But what does that amount to in practice? How are we to justify what I have just said? Can one reach back into the past and destroy seed and crops there, make something as though it had never happened?

The answer is yes and no. In fact this is impossible, since what has happened has happened. But one can extinguish the past in oneself as a conscious human action, and it is on this spiritual level that redemption takes place. The tangible fact is the physical or psychological consequence of a completed action. This consequence is irreversible. It belongs to the past. If I break a precious vase, once the vase is broken there is nothing that can make it not broken. The deed is done, and the fact itself cannot be destroyed, cannot be suppressed.

But the action which underlies the fact, which is its meaning, its moral and spiritual significance, its profound and internal motivation, can always be modified, up to the point of death, by a change in my inner attitude, by a transformation in the depths of my being.

Let me explain.

Our life is made up of a succession of actions: this act, followed by another, then by a third, a fourth, and so on. But over and beyond this succession of actions there is the person who dominates them. This person, who stands above them, at the top of the cone, at the point of the pyramid, transcends the successive actions which he or she performs, transcends the unfolding of his or her life, transcends the flow of time. It is because human beings are, to a degree, beyond time, because they already belong to eternity, that they are capable of taking up the past, not by transforming a fact but by a spiritual reworking of their action at the level of consciousness. A fact may be a past reality, but the action which lies at its origin is not. It remains deep within me, and that is why it is capable of being taken up again, of being remade, of being recreated.

That is what I understand by repentance. Repentance is taking up an action at an intentional level. In regretting my past action I deny it, and by doing so the self which is at the source of this act takes up this past to suppress it. In other words, the significance of the past always depends on the future. It is precisely because human beings are beyond time that they are not eternally the prisoners of their past. So the question is not that of knowing what our past is, but of knowing what we want to do with it.

Here is an illustration. When you go by train from Cairo to Alexandria, in Mustafa Pasha you pass a vast dump belonging to the Chekat El Nahas steelworks containing enormous piles of all kinds of old automobiles, old corrugated iron, old boxes, all the metal of Alexandria rusting in the open air. All this debris of the past is taken by the factory, put in a furnace and transformed into glowing new ingots of steel. What this firm constantly does with its old iron, human beings can do with their own lives and their past. The problem is not to know what our past is, but to know what we are going to do with it, what we want to do with it. I can look sadly at all these rusty old sheets of corrugated iron, all these carcasses of cars put on the junk heap and say, 'What a pity, what a catastrophe!' That is how some people contemplate their past.

But on the other hand I can look at all the used, rusted, twisted past and say to myself, 'I am capable of transcending all this, remaking it, remoulding it, letting it flow into something new, recreating myself in a new being. Human beings can constantly remake themselves, time and again.' That is the good news, that is hope, that is joy, that is 'the redemption of time'.

The history we have to make delivers us from the history that we have made, and repentance delivers us from the determinism of the past. By 'determinism' I mean all the force hidden in the laws of physics, that is, the inevitability with which one phenomenon succeeds another and simply ends up at a predestined goal, inscribed in advance in the pattern of its unfolding. There is the determinism of the force of gravity, the determinism of falling bodies, and so on.

But human beings are capable of transcending what determines them if they plunge deeply enough into themselves, to the level of their essential being, their person. They can take up their past action and as it were remake it, reshape it. The German philosopher Max Scheler knew where the roots of action lie, and in particular he knew that they can be destroyed:

> Seize the fault, once recognized, by the roots, to eradicate it from the person and give oneself the freedom to do good.

The very meaning of the past is transformed by repentance, which is not simply repair of the past but transformation of the past. What is the difference between these two words?

Suppose I have an old pan with two holes in it. I go to the *sankari* (an Arab word which means tinsmith) and ask him to put two small patches on the holes. I get back home, and put the pan on the stove, but soon the holes develop again. I go back to the man for another repair. After about two weeks I have to go through the whole process all over again. It's always the same with repairs. If you have an old automobile, and put a spare part in here, a piece of wire there, the automobile may go for a while, but it will soon stop again. That means more tinkering about; the process never ends. That's the trouble with repairs.

If redeeming time, redeeming human beings, were like doing repairs, the prospect would be pretty grim. I don't need someone to repair my past; I need someone to transform me – and to transform is to recreate.

Transformation is a total remaking, a radical remaking – not a bit of patchwork, a botched-up repair. It is believing that my life can be taken up anew, that I can remake a child's heart for myself.

'Give us, Lord, a new heart, put a new spirit in us': a new spirit, truly new and not painted over, pieced together, patched. The illustration of all this scrap metal which becomes pieces of shining new steel is a telling one.

Human beings are truly capable of involving themselves in a most profound act of repentance which renews them from top to bottom. True repentance is a rebirth.

We emerge from repentance like a baby coming out of the bath, like a child with clean fresh skin, because we have gone so deep down to the heart of our fault and touched on the depths of our misery, guilt and responsibility. Often our confessions do not renew anything in us, beause they do not get to the level of true repentance. We come out of them as we went in, and absolution slides off us like water off a duck's back. For absolution is certainly not enough in itself; in confession, what counts is not so much absolution as the depth of repentance that one feels.

A thousand years before Christ, David cried out his fault, and expressed his misery in lament; he tore his clothes, he rent his heart, and from this emerged his feelings expressed in Psalm 51 – an eternal, unforgettable, immortal psalm:

> Have mercy upon me, O God, after your great goodness: according to the multitude of your mercies do away my offences. Wash me thoroughly from my wickedness: and cleanse me from my sin.

> For I acknowledge my faults: and my sin is ever before me.

The grace of God is commensurate to the abyss which repentance opens up in us. What we lack is the sense of our guilt, the sense of our sin – a sense, however, which is not despair or vain remorse, but true repentance.

We have to go to the roots of our being to rediscover the source. In repentance there is a secret of youth, a secret of life, a secret of extraordinary childlikeness. We usually live in the middle zones of our being. We half-sin and we half-repent. We half-look at our sin and we half-turn to God. Everything about us is half-hearted, and takes place in the intermediate areas of a frightful mediocrity. We are neither dead nor alive, nor hot nor cold, but lukewarm. So our repentance is not true repentance, but a formality – or worse, self-justification. We tell ourselves, 'In the end it's not as bad as all that – everyone does it.' We plead all kinds of mitigating circumstances. We dress up our sin in the best clothes, we decorate it, disguise it, and bring it to the Lord in the form of a very little fault, quite gentle, cute, touching. At heart we have already given ourselves absolution and feel justified. This refusal to take responsiblity for our faults is connected with the fact that we have no other alternatives than remorse and despair. For us, culpability takes on only one face – that of the bad conscience, the scruple, and this 'morbid universe of sin' evoked at every moment. It is because we are imprisoned in this false sense of guilt that we reject it.

But what I want to bring out is the other face of guilt, that of repentance. Repentance is not afraid to get down to the heart of a fault, to the depths of being. In true guilt I take my fault in my hands, I look it in the face, I recognize it, I accept it, I take responsibility for it while at the same time repudiating it.

Our ultimate dignity and greatness as human beings lies in the way in which we take responsibility for our actions. Human beings know that they are responsible, want to be responsible. When we seek to veil our guilt and deck it out with all kinds of more or less specious motives, with more or less imaginary justifications, we refuse this responsibility.

A while ago someone said to me in confession, 'Father, I have committed a very serious sin. I did so not by mistake but freely, deliberately and willingly. I accuse myself of it and I regret it from the bottom of my heart.' As I listened to this confession I bowed my head and said to myself, 'That's beautiful...'

Acute awareness of our faults and true repentance is what helps us to get to the bottom of things, makes us reach the source, and renews us.

To refuse to accept guilt is to refuse to progress and move beyond oneself. When guilt gets to the heart of being, it causes a rebound, like a ball falling to the ground. When it reaches the ground and makes contact with it, it bounces back. Human beings are not often capable of rebounding, because they do not want to touch the ground of their being, because they refuse to fall to their depths. So there is no reprise, no renewal, no going beyond.

As Jean Lacroix commented,

The true feeling of guilt arises out of a self-criticism which is the recognition of a deficiency, an incompleteness, and at the same time an awareness of the effort by which we can pursue our achievement.

So repentance involves recognizing a deficiency. How can one remedy this deficiency without first recognizing it? The self-examination of which I spoke earlier is precisely this recognition of a deficiency, and once that has been done, the deficiency can be compensated for and made good. But if there is no awareness, no self-criticism, we can no longer rise above ourselves and we are stuck in our mediocrity.

A refusal to recognize that one is a sinner is one of the most frequent causes of a state of lukewarmness and essential mediocrity.

How was it possible for the robber crucified alongside Jesus to be able to wipe out a whole life of crime by his one act of repentance? Jesus promised him: 'Truly, I say to you, today you will be with me in paradise!' (Luke 23.43).

It is precisely because this man penetrated so deeply into himself that in this sole act of repentance he was capable of renewing his whole life, of ransoming all his past. We may protest at this forgiveness granted freely and immediately by Christ, and say, 'But that's unfair.' Christ replies to us, 'No, it's fair.' For though this man may not be capable of obliterating all the evil actions he has done and all the crimes that he has committed, in his profound intention and his essential being he is capable of wishing himself otherwise, of choosing afresh to give his life a new dimenison. That is what conversion is. It is choosing oneself anew and wanting oneself anew. And that is also hope.

The good news given to us is that everything can be taken up again, everything can be begun again, everything can be redeemed, everything can be recreated.

This return to the source of our being, to the source of things, is conversion. Conversion is a return to the first morning of the world when the light shone from the darkness. Moreover, the word conversion (*convertere*) means resuming, turning round. I take up my life and turn it inside out, as one may turn a bag inside out. I make something new out of the old.

A young man condemned to death said before he died, 'I am worth more than my life.'

This amazing remark indicates that this young man, who had committed all kinds of crimes and atrocities, was aware at the moment of his death that they did not express his true life, his true self. In strictly legal terms he was guilty. But in the depths of his heart, he told himself, 'All that is not me.' Which of us, after a sinful action, has not felt deep within ourselves that what we have done is not us? True repentance does not consist in denying that we have done evil, but in standing above it and telling ourselves, 'Yes, that's fair, I've done wrong, but the wrong that I have done wrong is not the deepest expression of my life. I refuse to identify myself with it.' 'I am worth more than my fault.' I wanted it and at the same time I did not want it, as Paul was aware (Romans 7).

In other words, I repudiate my past, not by refusing to take responsibility for it, but by saying, 'I am worth more than my past: I do not want to be what I have been.' Conversion is a return to my original self, to the person at the roots. Conversion is going beyond the law.

If we wanted to make another comparison between remorse and repentance, we might say that remorse is at the level of the law, while repentance is at the level of grace. The law is fixed and firm: 'Did you do this?' 'Yes.' 'You will be condemned.' 'That's fair, I deserved it.'

There was transgression, so there will be judgment; that is penal guilt.

Repentance is another matter. Repentance is not on the same level as penal justice but is at the level of moral justice. It is not at the level of penal culpability but at that of moral culpability, and that is quite different: it is grace, it is conversion, it is rebirth.

Now while we are imprisoned in the law, while we are imprisoned in the Ten Commandments, while we are imprisoned in a kind of moralizing morality, we can only be encouraged in a feeling of morbid guilt and remorse. The majority of men and women are still in that state.

But let us look again at St Paul, at his letters to the Romans and to the Galatians: 'You are no longer under the law, but under grace' (Rom.6.14). The law is condemnation. The law is morbid guilt. The law is sterile remorse. The law is the past in which one is shut up and to which one is chained. But, grace is the future; grace is hope; grace is rebirth; grace is the remission of sins.

When Jesus is asked, 'Are you the one who is to come or do we look for another?' (Luke 7.19), he replies: 'Go and announce that the blind see, the deaf hear, the lame walk, the lepers are cured and the dead raised' (Luke 7.22).

What does that mean? It means that with Christ there is a new creation, a total remaking of this world.

All these cures and resurrections on a physical level are simply the sign of another cure, another resurrection, on the level of essential being, on the level of sin and grace. That is what Christ meant when he cured the paralysed man: 'Is it easier to say "Your sins are forgiven" or "Take up your bed and walk"?'

The forgiveness of Jesus is the very act which remakes a person, renewing him or her at the centre. Our forgiveness, too, is an act which can recreate others and renew them at the centre. It consists in saying to the other person, 'Your past is forgotten, rubbed out. I'm giving you a chance; you can begin your life again.' To this desperate, crushed, humiliated person I am offering the possibility of a ransom, the possibility of redemption.

In a school there are always bad pupils, trouble-makers. The danger is that these children will be classified as belonging to that category and in effect be told, 'Nothing can be done with you. It will never be possible to do anything with you. You're a failure.' Once this has been said, the child will always remain a failure. We have fixed the child in his or her past without offering any chance of a fresh start. This child is lost, cursed, condemned for ever, shut up in its past.

Husband and wife, or friends, will often remind each other of past faults: 'Remember, you did that to me, you said that to me. You did the same thing again last year, last month.' 'Yes, I remember, that's right. So I did.' You hang your head while the other person attacks you even more, tramples on you even harder, vilifies you even worse, enjoying the revenge. Then you say, 'Yes, that's right, I did that, but what about you? You did that to me; you said that to me.' This quarrel is war, the vicious circle of morbid guilt.

Forgiveness consists in saying to the other person, 'I know that you did all that, but you did it in spite of yourself; you weren't the one who was doing it; someone else was doing it in you. Basically you didn't want to do it. Everything is forgotten, blotted out, forgiven.' And at that moment there is the possibility of ransom, the hope of redemption.

That reminds me of a little incident which happened when I was teaching at a preparatory school. One of my pupils, who had had polio, full of complexes and crushed by a terrible feeling of inferiority, had become tough and aggressive with his friends. He pinched, pulled, hit, insulted them, watching them enviously as they played football or rushed around, while he remained in his corner, condemned to immobility by his infirmity. That had made him naughty and he avenged himself for it. One day I called him and said to him. 'You're being naughty like this despite yourself. Basically you've a heart of gold. Deep down you're good, very good.' The child then burst into tears in my arms and cried as though he couldn't stop. Beyond all his hateful behaviour he felt that someone understood that he was basically good, that his soul was overflowing with tenderness and affection. And from that day on he made progress; he was transformed and became sweet, gentle, smiling, affectionate, because I had been able to show him his other face.

That is what Christian forgiveness is: drawing a veil over the past, beginning on a new page, giving the other person a chance and allowing him or her to begin afresh.

The gospel says to us, 'Do not judge' (Matt.7.1).

Yes, do not judge, do not condemn, for you do not know what is hidden in a person. What you know and what you judge is the past, but you do not know the future, and the past is full of promise. I've known desperate people who have said to me: 'I'm ruined, there's nothing I can do, I've spoilt my life.' But given an attitude of patience, attention and hope on our part, such people can change, can be radically changed, profoundly changed, and become new creatures.

To act in this way is to open up a gateway of hope, to offer redemption. We are responsible for one another, and by a certain faith, a certain attitude, we can recreate and raise up those who come to us, those around us. Redemption is possible: the redemption of time, the redemption of the past, the redemption of faults.

If we are truly to arrive at this level of forgiveness we have to begin by recognizing that we ourselves are sinners and are ourselves in need of forgiveness. It is often because we cannot recognize our own faults that we cannot excuse the faults in others. In the Our Father we say, 'Forgive us our trespasses, as we forgive them that trespass against us.' It is in recognizing our own sin that we become capable of pardoning the sin of others and bringing about reconciliation.

Jean Lacroix has expressed his vision of a new sacrament, the sacrament of the future, conjugal confession:

Conjugal confession is the essence of marriage, because love consists in constantly giving the other a chance to start again. Love is continual creation and recreation.

That is why the Dane Kierkegaard says that basically, at the very heart of guiltiness, there is forgetting. His God, like the God of the Bible and the gospel, is a God who forgets. There is no true love without forgetting.

This is not a forgetting caused by old age or infirmity, but a deliberate, agreed forgetting. We often carry around in the depths of our hearts grievances which go back to childhood, to adolescence, to the beginning of our marriage or some such period of our life. We have made a list of other people's mistakes that we never stop mulling over. But forget, forget! The other person has changed, is no longer the same, and is basically better than we think. He or she must be given a chance, be healed and reborn. We should not keep harping on the past; we should turn the page, and then we shall see a new being in front of us. To know how to forget is one of the supreme virtues.

There is no true love without forgetting. That is what forgiveness is.

Let us look at the way in which Jesus regards sinners. This is not the Sartrean look of God which fixes, judges and condemns, but the look of hope which gives courage, and confidence. Jesus looks at the woman of Samaria and says, 'You have had five men and the one you have at present is not your husband' (John 4.17-18). He looks at her, and yet she does not feel either judged or condemned. And Mary Magdalene, the sinner, the courtesan, the public woman, sits at Jesus' feet while he looks right into her heart. She too is not obliterated by this gaze, but she cries tears of repentance, and her heart is transformed.

And the adulterous woman: 'Woman, I do not condemn you.' Her accusers are there, full of hatred: 'She has sinned.' 'Yes, she has sinned.' 'She has committed adultery.' 'Yes, she has commited adultery.' 'She must be stoned.' But Jesus answers: 'Let him among you who is without sin cast the first stone' (hypocrites!) (John 8.7-11).

We are all hypocrites, because we excel at accusing one another in our well-educated society, and as we sit and talk, calumny is often distilled like a poison. Let the one who is without sin cast the first stone at this fallen woman, at this man who has gone wrong, at this other person how has dirtied his hands. You who find fault with the dirt of others, are you aware of all the rottenness deep within yourself? It is in recognizing your own sin and guilt that forgiveness will become possible for you.

The look that Jesus gave to Judas and to Peter was the same look that he gave to the woman of Samaria, to Mary Magdalene, to the woman taken in adultery. Judas did not understand, but Peter did, and it was this look which broke his heart and called forth a torrent of tears.

The look which Jesus directs towards us is a look of compassion, a look of redemption, a look of ransom, a look of resurrection, a look of hope. And as Fr Baudiquey said in a famous poem, 'The only glances of love are those which make us hope.' Only the look that is capable of discerning the new person behind the lowest, most vilified, the most ravaged being, waiting for rebirth and resurrection, is a creative look, a look of redemption, a look of hope.

That is the redemption of time.

But this look and this redemption are possible only when my sin is a sin not confronting me, but the one who can save me.

I quoted earlier a phrase from Psalm 51, 'My sin is ever before me.' My sin can be ever before me like a foul and morbid obsession, but it can also project me forward towards the one who can rid me of it, tear me away from it. That is why the psalm also adds, 'Against you only have I sinned.'

Those who sin before God do not sin against themselves, do not debate with themselves in a sterile and exhausting fight, but place themselves before the one who alone is capable of extricating them from sin.

Nothing is finished, nothing is lost, nothing is to be regretted. All is grace, all can be saved, all can be redeemed. The blind see, the deaf hear, the lame walk, the lepers are healed, the dead are raised. Through all these signs, God tells us: 'I who can cure the body and recreate it can also cure your soul and recreate it. Little person, I can remake you, create you anew. The ultimate sign of the kingdom is the resurrection. And the resurrection is a new person, a new heart, a new spirit, a new being.

The resurrection does not consist in rediscovering a body doomed again to death. I am not interested in living another life which will end in a new death, in that eternal beginning-again of successive resurrections and indefinite reincarnations. No, I dare to hope for something else, something different from this life which keeps getting longer and longer and which doctors promise us will develop until one day soon we shall live to be a hundred, a hundred and twenty, a hundred and fifty. No thank you, Lord! I dare to hope for something other than this indefinitely prolonged old age, going on and on, or the slow death which never seems to come.

What I want is eternal life, life which does not die, life with a capital L, which is continual rebirth, perpetual flow. What I want is a body which does not decay, a body which does not perish, a resurrection body. That is our hope, when the Lord takes our flesh and bones to make us new, like the scrap iron which the furnace transforms into new and shining steel.

This was the hope which the French poet Charles Péguy celebrated in a famous hymn. In his enormous verse epic *Eve*, almost two thousand strophes long, depicting the salvation history of humankind, in a vision he depicts the coming into being of another, new, world involving the material of the old and the resurrection of the dead.

This new world will contain our past reshaped, fused in the glowing love of a future which will never fade, which can never be extinguished, since we shall be eternal, and there will be no more death.

In a providential way, the text of the mass for the day on which I am finishing this chapter coincides with the idea that I have just been developing. So let me take these words from the Revelation of John as a sign for us and as the end of this chapter:

> I saw a new heaven and a new earth, for the first heaven and the first earth had passed away (Rev.21.1).

We shall no longer remember the past and our life on earth, happy, but also full of mistakes; it will no longer come back to us on that level, but we shall delight in the joy and eternal happiness of what God is to create. There we shall not see but *taste* with happy hearts and in ardent joy the transformation and consummation of our life rediscovered for us by the divine hand.

On many occasions priests accumulate the concerns of desperate people in their prayers. So I have summed them all up in a prayer to focus our meditation on feelings of guilt and redemption:

To the Master of the Universe

Lord, your sovereign power conquered nothingness
when you brought the universe into being.
Help me to believe
in your infinite power,
which creates each day in a new realm.

Lord, your spirit went over the primal waters of creation
to make them fertile.
Help me to believe

in the lifegiving power of this spirit,
present in my heart and in the heart of the world.

Lord, you conquered the darkness
and made the primal light shine at your bidding.
Help me to believe
that your word will make a sun rise
from the depths of my night.

Lord, the gleam of your light breaks through all nights
in its fullness, its clear shining.
Tear off all the veils in me
and make it day,
your day in me.

Lord, you willed and created teeming life
and enabled it to inhabit the material earth.
Help me to believe in this wonder,
because it will conquer death and decay.

Lord, you made trees and woods grow,
buds spring up and flowers bloom.
Help me to believe
in this eternally new mystery
in its never wearying power, because it is you yourself.

Lord, you ordered chaos, by forming in your hands
a universe in beauty and harmony.
Help me to believe
that you can correct our errors
and can change our uglinesses into masterpieces of grace.

Lord, at the beginning of time you bent over us
and lovingly steeped us in your spirit.
Help me to believe that you will not stop
bending over our guilt
so that we can be born eternally new in you.

Lord, you have created me in your image
and according to your likeness.
Create anew once again
the countenance that I lost,
and make it like yours.

Lord, you have called me your son,
your only son.
Help me to believe inwardly
in this fatherly heritage
and surrender myself to your motherly arms.

Lord, you tested Abraham but did not forsake him
when he went through this night.
Help me never to doubt
in your presence,
and preserve me victorious in my faith.

Lord, you snatched your people from slavery
and freed them from pressure and servitude.
Help me also to become free
from all that chains me, fetters me, binds me.

Lord, you made a firm way for your people
through the depths of the sea.
For me, too, in the sea of my sorrow
open up a way to salvation.

Lord, you went with your people
through wilderness and solitude.
Help me always to feel your presence,
when every support and all help fails.

Lord, you will prepare for your people
a land where milk and honey flow.
Help me to believe
in this kingdom of gentleness and love,
your promise at the end of our way.

Lord, you have made the blind see
and the deaf hear.
Open my eyes, too, to your light,
and my ears to your truth.

Lord, you healed the sick
and lepers became clean.
Heal and purify me also
from my weaknesses, suffering and infirmities.

Lord, you forgave the adulteress
and freely accepted the sinner.

Accept me also in your understanding heart
and save me by the power of your love.

Lord, you opened your arms to the prodigal son
and took him to your heart.
Accept me also in my poverty,
and have mercy on me in the grief of my failure.

Lord, you bade the storm be still
above the turbulent waters, and calmed them.
Smoothe the waves in my sorrowing soul
and give them your peace.

Lord, you strode safely over the waters
despite the challenge of the elements.
Deliver me from the power of evil,
and rescue me from its undertow.

Lord, you enabled Peter
to do as you did on the surface of the water.
Help me, too, to conquer doubt which holds danger
and anxiety which paralyses me.

Lord, you resisted temptation,
strengthened by fasting, fortified by prayer.
Help me also to withstand my test
by rooting myself still more firmly in you.

Lord, you drove out demons
and rescued people from their attack.
Preserve me also from negative influences
and alienation from myself.

Lord, you fettered and cast out
the prince of this world.
Help me to feel your powers within me
and remove me from the sphere of evil.

Lord, you said, 'Behold, I make all things new.
These words are true and faithful.'
Make me today a new heart
and fill me with new spirit.

Lord, it is written,
'Behold the tabernacle of God is with men.

He will dwell among them.
He will wipe all tears from their eyes
and death will be no more,
nor sorrow nor lamentation nor tribulation,
the former things are past.'
Help this tremendous hope to gain strength within me
when suffering seeks to suffocate me
and death embraces me.

Lord, you have said,
'He who believes in me will live,
even though he is dead.'
Help me to believe inwardly in your life,
your final victory and your triumph,
over all that is evil.

Lord, you have said,
'I am the resurrection and the life.'
Help me now and every day to rise in you
in order to live from you – wholly from you.

7   All is Grace

'Do not fear evil, for it may bring you good'
(*Arabic saying*)

All is grace. From the very beginning of cosmic existence all is grace, since creation is a free gift. Creation is grace, the first of all graces – a gift of God.

'But sin came into the world, and with sin, death' (Romans 5.12). Evil manifested itself in space and time, entered history and took part in it. The gracious gift of creation became stained. Evil grew, multiplied, raged, and culminated in the greatest of all human sins, which is called the 'cross', or Golgotha.

'But where sin increased, grace abounded all the more' (Romans 5.20b). Thanks to this cross, this crucified man on the cross, universal redemption took place and our fallen world was established anew. The free gift of creation was followed by the free gift of redemption. Since then, countless members of a new human race have looked towards a different goal of creation, 'a new heaven and a new earth' (cf. Rev.21.1).

This new humanity took its beginning in the days of the death and resurrection of Jesus. The moment of its birth was the time when a promise recorded in the book of Isaiah was fulfilled, 'Behold, I make all things new' (43.19).

The redemption of Golgotha is this new creation, and in particular it is a new creation of humankind. This process is taking place as a result of the workings of grace, through which the whole of creation since the moment of the dawning of light up to the complete transformation and consummation of the history of this universe is taken up into the divine stream of grace. We recognize the free gift of God as a source at the centre, flowing out in two directions: back to the origin of all things and forward to the new goal of creation. This source of grace sprang from the hill of Golgotha, as it had sprung from the rock in the burning wilderness when Moses touched it.

It is interesting to read in the legend of creation that God begins with the creation of heaven, earth and light. Then God brings into being plants bearing seed and fruit trees, and sets 'lights in the firmament'. What a glorious fresco is painted here! After that, 'swarms of living creatures' are said to have been created in the sea; then God created fowls, wild animals and cattle, and finally, right at the end, human beings, who were to inaugurate a new era. They are completely different...

By contrast, the New Testament begins with the last member of this human race, again opening a new era. Now, through him, the new Adam, a people of God slowly begins to develop and to strive towards a goal of development through history, that 'new heaven above a new earth'. One has the impression that here something is incrasingly narrowing and becoming concentrated on itself, so that it comes to a focal point in the midst of this tremendous history. From there it develops outwards and extends further, to become a multitude of 144,000 people – a symbolic number which means 'tremendously great'. The focal point through which history runs is called Jesus Christ. When the new heaven appears over a new earth, we recognize the significance, the goal and the end of this grandiose saving event which began with the redemptive death of Jesus Christ.

At the heart of this movement in history we find the mystery of this death, but we know that this mystery is at the same time a mystery of resurretion. The two are identical, since they mean resurrection in death and resurrection for death. 'Death has been destroyed by death,' sing believers in the Byzantine Easter liturgy. 'Death has trampled on death and opened up the way for those who rest in the grave.' This powerful impetus, this brilliant dawning of a completely new life, born out of the mysterious depths of this crucifixion, is the paradox and apparently insurmountable contradiction in our Christian mystery. Death means life and life means death.

Deep within this death there is a fertile field in which human salvation takes root and puts down shoots. From this miraculous earth, eternal life now grows up in all its strength. It germinates and grows out of death, presses towards development, and will blossom for us all. Golgotha, a crucified man, an opened side from which the source of grace sprang, to permeate and heal the world! The fruit of redemptive death is grace.

What is grace? Grace is the life of God's own self. Grace means life, but far more than the ordinary life that we know. We know that the ordinary life of Adam most certainly leads to death. His life bears him there, just as the whole of the first creation falls victim to death. But there is already a second creation which we call the history of redemption, and this leads beyond death to another goal: it leads to eternal life. It leads to eternal life because it now has its source in the new Adam, in the divinized human being who bears this lifespring in himself. So the mystery of grace means boundless light, hope, deep confidence, for eternal life means life in God.

What does grace mean in everyday life? We find almost the same word in many languages and with the same meaning: *gratia, gratis, gratuit*, and so on; it always means 'free gift', a present. In our human society, a world of trade and business, everything costs something; it all has a price that has to be paid. But at the same time we also form a human community of the children of God in which we receive freely, *gratis*. In and with God we live *'en famille'*. Are there any families in which payment is expected before anyone can have anything to eat? No, one may take without payment or hesitation, quite naturally, since at home everything is gratis.

God's offer is of the same kind, for our relationship to this offer is that of being children of God, and our life in the community of the world is *en famille*. Everything is free. Unfortunately modern men and women have lost the sense of this free approach of and to God, since they are utterly dominated by the commercial thinking of a world of painfully accurate calculation and correct bookkeeping. Our conception of a life with God, a spiritual life, has become distorted, as have our human personal relationships. How rare is the kind of relationship which is so free and authentic that everything is free on both sides!

In a European country I saw a young girl visiting her mother and eating lunch with her. Before she went, she paid her mother for the meal. But there is no need to resort to such extreme cases to be aware that our mode of existence is basically a calculating one. Our life is one long transaction: I give you this – you give me that. I gave you a splendid present, so you should have given me one in return. Since I'm still waiting, don't expect any more of me... These are really impossible conversations, and yet they happen so frequently in the quiet secrecy of a speculating heart. But a gift which is not a completely free offering to someone else ceases to be a gift. The good relationship between two human beings can no longer be called 'good', since often the cost of a gift is carefully worked out and compared, and woe to anyone who has bought and given below the other's price level!

By calculating, we allow deep shadows to fall upon our human relationships, which prevent them from growing. Gently but clearly, ugly tensions become evident, and the pressure of this reciprocal having-to-give dominates; it is almost impossible to find that bright sphere of pure joy which goes with a real present. I know what I am saying, because I myself belong to this bourgeois society in which people put one another under pressure with their gifts. I am delighted only by truly free presents, when I know that there is no hidden calculation behind them, for I long so much for another world, a world of mutually free gift.

Among free gifts I also include all contributions towards mutual help and service, spontaneous self-giving without expecting anything in return. That already begins in schools where brave teachers work year in and year out with difficult pupils, never getting anything back in recompense. Let us take that as the best example, and all work in this attitude of sheer giving. Let us become sons of the one 'who makes his sun rise on the evil and the good, and who sends rain on the just and on the unjust' (Matthew 5.45).

The one of whom we are thinking here is the one who certainly does not look for anything in return. I was always an opponent of the so-called spiritual payment of God through litanies. I simply cannot believe that God wants to be paid, either after a gift of grace or before it, by being begged for it. I have always been saddened when watching people trying to do business with God. For great graces a novena or a triduum, for smaller favours of heaven less would suffice – perhaps a rosary. As if there were a heavenly tariff which we human beings could set!

This is a lapse into the trade in indulgences from olden days. I had a dear old aunt who spent her time sitting in a pew with her rosary. She ardently sought to liberate this or that soul from purgatory and incessantly paid the tariff in the form of countless prayers and appeals. That was her religious mentality, and she acted with the best intentions, so I won't criticize her here. But that sort of thing led to excesses in our churches which make your hair stand on end, and one feels sympathy for the Protestants who at one point reacted so strongly against the system of trafficking in indulgences, especially as unfortunately it had also developed into a thriving business. No, God really does not need to be paid by us, nor does he want to. How could God be bought? All is grace.

People also seek to secure divine favour with works; they try to redeem themselves or keep in God's good books by what they do. This commercial way of thinking is very widespread, and extends right into our modern spiritual communities. Certain of good will and with the utmost generosity, with growing zeal people offer God more and more hours of work and promise to spend them in pious service for him. An eight-hour day becomes a twelve-hour day; soon it gets up to fourteen and attempts are made to make it sixteen. 'I will sleep less and work more, eat less and pray more. Lord, you must be pleased with me!' But we must listen carefully to the words of Jesus when he was the guest of two very different sisters: 'Martha, Martha, you are anxious and troubled about many things; one thing is needful. Mary has chosen the good portion, which shall not be taken away from her' (Luke 10.41f.).

The time comes when God speaks to the overzealous, for when they do too much of his work, it destroys their inner peace: 'That's enough! Stop! Break off! Relax and find rest with me. Smile, let yourself go for a while and feel that I love you. I love you. Can't you feel it? I love you. Can't you accept it?'

The true Christian attitude does not consist primarily in loving so much as in knowing and accepting the love of God. Let's look at that more closely. It is always much simpler to give than to receive. We don't understand that properly. In the zeal of our faith we grit our teeth and go on working, but letting go and surrendering to God is also an attitude of faith, since it is evidence of trust; indeed it is already prayer. At that moment people cease to give and only receive, in other words, contemplate God with their whole soul and listen to his word, as Martha's sister Mary did.

Human beings should not degrade themselves to the point of becoming machines, but they should be receptive souls. God does not want us to kill ourselves with work; that is certainly not his will. He did not create us to kill ourselves in that way; in everything that we have to do we need to be able to be quite relaxed, to pray with a smile and to keep silent – the signs of deepest spiritual relaxation. Then our being can adjust itself to the being of God. But think of all the misunderstandings there can be here. People rush through a series of prayers because they only have fifteen minutes to spare, and at the end they have frustrated God by not letting him get a word in edgeways. A prayer is not a monologue but a dialogue, a dialogue of love. Let us be sensitive to our creator and feel his call: 'Be silent and listen. Rest and let me be active now!'

This experience of emptiness and radical poverty bears witness to the deepest attitude that we can adopt before God. At this moment we share in an experience of grace. Without any visible reason, without any previous effort, quite contrary to our expectations, we are given a gift, a pure gift. 'If only you knew the gift of God...'(John 4.10).

That saying comes from the episode in St John's Gospel in which Jesus drinks from Jacob's well. He is speaking of grace. Just as the Samaritan woman gives Jesus water here, so we human beings give God water in the form of human friendship, human work, human love. He even asks for it and accepts it gratefully. But the moment comes when he wants us to be on the receiving end, when he wants to give us something, to give quite different water: the water of eternal life as a free gift to us. This is the experience of the grace of God.

Prayer, too, is ultimately a gift to us, a gift of God, so it is better to go to prayer with empty hands. For if our hands are full of good works which we joyfully offer up to God, there is no room for God to put anything in them. At times we have to be able to set everything aside and forget it: all our duties and tasks, all our own plans, in order to be able to go to God completely naked, simply to receive. Then the Lord will surprise us, astound us, shake us, for he will fill our hands to overflowing. We shall receive treasure beyond our dreams. But in prayer one first has to have the experience of radical poverty.

Here I would like to distinguish between faith and love for God. We are accustomed to hearing that our love stands right at the top of the table of values, for in his great hymn of praise in I Corinthians 13 Paul writes that of faith, love and hope, love is the greatest.

From this text people have inferred that the love of neighbour is our most noble impulse and our most noble action. I may indeed attempt that. I may work hard to love God and others as much as I can; but I know that there is another attitude, which consists in letting oneself be loved. Perhaps this attitude is the greater and more important one; as John tells us in his first letter, love is not that we loved God but that God loved us and sent his Son (I John 4.10).

Even more profound than love is faith, faith in love. Of course it is noble and praiseworthy on our part to love God, and we should certainly try to do that; but it is more, better, greater, to know that we are loved most deeply by God. For what is my mere human capacity to love compared with the immeasurable power of the divine heart? By contrast it can only be a dull glow, since it shines from a limited human heart, no matter how much that heart loves. And how often it is lukewarm or dried up, cramped or cold! If that is the case we are not to engage in psychological gymnastics in order to arouse feelings of love which warm our hearts to the love of God, but must set our being on receiving love, and allow ourselves to be warmed by it.

The experience of radical poverty of which I spoke then turns into an experience of fullness: the initial emptiness is the presupposition for the later fullness. The poorer we make ourselves, the richer our prayer. Those who have completely stripped themselves can have the experience of the over-abundance of a divine gift which grace brings about in them. It is those whose prayers are very modest and simple who experience that, for in quite natural humility they already know in advance that God will get to them first with his love, indeed that God has already got to them. They accept that God's love is infinitely greater than their small human love can ever be. They do not want to get above God's love, nor do they want to promise anything in return for the divine love. They will not promise anything either before or afterwards, since they know that they may go naked and poor before God at any time.

'Ho, everyone who thirsts, come to the waters; and he who has no money, come, buy and eat! Come, buy wine and milk with no money and without price' (Isaiah 55.1)

'This spring is free, free to refresh you,' says our heavenly Father. 'And to please me take, receive! Drink! It costs you nothing. It is my delight to give it to you.' I think that we need to recognize that clearly. In my view that is authentic Christian life, for people recognize God as the source and origin of love.

I grant that this attitude calls for a good deal of boldness in everyday practice, not to say audacity. Nevertheless, we must not balance God's possibilities against a gift of grace, but count on it right from the beginning. Let us be bold enough to have the most extraordinary wishes and to ask for the utmost grace for them. Let us be confident of being heard, not fear the magnitude of a grace but dare to ask for everything. We may have impossible wishes and count on their being fulfilled. We may go to God with our deepest longings and most urgent requests, and count on improbable promises, since they are all probable. That is Jesus' promise: 'Whatever you ask in prayer, believe that you receive it, and you will' (Mark 11.24).

That is my attitude to God. I have no time to consider and calculate all the things that I will promise to do, nor do I want to, since in any case I should have no time to keep this promise. So my hands remain empty. I have often asked God to solve a problem for me quickly because with the best will in the world I can't do it myself, and I find that it is solved spontaneously without my having to deck it out in ceremonious requests and solemn thanks.

Here is an example.

Some time ago I was back in the Sudan and urgently needed a car for the mission which we had started there in 1980. I had no money to buy one; the whole mission lives on Egyptian gifts dropping on hot Sudanese stones.

What a prayer! Lord, I need a car and as quickly as possible. Please see to it!

The next day I had an inspiration and went to a very rich Syrian Lebanese businessman in Khartoum, who owned a soap factory, an oil refinery and much more. I put my request to this stranger, told him of our group of young Egyptian volunteers who are strengthening the poor Sudanese Christians – moreover, four million animists live in the south of the country. I told him that there are only fifty priests in the largest country of the African continent; the diocese of Lome, which is as big as France and Italy put together, is looked after by a bishop and thirty-five priests. I told him how I had visited a priest whose parish was as big as the whole Nile delta and how he was one priest looking after forty-six churches and seven schools, caught up in a chain of insoluble problems. Moreover, in four years it might be too late for the Christians in the Sudan.

The man listened to me in silence, and someone else next to him nodded. Then I was asked when, how and in what currency I wanted to pay for this car and whether, as he assumed, I would get it at a much reduced price.

'No,' I said, 'I'm looking for someone to give me a car.' The two men were amazed, then they thought about it and talked together. A couple of days later I got the keys and became the owner of a Datsun which had hardly been driven.

And yet again I thought happily that it is true that one can put the most immodest requests to God. How glad I am that I had not asked God for a bicycle...

I am convinced that God wants us to ask for big things and not anxiously for trivia. For he wants human beings to think of greater things. The creator is generous; he is generosity in person, and he is pure love – and a Father! So let us delight him and put our trust in him.

In my daily work in Cairo and in my ministry as a priest, the problems pile up before my eyes, each more insoluble than the last. In addition there are the cares and needs of individuals seeking help, for first they go to their best friend, then to the doctor, then to the psychiatrist, and finally, with the problem still unsolved, come to the priest. How can a poor priest cope with such private matters, and such an infinite number of them?

There is one thing that I always do: I hand over this problem to the Lord in boundless trust and faith with a prayer for grace. And then I say good-bye to the poor person who has looked to me for help with the words, 'Go in peace. Your problem will be solved,' for I believe that. Now I have no statistics, but it seems to me that the Lord is gracious to me. Sooner or later, the person involved returns or calls me, overflowing with gratitude, for something with which I have had absolutely nothing to do. I have not achieved anything, but only believed that grace will be given to those who seek grace. All is grace.

God loves our empty hands and our hopeful, all-expectant hearts. He loves a boldness which aims high and can ask for everything. He delights in a faith which will take risks. This is how we can also slowly recognize that grace is not a flow nor a stream nor even a flood, but in its depth and breadth a boundless ocean. If you knew the grace of God – the infinite gift of God's grace! If only you knew how much God is ready to give you, is ready to give himself, if you open yourself to him! We need to know God's freedom, this generosity of the Lord of glory. If we have deep faith in his grace, then we can solve the most decisive questions of our existence in the simplest way. Faith is action. We need to repeat in our hearts, 'I believe in grace', for we are children of God and receive freely. In the house of my earthly father, everything is freely at my disposal, but in the house of my heavenly Father there is even more: I have received a share in the divine riches, a share in the fullness of God. That is unimaginable, but it is a starting point, something that we can believe. Here is a source to which we can turn.

Now that I have tried to answer the question 'What is grace?', I shall return to the redemptive work of grace, to its saving activity over the space and time of history, because it embraces and permeates everything at the same time.

If we look very deeply, we recognize that all is grace, even evil, death and sin. I have already said that the culmination of all sins in human history is the crucifixion of our Saviour. Human beings never did anything more reprehensible than that – one could almost call it original sin. There are theologians who do not locate original sin back at the origin of human history, as the guilt of the first Adam, but at a later time, the time of the second Adam. They see original sin as the act of rejecting the divine light which came to lighten the darkness but was misunderstood and rejected by it. The darkness crucified the light.

The light has come into the world, and men loved darkness rather than light, because their deeds were evil. For everyone who does evil hates the light (John 3.19f.).

But we can leave that aside. I don't want to get into a theological discussion about it. However, one thing is clear. The most abysmal of all crimes became recognizable as a source of all salvation and all blessings. The thrust of the lance which also wounded the crucified Son of Man and Son of God at this time released a flood of grace which from then on streams into the world to reach all things: it is the source of eternal life for all. Since this hour of grief, the darkest and most terrifying thing in this world, the cross, has become an instrument of grace for our redemption and sanctification. The symbol of evil and death has become the symbol of life, of eternal life: it is the mathematical plus sign *par excellence*. What a remarkable dialectic – good and evil, salvation and disaster, grace and sin!

So if the supreme happiness can derive from the deepest misery, the richest blessing from the fatal wound of evil, then we should all lift up our hearts and have the unconditional confidence to be unshakeable optimists. Let us remind ourselves again that the greatest of all news, the really good news, is that all is grace, even death, evil and sin, for Jesus' death was a saving death which burst the bonds of evil. Through this grace of all graces *everything* has been ransomed, paid off, saved – everything. Through this death came the turning point, the dawn of the new time.

The cross has overturned the values of the world and stood history on its head. Where evil gathered and seized its supreme power, goodness shone over the night like a sun, because 'where sin increased, grace abounded all the more', as Paul told the Romans. Christ should not have had to be tortured to death at human hands, but on the other hand it could not have been otherwise. It had to happen that the supreme good sprang from the depths of evil, so that the new creation became even more wonderful and amazing than the first. The new man – created anew in Jesus Christ – towers in his true greatness above the old, for he was restored to a state of grace: his beauty will become slowly evident above the abysses in the process of history.

The old Latin liturgy of the mass conveyed this word for word. In the offertory we spoke of the creation of human beings in a wonderful way, and of how the new creation formed them even more wonderfully. It is the grace of God which here becomes active as a new process of life for men and women, which becomes powerfully effective. God not only forgives in his boundless love, but he reshapes men and women, better than before. God's will for salvation succeeds in bringing good out of evil – and if we try to imagine it, the sheer size of it takes away our breath completely. Saint-Exupéry penetrated to the heart of the matter when he said: 'The conviction that there is nothing to lament and nothing to regret is a great comfort for me.'

Here the stress lies on the word 'nothing'. We cannot in any way understand how the good could ever emerge from some kind of evil – and especially sin. But that is the challenge of faith. It is the conviction of faith that the impossible is possible because God is stronger than all the inadequacies of our world and all devilry.

Here I want to quote some fine texts from Nietzsche's Zarathustra in which Nietzsche says the same thing in his own way. He speaks of the 'foaming mixing-bowl of spice, in which all things are well compounded... the furthest to the nearest, fire to spirit and joy to sorrow and the wickedest to the kindest', and of the 'redeeming salt that makes everything mix well together in the bowl, for there is a salt that unites good and evil; and even the most evil is worthy to be a spice and a last over-foaming'.

Elsewhere he remarks, 'My brothers, it is wise that there is so much evil in the world,' or ,'Wisdom wills there to be things in the world which feel evil.' And he follows his remarks with thoughts like this:

Did my disgust itself make me wings and strength to find new fountains?

The transformation of values is the transformation of the creative.

He who must be a creator always destroys...

So the supreme evil belongs with the supreme good,but this is creative.

Evil is man's best strength.

'Man must grow better and more evil' – thus do I teach.Evil is necessary for the Superman's best.

That is a harsh paradox – and yet a fantastic source of hope for our existence. Despite everything Nietzsche remained an atheist, but he recognized particular Christian truths which many Christians have not yet understood. He makes another comparison with the effects of an earthquake which buries fountains here and there but opens up new and stronger springs in other places. To put it more profoundly: earthquakes are needed to bring to light the inner powers of the mysteries. New springs burst out in the cataclysm of the old.

Christian optimism is Easter optimism. Christian optimists do not assert in naive tones that all will go well, but they believe in holy earnestness that even if something ends unhappily or tragically, this negative will be transformed into a positive in an unfathomable divine way. When everything goes smoothly it is easy to be an optimist; at that time no one deserves to be called an optimist. Our Christian optimism is paschal: that is, it is no easy fair-weather optimism, but a resurrection optimism which has gone through storm and hail and has survived death. It is an optimism beyond night and mist, beyond evil and death, and beyond time – an optimism which has an even stronger name, confidence.

The great among us have grasped this mystery. We heard Saint-Exupéry and Nietzsche. There are also the comments of the great German Protestant theologian Dietrich Bonhoeffer, who was executed a few weeks before the end of the Second World War after two years in Berlin prisons: 'Over the heads of the men who make history the ruler of history continually brings good out of evil... I believe that God can and will bring good out of everything, even the worst.'

That is very clearly seen and said. Evil will turn to good. But that is continuous creation, uninterrupted new creation through a change for the better. God has not only made being arise out of nothingness, but he also works incessantly at it, at this human world with all its follies and weaknesses, and at its deepest sins – starting from human sin. That is God's work of redemption and Christ's message of redemption.

Our wanderings and our errors... We all experience a fiasco at some time in our life; there is no biography without this experience of shipwreck. At that point a person may either describe the failure as catastrophe and perhaps even give up, or understand it as a blessing and a starting point for all that is essential. Words spoken which it would have been better not to utter, actions which would have been better left undone, all that we lament, that burdens us, causes disquiet, anxiety or bitterness, has been put before God in quite a new way and can be to our gain. Catastrophes are then no longer catastrophes, mistakes are no longer mistakes – so long as we believe that the creator is capable of changing everything, even evil and falsehood, into what is good and right.

I imagine that it is infinitely easier for the creator God to make his creation shine forth out of nothingness and bring a perfect world into being than incessantly to take up, change and recreate our failure towards him and creation. God forms and shapes, collects and builds up, but human beings tear down, scatter, alienate and destroy. And then God picks up what has been destroyed and reshapes it in his hands, creates it anew in a thousand ways. No matter how much human beings also damage and degrade creation, and even threaten to lose themselves in the process, they never fall out of God's hand, and in God's hand they do not remain in this state. We should certainly not believe that redemption is that unique historical act two thousand years ago in this corner of Palestine. We should speak, rather, of the redeeming event, since it continues over the course of time. Redemption is a continuous action of God in our present.

And there is our baptism. This short moment in our early life, too, does not mean our once-for-all ransom from the fangs of evil; rather, God baptizes us uninterruptedly, so that we are constantly released newborn from his creative hand. That is redemption beyond our measure of time, and not an event fixed in space and time and thus a purely historical action. Redemption is the ongoing process of recasting the world and thus above all of reshaping men and women – God's constant re-creation. God takes us and immerses us in the water of baptism, floods us with this source of renewing grace. Grace is effective in the present, at all moments. We should not say that we have received grace, but we should get used to saying that we receive graces, now, for they are at work in the depths of our being.

We also find this sign of divine alchemy, of creating good out of human powerlessness and filth as the alchemist creates gold from the meanest elements by the transmutation of metal, throughout nature, and very near to us in our own gardens. Roses spread their fragrance and blossom over the decay of a family household when this has turned to corruption and been transformed into good earth. Divine alchemy – what else? We should seek these signs, and wonder with reverence at the most remarkable metamorphoses in the sphere of nature; we should let it be an indication of redemption, for redemption is a metamorphosis of this world.

All is grace: the historical process of the church is also grace, since the deaths of its martyrs are grace. As the church lives and matures and constantly reshapes itself, it certainly does not do so, as some might assume, on the basis of the intellectual capacity of competent theologians; these merely contribute to it. Nor does it do so on the basis of its financial resources, since such success cannot be bought. No, we find the mystery of its growth in the phenomenon of weakness and death, martyr death, ongoing martyr death in the past and the present, through time and history.

Three hundred years of the persecution of Christians at the beginning of our church history is a long time, full of tragedies. The first Christians hung, like the Saviour himself, on crosses and gallows, were reviled naked in the circus or thrown to the wild beasts, were publicly flogged, tortured in prison, put on the wheel in the market place, quartered or dragged to their deaths; they were hurled into boiling oil or burnt alive. But again we observe the mystery of death and life: this fearful field of dying was a fertile field of life in which the true church grew and gained stength. Down to the present day it has its roots in this sacrificial field, in the blood of the martyrs, from which it drew its first living power and could become firm, secure and strong. Therefore it also became a sacred custom to put the relic of a martyr within the altars of the world, for the sacrament of Christ is very closely connected with the sacrament of human beings; the sacrifice of Christ is very closely connected with the sacrifice of human beings. The source of the church's life eternally remains 'three hundred years of the persecution, suffering and death of Christians'.

Consequently, the founder of our Jesuit order showed himself to be deeply concerned when the missionaries who were sent out suffered no persecution, but he received the good news that things were going well with them under emperor X in land Y, or particularly well under marchioness Z...

No, they really lacked nothing. They were given splendid villas which even the king visited. Doesn't that say it all? And the financial resources for the building up of missions flourished. All this was very unwelcome news to St Ignatius, since he felt that something was wrong here. But if someone on the other hand whispered to him that his Jesuits were being arrested and tortured, then he was reassured.

'Excellent,' he would cry. 'In that case I'm certain that they are preaching the gospel without compromise, not watered down or falsified, rather than something quite different. The proof is the obstacles that the gospel comes up against and will always come up against.' So St Ignatius. Persecution is always a sign that the kingdom of God really is the kingdom of God. Without opposition and persecution there is a danger that the preaching is only about a better kingdom of this world. That has been the experience of those who have proclaimed the gospel for almost two thousand years.

And when I send my young people to the Sudan, as I say goodbye, I don't add, 'All the best.' No, I tell them that I hope it will be tough. Terrible tropical thirst and sometimes hunger and extreme exhaustion, the strain of travelling on bad roads, nerve-wracking cancellations of flights, the indifference of the Sudanese to their words, rejection, repudiation, obstacles to their mission... That is what I tell them to hope for – and such hopes are immediately fulfilled in the Sudan.

I have to say that to them, since most of them set out with a flower behind the ear and a religious song on their lips, delighted at the adventure, enthusiastic and certain of victory. But first of all they must be milled like grains of wheat, so that they can give the Sudanese spiritual nourishment and strengthen them. Unless they are caught between the millstones there, they can give no more than their own human dedication and enthusiasm, their human words. But anyone can do that; any man or woman is in a position to do good voluntarily, to give his or her best and practise love of neighbour to the full – especially at this idealistic young age. However, for the kingdom of God quite different work is needed, and the Lord purifies these souls which he sends out accordingly. For many years our Sudan mission has been experiencing in body and soul how the Lord lets it taste the grace of suffering. The unbelievable obstacles and cares have to be welcome to us. I hope that these obstacles will always accompany us; I wish for that and ask it in prayer, for only with this blessing can a mission get going, can it be given substance and importance, duration and success. Mission needs the positive effects of suffering in time. The suffering of today is the joy of tomorrow.

So, too, only a fighting church is vital and fruitful in the world, but it wilts as soon as it has settled somewhere in perfect prosperity, as soon as it is celebrated, receives recognition and honours – as soon as people flatter churchmen and give them privileges. The era of Constantine put the church in the limelight on the stage of time and removed all its problems. One new gateway after another opened up for the church – and then what happened? When the church flourished under Constantine, its decadence began.

There is nothing worse for the church than to be firmly established. There is nothing worse for a spiritual community than to be 'well provided for'. There is nothing worse than easy access to the necessary money, nothing worse than if one can say contentedly, 'All is going well'. The decadence of the religious orders always began on the day when they had grandiose monasteries with great lands and worldly regard. Then the life stopped flowing through their veins and decline began. Without struggle and tears there is no church; it has to go the thorny way of the cross. There must be obstacles; suffering is the spur. Without suffering there is no church, and without poverty no gospel.

I would also add that all the heresies and schisms and all the other errors of the church are also graces working beyond time; in other words, they work for the success of the church of the future without its always being aware of the fact or intending that result. For at all times heresies encourage progress in the inner growth of the church, and some people claim that the church only moved forward through its grossest errors: they were a stimulus towards the better. The French for a mistake is 'la gaffe', which has two meanings: 'blunder', and the 'long pole' with which one pushes a boat from the bank, stirring up a good deal of muddy water in the process. I don't think that God is particularly bothered when the church even now makes gaffes, as long as it learns from them, and here and there is prepared to take a new course. Even the mistakes of popes and bishops don't disturb me, and there are undeniably mistakes at all times which cry to heaven. Priests, too, make many mistakes, but it is precisely through these that the church grows. All is grace!

The Second Vatican Council, the place of the resurrection of our Catholic Church, would have been neither conceivable nor practicable without the Protestant Reformation and the French and Marxist revolutions. These explosions had to take place first. So in the end it is true of every contemporary phenomenon that all is grace. This insight should give us comfort and open our eyes. In that case there should be nothing more to lament, for all that we call evil particpates in the building up of the new, future people of God.

War is one of the cruellest evils of all: the earth weeps under it, and human beings should never have invented it. But paradoxically history teaches us that war gave the impetus to greater changes which brought us human beings authentic progress as well as terrible losses in all spheres. And here I am talking about progress at a very deep level; as progressive inner growth. In some cases war can work as a powerful catalyst with evil side-effects;

it drives humankind forward from within so that it takes not only timid steps towards its goal but also great leaps which save time.

My view is that, on the whole, humanity learned more in the six years of the Second World War than in all the previous six hundred years put together. Are we not all witnesses to a fantastic firework display of international discoveries and inventions in our firmament? And where were these fireworks set off? Was it not at the pinnacle of evil – in the Great War and the subsequent distress of total collapse? Under the pressure of time the human spirit had to invent a thousand instruments of evil and develop them with science and technology, so that this spirit, aroused, sharpened and trained, could soon also create instruments of good which today serve all men and women. I see that as having happened generally in international confrontations, which for all their terror and human tragedy were nevertheless encounters that, after the conflicts died down, turned into honourable mutual efforts and true human encounters.

The best example of this today is provided by the European nations. Since the end of the Second World War they have been acting – slowly to begin with, but then increasingly so – with marked courtesy and friendliness towards one another. Asia, too, is involved as a brother, and hands are stretched out over land barriers and seas. This worldwide drawing-together cannot be overlooked; we are growing out of the heartache and ruins of the Second World War into a world community. Through war we are unlearning war. And in this connection we might also think of the quite different relationship today between white and black citizens in the United States of America, and all that had to precede this new development. Evidently this is the only way in which people learn really to reach one another, to create and sustain a brotherly and sisterly world together.

The concept of peace has a variety of aspects, not all of which are necessarily always seen together. Unfortunately peace can also act as a narcotic with ultimately negative consequences for true human well-being. Deep peace makes us go to sleep, and then acts as an anaesthetic for civilization and its progress. In times of golden peace and universal prosperity, human souls atrophy to such a degree that for fifteen years people can live on the same floor of a house and not have more to say to each other than a barely audible greeting, uttered from a closed mouth. But when we hear reports of prisons, penal camps, political arrests, and so on, over and above all the cruelty of evil we also hear of people who precisely when there is no carefree peace become brothers and sisters overnight and remain so for life, bonded together in unity through their shared bitter experience of suffering. Wherever human beings have to put up with one another in extreme situations, they do not draw away from one another but their souls become welded together – while in ideal times they tend to lose themselves, become separated, avoid one another.

The suffering of poverty also has an aspect of grace which cannot be argued away. Most people have already had this experience in dealing with the poor or living for a time in poor countries. The solidarity of the poor is a light in this darkness, which the rich neither know nor suspect. How closely the poor come together in human terms! How transparent their hearts and feelings for one another become! And war, too, creates temporary poverty.

War also deepens spiritual life: a buried religious life is uncovered and begins to stir again. Not, however, as a cheap search for comfort; something much deeper is happening here. In their care, in acute anxiety and the common experience of suffering, human beings not only draw closer together physically and practise spontaneous solidarity, but also bond themselves in a still deeper dimension to become the people of God. How many conversions were there during and after the last war, known and unknown? What is the explanation for them? Is not the reason that in such times the masks fall everywhere and men and women find their true faces in the mirror? In this situation they become truthful to themselves and to their God overnight. In suffering of every kind the unworthy comedy comes to an end. Painful though the effects of war are to experience, it is also certain that they bring out the truth about men and women. The individual is purified and becomes transparent in this furnace. All is grace.

There are Lebanese today who confirm all this for me. They tell me something like this. 'Of course our civil war is sheer madness, but on the other hand this change of climate is doing Lebanon good. We were on the point of losing ourselves; pleasure was undermining all values and devouring us. There was far too much money in this country. Couldn't we understand what has happened and what is still happening as a blessing? Nowadays, amongst the ruins of Beirut, there is a rediscovery of human depths and a new understanding of existence.'

I believe such authentic reports from the Lebanon; they seem to me to be quite true. They are reflected in the great variety of spiritual movements which blossom from this suffering earth like fresh shoots. In particular the number of young people in the Lebanon who now deliberately want to confess God was never so high, and it is constantly growing. They have found the sense of a much more authentic reality, and from now on they want to commit themselves to it. All is grace, and ultimately nothing can be pulled out from the flood of history, not even if we fail to learn otherwise, not even a war, which represents the embodiment of evil, and not even death. For redemption began with a crucifixion. That stands at the heart of the 'good news'.

Now let us look into ourselves. In the quite personal sphere we sigh or shrug our shoulders and talk of our mistakes and weaknesses. How often have we been told that we should have declared war on them and exterminated them root and branch! There is no objection to this noble principle, but it cannot be realized; it remains utopian. I have only to remember the time when I was a novice in Lebanon! Systematically, week by week, month by month, we had to discard our errors, discard them one after another, like a garment. The whole of spiritual life can be understood as a war with our errors, with perfection as the aim of the battle. But a person without faults is not a person. Human beings without faults would be the most boring creatures under the sun, and God seems wisely to allow us this or that mistake so that we remain interesting to one another.

Fortunately we all have our drawbacks, and will take some of them with us to the grave. Happily we keep them all our lives, for they are facets of our basic personal being. They also have a role. Our mistakes are the other side of our virtues, the counterpart to our good properties. One can say that we have the good properties of our mistakes, and we have the mistakes of our good properties – it amounts to the same thing.

So quite a nervous person may be full to bursting with good ideas and try to put them into practice with great energy and much dynamism; a somewhat tranquil person whose sluggishness one laments may be goodness personified, with loving readiness to accept the concerns of his or her neighbour, a person who can listen and whom one trust. But in that case how do we judge nervousness and sluggishnesss? Are these good or bad properties? Are they advantages or disadvantages? Above all, how should we behave? Always in the same way: by accepting – by accepting people as they are.

We must also accept ourselves with the weaknesses which get in our way, great or small, and with the faults that we cannot get rid of. We must be able to laugh at ourselves. A sense of humour is a good help towards accepting ourselves. We need to laugh at our failings and limitations and not be afraid, for our faults are not bigger than we are. If we do that, others too will laugh with us at ourselves and our faults and like us as we are. Unfortunately the art of accepting ourselves seems to be a difficult one. However, our motto must be: 'Begin by accepting yourself, and you will be accepted; begin by loving yourself and you will be loved.'

We need above all to give up our enthusiasm for developing a faultless, unobjectionable nature: that applies most particularly to those called to the religious life or to the priesthood, since this is an illusion. We have to learn to develop along with our defects and within our limitations, and especially through them, since they may prove important equipment for us. How do we derive any advantage from our mistakes, defects and limitations? That, too, needs to be learned. To create his famous David, Michelangelo used a piece of marble which to begin with seemed to him impossible: it was too small. But instead of waiting, or looking round for a larger block, he set to work. And so his David was created within these limitations. To his genius were added these difficult circumstances, which compelled the artist to create a masterpiece. We are now convinced that there would have been no David had circumstances been easier for the master. Works of genius always arise out of a compulsion, a pressure. Here the great achievement derives from an overcoming of the obstacles. That is the thorny law of life. Obstacles and limitations make extraordinary things possible. Did you know that the great Moses and the great Jeremiah were miserable speakers (Ex.4.10-13; Jer.1.6-9)?

We have thousands of excuses to give God, so the Lord once called twelve weak and ignorant people as an example and an encouragement for us. At least ten of the apostles were very simple and uneducated men, but he called them on account of their poverty and weakness. Most significant events in world history are continually brought about by people without academic qualifications. So there is no need for us to have a complex about our intellectual background if we want to become active and make

[139

our personal contribution to society. The decisive thing is for us to have trust and to get to work. With the little that we have inherited we can work wonders and change the face of the earth. We have only to believe.

Above all, we have to accept what we were yesterday: we have to accept our past fully, along with our education, the social environment into which we were born, our health and our appearance, with all their defects and disadvantages. We must not dream of being otherwise. I know people who waste their lives burning with envy for others – and for so many reasons! Then comes a time when they become embittered or get stuck imitating people. If only they knew that they had enough good stuff in them to make a wonderful person who could have amazing success in life! But the spirit of the age dictates in us admiration for particular people who seem to us to live in splendour and glory, though when we get closer to them they are deadly boring. And there are the unknown, the insignificant, the unattractive people who captivate us precisely because of their inner being. God gave all of us many positive characteristics which make us lovable if only they can be brought to light. And we should work with this 'best part'.

However, in personal conversations I often hear nothing but the word 'if'. If I had more energy, if I had more time, if I had more money, if I had a diploma, if I could study in America, if I had contacts... This word 'if' saps people's energy and they never get started. But think of all the people whom we call great who were neither well-educated, nor in perfect health, nor so rich as to be able to carry out their plans quickly and smoothly. Many great people had very little at their disposal: only empty hands and a frail or even suffering body. But in their weakness they mobilized in the spirit the little that they had, as does everyone else, and then they believed unshakeably in their goal.

The whole secret of working wonders lies in faith. Those among us who do not believe are those who stand before us chock-full of knowledge and education but who clearly have not developed any personal life. They have no sense of even the most natural things in life, often not even of that relationship with one's neighbour which is so important. They either stand around helplessly or go off in the wrong direction. At home, framed diplomas hang on their walls, a promising future under glass, and in addition they enjoy brilliant health; some of them even have private fortunes. But nothing comes of all that! They do not desire, want or dare anything. Or they wait... They keep waiting for a still better opportunity and want circumstances to be even more favourable. They wait and demand – that is all that they 'do'. But real action would be their faith – and in faith that would be a start. Those who hesitate with their eternal excuses age very quickly: how quickly the inner person dies without plans! As Emmanuel Mounier commented, 'One should not wait until something is ripe before beginning an undertaking.' We need to begin with the little that we have been given and believe in it; if we do, then grace will be given us with which to work wonders.

Five thousand people once followed Jesus into the wilderness 'like sheep without a shepherd', including many who were sick, 'and he took pity on them and healed them'. Towards evening the twelve disciples worried about how this enormous crowd was to be fed, far from the city. When a child was brought to Jesus who had five loaves of bread and two fishes, Jesus said, 'Make the people sit down.' Then he held the child's basket, took the bread, prayed softly, and broke it and divided it, and afterwards the two fishes. At the end of the feeding of the multitude he told the apostles to go round and gather up the fragments so that nothing was left, and they came back with twelve basketsful. This is a story which is told in all four Gospels.

All is grace! We should reflect as often as possible on this miracle of the multiplication of the loaves. We need to offer the Lord the little that we have and ask him to bless it. Perhaps I, too, can feed thousands with my five loaves and two fishes, for in that case the one involved is not myself but the one who has blessed the little that I have.

Grace proves increasingly fruitful. It turns our natural gifts into supernatural, wonderful gifts. 'If only you knew the gift of God.' Those are words of Christ. If only you knew the power of grace, if only you could accept your poverty, if only you had sufficient faith! 'Believe in the power of God which is perfected in weakness' – that is the testimony that Paul left behind for us like a legacy. Paul complained a great deal about the thorn in the flesh which made things so difficult for him. He urgently prayed God to remove this thorn. We can no longer even guess what kind of a thorn it was. Paul was short in stature and unimpressive to look at: he complained about this in one of his letters. He could well have said that he was not very suitable to be an apostle. 'God, for heaven's sake choose a large and impressive person to proclaim this message to the world. I am incapable of doing what you want of me...' And then there was his thorn in the flesh which tormented him so. Was it a chronic illness? A psychological weakness? A temptation of some kind? Whatever it may have been, it seems that God thought this goad necesary, since Paul still got the same answer: 'My grace must be enough for you, my power is made perfect in weakness' (II Cor.12.9).

Presumably he would not have become 'Saint' Paul without the goad of his suffering which the Lord gave him like spurs for the race. We should feel our weaknesses and know our limitations before God – that makes us keen of hearing, sensitive, humble. We must be poor before God, but know that all is grace. Ill health can sometimes be the condition for a spiritual revival and flourishing, for full awareness. We have plenty of instances of this. There are infinitely many things which robustly healthy people cannot grasp, which they find so difficult. But think of the power there is in the mystery of suffering! From antiquity down to our day these great sufferers have lived among us. Pascal, one of the most profound and versatile thinkers in human history, was infirm and soon fell sick, but he left us his *Pensées*, which are among the finest pearls that human genius has ever produced. These pearls of wisdom occurred to him between migraines and fearful liver disease, and he died at the age of thirty-nine. So defect or loss on one level becomes gain on another, higher level. All is grace. The state of our health never determines our spiritual productivity.

We might think of the invalid Blondel, or Bergson, the Jewish Nobel prizewinner. Or the blind Lazarist Pouget, to whom the young intellectuals of France went for counsel. Or the Egyptian Muslim Taha Hussein, one of the most significant scholars and writers in the Arab world. He would probably never have become the great Taha Hussein had he not been blinded at the age of seven. His work of staggering sensitivity, refinement and depth is rooted in this life of suffering. His eyes were closed to our sunlight, but were opened to another light and saw things which we are not able to experience. He wrote forty books, and his finest, *Al-Aijam*, has meanwhile appeared in Russian and Danish, Indonesian and Chinese, among other languages. He died in 1973.

Let us remain in Egypt, but look back to the time of the Pharaohs, to the year 1350 BC. Not many people know much about Akenaton, the social pharaoh, religious genius and founder of monotheism. Moses was influenced by him, and many psalms in our Bible go back to his inspiration. This great man was a physical wreck; he lived, thought, wrote poetry and worked with his health completely ruined: he died at the age of thirty.

Geniuses in particular and spiritual figures generally do not need health or special privileges. We should never let a weak condition be an excuse for sitting back, but rouse ourselves and offer our intention to God. Then he will help us to begin it, and bring it to an end.

Think of the simple spirit of the Curé d'Ars, later St Jean-Marie Vianney. Despite his ardent desire to become a priest he was virtually incapable of grasping arguments, though he was borne up by a rocklike faith. Although the academically-minded advised him to abandon his dream, he made the attempt. Then by grace he passed the examination, was ordained priest, was allowed to give absolution. And the Curé d'Ars became the best-known and most beloved spiritual advisor of his century, if not of all centuries. People flocked by the thousand from all over Europe to his simple sermons – especially the intellectual world, including learned men and philosophers. Could not this man have said to himself, 'Priest? A splendid idea! Unfortunately I don't have the equipment'? But he said something else, perhaps, 'The little that I contribute will bear fruit if grace touches it – and that is what I shall ask for.' He offered his five loaves of bread and two fishes to the Lord, and asked him to bless these gifts. And God's blessing fell on this paltry gift a thousandfold and a hundred thousandfold – beyond all expectations. Here is the wonder of grace: great things can perhaps perfect themselves in weakness, as Paul writes – through the simplest instruments by means of poverty.

Is understanding other people also a gift? In understanding one 'gives' something. And it is very often those who have had to drink the bitter gall of suffering who now understand their fellow human beings. If you want to sense someone else's suffering and understand the particularly deep realities of existence, then you must be made porous to it by undergoing suffering. If God wants to shake people awake to teach them a particular lesson, then he often begins by blessing them with what in Arabic is called a *mussiba*, a piece of misfortune. So the Jesuit order begins with the broken leg of a man called Ignatius Loyola. Had he not had this painful leg with its unpleasant consequences at a particular point in his life, then today there would not be a single Jesuit in the world, instead of the 26,000 that there are.

In the end, all is gain. Look through your personal life to see whether you can find any roses blossoming among the refuse. If we lose something at one level, we gain it at another. At one point I prayed to the Lord to shake a particular person by a *mussiba*, to scare him out of his permanent coma. He had sunk into himself and was blocked off by his egotism, too dull and incapable of feeling and understanding the most basic need in his surroundings, and was acting accordingly.

What can we really know about the nature of a misfortune, about its essence, its meaning, its message and its consequences? And what do we really know of happiness? What is ultimately good for us or bad for us? Only God knows. There is an Arabic proverb which goes, 'Do not fear evil, for it may bring you good.'

In the context of this Arabic wisdom, here is a legend, a parable from China.

A wise farmer had a son, a horse and a neighbour. One morning the son rode off to market in the city, but in the hills the horse threw him and wandered off. So the son came back by himself. 'What a misfortune,' said the neighbour. 'How do you know?', said the farmer.

The next day, the son set off to look for the lost horse. He found it, and in addition brought back a splendid wild stallion – proud at his skill in catching him. 'What good fortune,' said the neighbour. 'How do you know?', said the farmer.

The next morning, the son began to break in the stallion, but it threw him, and the son broke an arm. 'What a misfortune,' said the neighbour. 'How do you know?', said the farmer.

The next morning the king's recruiting officer came to the village to conscript the young men for war. Because of his temporary incapacity the son escaped military service. 'What good fortune,' said the neighbour. 'How do you know?', said the farmer.

The next morning... The next morning...

Fortune or misfortune, how do we know? We need to accept in faith what God has planned for us. The saying 'all is grace' comes from St Paul, and St Augustine added, 'even sin'. In fact sin, evil *par excellence*, can become the source of good, indeed the greatest good; and we believe that and understand it when we look on the cross.

Do we not find the story of many former sinners even among the saints? Only grace can bring about such a transformation. St Augustine, whom I have just quoted, did not write this sentence while theorizing and theologizing between his tractates, starting from a purely intellectual concept, but from the abundance of his own practical experience of life and suffering. In his famous *Confessions* he records more than thirty years of his life which in his estimation he spent as a sinner. The founder of our Jesuit order, too, was bent on pleasure until his conversion, as was Francis Xavier, who was later to become the great missionary to the Far East. And there was Charles de Foucauld's loose life-style in Paris, with all his diversions. And all the rest... Perhaps many of them could not rise to the state of holiness unless they had experimented in their lives with sin and subsequently had tasted the misery of the sinner. It seems to me that sin tears something open in the human heart; it opens up a division through which grace finds entry. Then those involved experience a radical spiritual transformation, a conversion. Whether they would ever have been capable of discovering the same depths of God, the same nearness of God, of discovering love, without the background of their experience of sin suffered in body and soul, is something that none of us can know – nor did they themselves. If we are really convinced that sin – and nothing worse can happen to us – can be a way that ends in God, then we no longer need to be anxious, since all is grace, all is gain.

But we are so often Pharisees! We fancy that we are free from sin... and then an armour of self-satisfaction encloses us and cuts us off from the light of grace. We think that we do not need anything. The crust on the essence of our being shuts us off from our environment and is so impenetrable that not even grace can shine through it. Withdrawn into our self-satisfaction, we do not even long for redemption, for otherwise we would open ourselves to it. How can grace reach us? It will not break our free will. So presumably it is sin which creates this salutary wound. The Lord allows it as a divide through which he can find access to our hearts. Formerly we were too smooth and too orderly – so much so that we pleased ourselves.

But if we are going to offer ourselves to God, we need to do so soon. We must not wait for the day when we are spotless and worthy of this encounter, since there are the morally bent among us who have no self-confidence (or not enough) and a distorted relationship to God, the Father. No, we must not wait. Some people tell me that they won't start praying until they have got rid of their faults and weaknesses. And then I prophesy to them that they will spend their lives waiting. But above all, God is wholly other. He is not someone whom one visits in a dinner jacket. So we must go as we are, now, straight away. And if we fall, we must get up and keep going towards him. We must be like the prodigal son who heads home and considers what he will say to his father: 'Father, I have sinned against heaven and before you, and am no more worthy to be called your son.'

But it is not like this. The Lord will receive us as his children, always and in every situation, precisely as we are at this moment. The love of God which we experience knows no deeper relationship and no higher quality than the concept of our childlikeness. We are children of God. We stand before him with empty hands and sometimes like the prodigal son, stained and broken, exhausted and guilt-ridden. But beyond the shadows, within we remain profoundly God's children. We have no higher quality than this: it is the supreme quality that we can possess as human beings, and grace gives it to us. The love of the Father is pure grace.

We need always to compare this inner relationship with the father of a family who is cuddling a child which has a bad conscience. The fact of the father-child relationship is enough to show that the child is accepted, is loved; that it is understood at critical times and, if necessary, is given its father's forgiveness. A loving father does not just close one eye, but both – we have all experienced that.

The prodigal son had squandered his father's money and property and abused his trust. But now the father was not interested in any discussions about the cirucmstances and reasons for this breach of trust, but in unbounded joy ran to meet his son when he saw him coming, and embraced him.

There is no doubt that the father loved his son greatly, for the son had caused him infinite pain, anxiety and suffering. That is always the case. If you are a teacher or have children of your own, there will always be the *enfant terrible* who is closest to your heart. While grieving you he will raise your spirits. By contrast, the other son in the Gospel, the loyal and diligent one, had claims on his father: he thought that his loyalty and obedience gave him rights. This son will never have understood what was happening here, what the prodigal son was now experiencing. He himself was too clean, too self-satisfied and too loyal to understand the absolute and free offering of a father's love which the prodigal son was now enjoying. He could not have this experience of grace.

We need to reflect quietly on this parable, since in my view it is the most profound of any in the Gospels. It is our story. Nevertheless, all too many of us believe that we have to prepare carefully for our encounter with God, that we have to smarten ourselves up and above all purify ourselves in penitence before taking part in the mass and communicating. People think that only then will the Father embrace them: only if they are pure. But what a mistake that is!

Suppose that on his journey home the son had been told in a distant welcome from his father that first he had to clean himself up and put on respectable clothes before he came to give a detailed explanation of himself! It is just not true that we may not appear before God unclean; that is not said anywhere. Moreover, not only may we come as we are and God will receive us immediately, but God will take us to his heart spontaneously and embrace us, as in the parable, and we shall be clean, through him. For it is not human beings who cleanse themselves before going to God, but God who cleanses human beings if they come to him.

The love of God is absolute love. We are not given it by making ourselves fit for it, but it is directed towards us, shines through us and purifies us; it not only purifies, but ennobles and changes. So I would stress once again that we need to avoid those who want to drum into us that we must go to confession before communion, which I know is still the strict demand of a number of churches and certain priests. We all have particular weaknesses and particular faults. I too go to confession now and then, but I allow myself the freedom to choose how often. In earlier times compulsory confession tormented all of us, but that is past. No, I go to confession with the aim of being transformed, for the love of God precedes everything.

'Lord, I am not worthy', we say before every communion. No, I was never worthy to receive the host, God himself, on any day of my life. If I wanted to wait until I was worthy of this pure and infinite love of God I would have to wait to the end of my life and beyond – to the end of time.

So in the Coptic mass the faithful say before communion, 'Given to us for the forgiveness of sins'. The body of Christ is *given* to us, for all is grace. The Catholic priest chooses between the words, 'Whoever eats of this bread will live for ever', and, 'Blessed are those who are invited to the marriage feast of the lamb'. Those who receive communion are blessed, blessed in the working of divine grace. The word was revealed to John as the 'true word of God' (Rev.19.9). Contact with Christ in the host has a purifying, transforming, ennobling and redemptive effect. We do not go to him because we are pure, but because we want to *become* pure and worthy of him. He is the one who saves. The name Jesus is derived from the Hebrew *Yeshua* and means YHWH helps, God saves. Jesus is called the Saviour because he *is* the Saviour; it lies in his nature, his being, his person, his personality that he is the one who saves us. We do not go to a vague cosmic creator spirit, but we go to the Lord of the world who has revealed himself and who loves men and women, revealed and manifested in Jesus Christ. He showed himself to us as gentleness and meekness, as mercy and loving forgiveness. He is the God who saves men and women.

That is the revelation of the working of grace; that is redemption and sanctification. However, unfortunately we are all still too caught up in the philosophical, intellectual Old Testament, and in addition pharisaically think that we are more or less free of sin and in accord with God. But in truth, as human beings we shall never be in accord with God, but will remain debtors who are unable to repay him.

Still, all is grace. Let us remember the parable of the servant who is deeply in debt (Matt.18). He was in the red to his king to the tune of ten thousand talents, and he would never ever have been able to repay this debt. So in desperation he threw himself at his master's feet, and asked for forgiveness – and his master forgave him the debt! That is the gospel! And if we do not understand it in any other way, at least let us understand it in terms of these parables, which are strong and crystal-clear, for the Lord composed them for us to grasp and understand the message of salvation. Word for word we find in them what grace is. If we have the courage to encounter God not only with empty hands but with hands stained with guilt, with a long past, laden with the weight of faults of every kind, with mediocrity and weakness of character, then we are on the right way. Believe!

Here I think above all of Martin Luther. He was a man with very deep intuitions. To a certain extent he was right to oppose the Catholics by stressing so much the completely free gift of justification, that concept in Christian theology which relates to the restoration of the unity of human beings with their creator, which has been destroyed by sin. Since then, Protestant theology has called this pardon a pure gift of God which is given to human beings only in faith. Christians are justified solely by the grace of God, without any merit of their own. Luther, too, says that all is grace. Protestants believe that human beings cannot of themselves re-establish contact with God, but only on the basis of the divine forgiveness which they receive as grace in faith, 'by faith alone, by grace alone, *sola fide, sola gratia*'.

We also find the same thing in Paul. In several splendid chapters of his letter to the Romans he urgently writes about the value of grace; there we find his marvellous doctrine of justification. Paul proclaims the grace of God, that we are justified without our own doing through his grace, thanks to our redemption in Jesus Christ. He also writes to the Galatians to the same effect. Human beings are justified by faith and through grace, and not on the basis of their works. So-called good works then flow from grace as the fruit, the consequence of justification, as the outworking of divine forgiveness and purification; they are not its condition. This theological view, which was also that of Luther, is very deep and very important. Luther gave a great deal to the Catholic church, and especially since the Second Vatican Council we are in a position to appreciate the full depth of his teaching.

And while we are talking of Protestants, here I am reminded of another important theologian and philosopher, Paul Tillich. He was born in Germany and emigrated to America in 1933. This is what he had to say about grace.

We cannot transform our lives, unless we allow them to be transformed by the stroke of grace. Grace strikes us when we walk through the dark valley of a meaningless and empty life. It strikes us when we feel that our separation is deeper than usual, because we have violated another life, a life which we loved, or from which we were estranged. It strikes us when our disgust for our own being, our indifference, our weakness, our hostility, and our lack of direction and composure have become intolerable to us. It strikes us when, year after year, the longed-for perfection of life does not appear, when the old compulsions reign within us as they have for decades, when despair destroys all joy and courage.

Sometimes at that moment a wave of light breaks into our darkness, and it is as though a voice were saying, 'You are accepted!' If that happens to us, we experience grace.

After such an experience we may not be better than before, and we may not believe more than before. But everything is transformed, changed. In that moment grace conquers sin, and reconciliation bridges the gulf of estrangement. And nothing is demanded of this experience, no religious or moral or intellectual presupposition, nothing but acceptance.

This splendid text is illuminating for me in its greatness and beauty, and it expresses to me the innermost depths of Christian teaching. I am accepted as I am, in my poverty and emptiness, in my distress and anguish and with all my mistakes. 'Yes, you are accepted.' I believe that what has been put so simply here relates to the most important experience of grace which we can have in our existence, and this message may serve men and women as a source of liberation. We are all brothers and sisters of Christ, we are all children of God, and therefore we are accepted. The revelation of grace is a shattering one.

But we should note one thing. Justification by God means not only that God receives in grace sinners or weaklings and turns to them in love but essentially leaves them sinners and weaklings. It means infinitely more. It means transformation. And here unfortunately we find the difference between the Catholic and the Orthodox Christian conception on the one hand and the Protestant conception on the other. Our brothers and sisters who are Protestants believe that human beings are illuminated by grace or veiled in it; a cloak comes over sinners to cover their sin. But that means that their sin continues under the cloak and that despite the divine working of grace and being accepted by the Father, men and women nevertheless remain sinners. The confidence of Catholic and Orthodox Christians in the efficacy of grace extends still further; they do not believe that their guilt is merely covered and their soul illuminated by the light of God, but they firmly believe that they are newly created by the grace of Christ:

My legal status is restored;
The initial state of holiness is restored;

I am raised up as a new being.

This miracle which makes people righteous takes place in a constant dynamic process of the working of grace. Catholic and Orthodox Christians believe that sins are really taken away; for them that is the embodiment of redemption, the comprehensive meaning of the message of salvation. Grace transforms, recreates, renews, brings completely new children of God into being. Damaged, weakened, marked, we were taken into the furnace of the heart of Jesus and left it as gleaming gold bars. We are truly redeemed.

Redemption is a new creation, a radical change of being, a transformation at the heart of our being. God creates us with his own hands for the second time, for grace transforms men and women to the roots of their being. It not only covers all evil, lovingly enwraps the former person we were, but it says, 'Behold, I make all things new' (Revelation 21.5).

And that is the new and in fact redemptive element in this message to the world, which is why we call it the 'good' news that we are to proclaim to all men and women. And we should not do so timidly and irresolutely or in passing, but passionately and very directly. In the cross on Golgotha the whole universe was poured into the furnace and remoulded. That is why the Gospel of Matthew reports that on Good Friday darkness came over the whole land for three hours, the earth quaked and the rocks split. Elsewhere we read of such signs only in the Apocalypse: they are signs of the downfall of the old world. Here something breaks, something dies. On the death of Jesus the whole universe collapsed inwardly and died with him. It is the hour of the death of the old creation, and the hour of the birth of the new creation, which one day will shine in splendour before us all: at the end of history, when a new heaven spreads over a new earth. This is what John experienced in a holy vision which transcended time and which he recorded for us in his Revelation or Apocalypse, in accordance with the words which he heard: 'Write, for these words are true and faithful'.

We can also read in the Second Letter of Peter, 'The heavens will be kindled and dissolved, and the elements will melt with fire. But according to his promise we wait for new heavens and a new earth in which righteousness dwells' (3.12b-13).

Righteousness – for all is grace, all is gain. To end this book I want to express the wish that this new life, promising light and harmony, may finally conquer the lack of peace in our hearts and spirits and give birth to a peace which surpasses all other forms of peace, all anxiety, all toil and torment, all questions and counter-questions, every kind of wisdom, every proof and counter-proof, every reflection, every doubt.

What I mean is a spiritual peace, a clear inner heaven. This is what Christ meant when he said in his blessing, 'Peace be with you'. And if we keep alive deep in our hearts the conviction that all is grace and all is gain, then there will no longer be any reason for fears of any kind, for the transforming power of the death of Christ will bring about this miracle of peace.

> Peace I leave with you; my peace I give to you. Let not your hearts be troubled, neither let them be afraid (John 14.27).

The peace which the world gives is based on human logic and the human capacity for judgment, on human motivations, values and possibilities. That is why it so quickly vanishes and leaves our spirits abandoned. But the peace of Christ is of quite another order; it lies beyond all human evidence and certainty. This peace exists beyond all possibilities, but also beyond our lack of capacity, since it is borne up on the wings of blind faith and the deep certainty that God is and always will be, that he is wiser than the wisest man and stronger than the deepest sin, and overcomes evil in his love. 'Be of good cheer, I have overcome the world' (John 16.33).

This peace which is to fill us is not based on what we do or do not do, nor is it based on what we are, but only on God, on God's grace and his love. So there can be no power in the world which could threaten or destroy this spiritual peace.

At the depths of the Christian revelation we find the message that human history is a history of redemption, a history of grace, in which everything is redeemed, transformed and shaped anew, for 'where sin increased, grace abounded all the more', as Paul preached to the Romans. Since then we may assume that all is grace – in the last resort, even sin.

We might ask ourselves whether things could not have been different. Could the love of God have flowed over us to this amazing extent even if we had not been abounding in sin? There seems to be a kind of time-conditioned historical necessity for the existence of sin. Perhaps that is what Christ meant when he said,

'There must be offences.' Is that perhaps the ultimate significance of what we call original sin?

For we must never forget that sin, too, and perhaps sin in particular, manifests God to men and women. We cannot experience and understand what sin really is unless we see it in the light of God. Only through redemption can we learn to understand it in retrospect. God's redemption of humankind is at the same time an uncovering and disclosure of human sin and its obliteration – through Jesus Christ. Human beings could not bear the burden of their guilt were it not revealed to them in the mystery of Christ. It is useless for men and women to know their guilt unless at the same time and to the same degree they consciously experience the grace and love of Christ which saves them.

Last of all, a meditation to remind us of the truth of grace:

Lord, give me to the full the knowledge of the work of your grace in this world. Then your grace will also begin to work in me as a source of peace.

Help me to understand that despite my faults and weaknesses, my defects and limitations, you have invited me to the greatest adventure of all – adventure with you.

I still hesitate to accept your offer; I do not dare to take your hand. But I feel your impulses which move my heart, and I hear your gentle call in me to be bold. Indeed you encourage me in these days to find a new beginning in my life and to want to commit myself for this world.

You know that I am poor in resources and bring little with me. I am nothing special. But with the little I have I shall be able to do all things, for you will bring them to completion.

So I give you my five loaves and my two fishes, and I give you my weaknesses and the little that I have. Take it, Lord, and transform it into food for many, perhaps for thousands.

Then let this cheerful faith dominate all my actions and thoughts, beyond the errors and mistakes which I shall certainly make. Set me up when I fall, strengthen me when I fail, and make me confident of finding a new beginning.

Above all strengthen my faith in your grace more and more. Let me draw strength from this source which sprang from the hill of Golgotha, and which flowed into the boundless ocean of grace.

Let the deep certainty of acceptance sink into my heart. Above my being and action let me at all times sense your love and find your peace, your divine peace which is beyond time, which transcends all other forms of peace.

You have left us peace. Help us to understand it. Let it fill my soul and guide me to the knowledge of the last word of the revelation of grace: 'The love of God is at work behind all appearances.'